The Bryce

Handbook

The Bryce 3D Handbook

R. Shamms Mortier

CHARLES RIVER MEDIA, INC.
Rockland, Massachusetts

Executive Editor: Jenifer L. Niles
Interior Design/Comp: Publishers' Design and Production Services, Inc.
Cover Design: The Printed Image
Printer: InterCity Press, Rockland, MA

CHARLES RIVER MEDIA, Inc.
P.O. Box 417, 403 VFW Drive
Rockland, MA 02370
781-871-4184
781-871-4376(FAX)
chrivmedia@aol.com
http://www.charlesriver.com

This book is printed on acid-free paper

The Bryce 3D Handbook
by R. Shamms Mortier
    ISBN 1-886801-58-4
    Printed in the United States of America

98 99 00 01 7 6 5 4 3 2

DEDICATION

To Diane, Mic, and Ania

Contents

Foreword

Bryce 3D is one of the latest tools in a legacy that started with pigments applied to cave walls hundreds of thousands of years ago. It is a physical manifestation of: "In my mind's eye I see this."

If you think about it, the source of inspiration in all the visual arts comes from natural shapes, forms, colors, and light (a good reason for preserving as much of the natural world as possible). This was the source of inspiration for Eric Wenger when he created the original Bryce One. It was a simple idea really, create 3D graphic software that as closely as possible follows the dictates of nature in the creation of shape, form, color and light. The execution was of course far more complex, but a truly beautiful and powerful new tool was the end result of his hard work.

When we first began experimenting with Bryce for the creation of landscapes for "Planetary Traveler," we realized that we not only had a powerful tool, but an amazing "virtual reality" experience as well. We began referring to the Bryce artists on the project as "BryceLords." With this particular quirky little piece of software, the artist literally becomes lord of a world. The artist dictates the parameters for a world with the same elements "reality" uses, then watches over the world as it unfolds (or in this case renders). You become the "BryceLord" of what feels like a virtual world. Using the power of the computer and the elegance of natural laws together feels to me like part of the dawn of a new era of expression as experience.

For more information or to order a copy of Planetary Traveler on VHS or DVD. please visit www.thridplanet-inc.com or call us at 206-230-8010.

Jan C. Nickman
Producer/Director of "Planetary Traveler"

Acknowledgments

A book of this magnitude owes its existence to more than the author— but also to the many individuals whose help, guidance, and support assures its completion. Many such individuals are to be thanked for their efforts.

To Eric Wenger, whose vision and hard work brought Bryce into this world in the first place, thank you for taking the time to craft your ideas into a truly unique and wonderful piece of software.

To everyone at MetaCreations, and especially Teri Campbell, thank you for your efforts at adding all of the new features, especially the animation capabilities, to Bryce 3D.

To the Bryce masters whose work illuminates the pages in Chapter 13, Cecilia Ziemer and Mark Smith, thank you for contributing work, ideas, and perspectives that demonstrate new and exciting territory that Bryce 3D users can explore on their own.

To Jan Nickman, whose film "Planetary Traveler" allowed for the creation of a cosmic vision and the contributions of a world-class group of artists and animators, thank you for taking the time to write the beautiful foreword to this book. I have printed it out, and a copy rests on a wall of my studio.

Thanks to my agent at Waterside Productions, David Fugate, for searching out a way that a book that I was obsessed with doing could find a home.

Finally, thanks to Charles River Media and my editor, Jenifer Niles, and all of the staff who helped to shape the book into its final form, for providing the means by which the book could be written and presented to the marketplace.

Introduction

Welcome to the most full-featured book on MetaCreations' Bryce 3D. No matter what your skill level or experience with previous editions of the Bryce software, this book promises to deepen and enhance your learning and creative expertise.

Preparations

To be able to use this book effectively, you must be working familiar with Bryce 3D. That means that you will have, at the very least, worked through the tutorials and references in the Bryce 3D documentation, so you have an understanding of the basic parameters of the Bryce 3D tools and processes. Chapter 1 of this book does reference tool usage and can be used to refresh your memory, but it is not intended to supplant information in the documentation. Most references to Bryce 3D tools and their associated icons or menu listings in this book are meant to stretch your working knowledge of Bryce 3D beyond the basic information in the documentation and to build upon your basic knowledge. So read the documentation at least once, and work through all of the associated tutorials. You will find that in making preparations for this book, your appreciation of what is contained here, and this book's value, will be many times more useful.

YOU MUST HAVE THE FOLLOWING TO MAKE THIS BOOK USEFUL

The following items are essential if you are to get as much value out of this book as possible:

MetaCreations Bryce 3D

Obviously without the software, your appreciation of the contents of this book will be either nonexistent or severely limited. It is suggested that you not only purchase a copy of Bryce 3D or upgrade your existing Bryce 1 or 2 version, but that if you are a brand new user, you diligently work through the accompanying documentation before opening this book.

An Appropriate Computer Platform to Run the Bryce 3D Software

You will need a PowerMac or Pentium system to make creative use of Bryce 3D. The systems used in the creation of the book were a PowerMac 100 MHz computer and a Pentium 200 MHz system. The author found these to be adequate, with the Pentium being better for rendering the animations on the CD-ROM more effectively. Faster is always better when it comes to generating computer art and animation, and Bryce 3D is a very demanding application when it comes to rendering. If you can afford an acceleration card, that's better yet. If your computer runs at less than 100 MHz, your Bryce 3D interactions are going to be severely downgraded.

RAM

The more RAM (Random Access Memory) your computer can access with Bryce 3D, the better. More RAM allows for larger scenes that in turn render faster. The systems used in the creation of this book contained 172 MB (PowerMac) and 128 MB (Pentium) of RAM, respectively. Running Bryce 3D with less than 48 MB of RAM is not advisable.

CD-ROM Drive

CD-ROM drives are so commonplace today that one is probably already installed on your system. A 4X speed CD-ROM is the lowest speed drive you should be using, with 24X CD-ROM drives now becoming commonplace. Since all of the animations referenced in the book are included on the accompanying CD-ROM, you have to have a CD-ROM drive to utilize the book's contents effectively.

New Features in Bryce 3D

Compared to Bryce 2, Bryce 3D is a major upgrade. The first thing that separates the two, and the one most generally mentioned, is the addition of full-featured keyframe and path animation capability. But that's not all. There are also all of the following:

- Changes to the Materials and Textures palette, including a vastly expanded and updated library or presets.
- Sky and Fog settings with extended choices.

- Hyper Textures that add volumetric properties producing penetrable atmospheres that objects, cameras, or lights can move through.
- Moons with actual lunar map textures; phases of the moon from waning to waxing and other optical effects.
- Customized random star fields.
- Rainbows that simulate actual water vapor refractions.
- An Infinite slab in the primitives palette creates an infinite plane, scalable in depth, width, and breadth, allowing any volumetric property or texture to be applied to it.
- An advanced raytracing renderer and a shaded animation/still frame preview that takes advantage of Direct X5, Open GL, and a proprietary software acceleration application developed by MetaCreations.
- Animation: The simulation of real-world camera motion with a choice of several movement modes, rotation, curves, dips and fly-over motions; a new keyframe animation controller that offers full velocity control over each object's timeline, setting the keyframes to fit each adjustment; motion paths that can be edited and saved as preset "Ribbon Paths" and imported or exported.
- Import File Formats: DXF, 3DMF, and OBJ import allows Bryce to import simple polygonal models from programs like Poser and Detailer while maintaining their texture maps.
- Compatibility: Image saves in the following formats: AVI, Tiff, BMP (Windows), QuickTime, and Pict (Mac)

Pricing and Availability

One hybrid CD-ROM contains both Windows 95/NT and Power Macintosh formats, with DEC ALPHA coming in the future. Suggested Retail Price is US $299; upgrade price to registered users is US $99.

System Requirements

Macintosh: Power PC processor, Mac OS System 7.1 or later, 16 MB of available RAM, 50 MB of free hard drive space, CD-ROM drive, 16-bit video, color display.

Windows: Pentium or Pentium Pro-based processor, Windows 95/NT 3.5/NT 4, 16 MB of available RAM, 50 MB of free hard drive space, CD-ROM drive, 16-bit video, color display.

**The Book's
Structure**

This book has been carefully laid out into three comprehensive sections: Mastering the Bryce 3D Basics, Animating Your 3D Worlds, and Advanced Topics. Depending upon your level of skill as an experienced Bryce user and/or as a digital animator, you may desire to skip one section or another. Please do not do so. The reason for working through this whole book, no matter your experience level with Bryce or computer animation techniques, is that each section contains new and useful material for optimizing your Bryce 3D work.

SECTION I: MASTERING THE BRYCE 3D BASICS

This section of the book includes the following chapters:

Chapter 1: Preparing a Bryce 3D World.

This chapter deals with setting up Preference files and other needed items before you immerse yourself in the Bryce 3D creative process. An overview of many of the menu items and tool icons is also presented, so that cautions and suggestions can be given in order that your creative endeavors flow more smoothly. Again, this is not a repetition of the documentation (which you should be familiar with), but a way to call attention to ways to get you up and running quicker and more effectively.

Chapter 2: 3D Models.

This chapter focuses on differences and similarities among various types of 3D models used in Bryce 3D, and how they are constructed and manipulated. Also covered are Primitive Modeling Elements, Imported Modeling Elements, Multiple Replication Array Modeling, Ribbon-Path Arrays, Object Substitution Modeling, and Boolean Modeling.

Chapter 3: Terrain

Terrain models are a separate type of 3D model in Bryce 3D. Terrain models provide Bryce 3D with a personality distinguishable from any other 3D application on the market.

Chapter 4: Materials

This chapter covers Material Presets, Volumetric Presets, and the Refraction Index and its use. This chapter also covers the Materials Lab.

Chapter 5: Camera and Lights

Other than sunlight and moonlight capabilities (covered under atmospheric Effects in Chapter 7), Bryce 3D users have a host of options for customizing light objects and defining their parameters. This chapter also covers Camera

Types, Camera manipulation, and Camera f/x, including the use and function of the new Director's View.

Chapter 6: Atmospheric Effects

This chapter covers the new environmental effects options in Bryce 3D, as well as suggesting new ways to achieve similar effects. These include the capability to direct and place sunlight, moonlight, starlight, rainbows, and other environmental sky f/x components in your scenes.

SECTION II: ANIMATING YOUR 3D WORLDS

A comprehensive and detailed look at the Bryce 3D animation controls and techniques, variants, options, and possibilities is the focus of this section. We look at everything that can be animated in a Bryce 3D environment, and how to do it effectively for spectacular results.

Chapter 7: Bryce 3D Animation Basics

This chapter covers path and camera animation, and their association with Links and Targets.

Chapter 8: Earth, Water, Air, and Fire

This chapter shows you how to simulate and animate natural phenomena.

Chapter 9: Animating Objects: Singular, Composite, and Boolean

This chapter covers techniques for animating both Bryce 3D object primitives, as well as native composite objects and imported composite objects (like Poser figures). This chapter details the process using Bryce 3D Boolean operations and illustrates project uses.

Chapter 10: Mastering the Motion lab

This chapter contains everything you should know about using the Motion Lab to fine tune your Bryce 3D animations.

SECTION III: ADVANCED TOPICS

This section is devoted to detailing new ways to use Bryce 3D in the creation of sometimes unusual and novel projects and scene content.

Chapter 11: Wrong Materials for the Right Reasons

After learning the rules and following the standard practice on the application of materials and textures to 3D objects, it is important to stretch one's creative muscles. Techniques and examples, as well as animated samples on the CD-ROM, are included.

Chapter 12: Advanced Animation Techniques

Animating an imported object's parts sometimes presents problems, because the connective joints can appear disconnected when animated. Here is a unique way to prevent this from occurring. The chapter also covers the uses of Null objects.

Chapter 13: Hints, Tips, and Master Users

Two Bryce 3D master users are quoted here with advanced tips and advice, as well as insights into their own Bryce 3D uses and projects.

Chapter 14: Special Projects

Ten unique projects are included on the CD-ROM for your exploration and customization. They are detailed in this chapter.

Appendixes

Appendix A: CD-ROM Content
Appendix B: Web Output
Appendix C: Useful Add-ons
Appendix D: Other MetaCreations Applications
Appendix E: 3D File Format Translators
Appendix F: Post-Production Utilities
Appendix G: CD-ROM Content Libraries
Appendix H: User Bios
Appendix I: Upgrade

How to Use This Book

The way that you use this book, and the priority of the information contained in it, will necessarily depend upon how much experience you have had with both Bryce and computer art and animation. Here are some general categories that look at classes of users. If you would put yourself in one of these categories, you may find it helpful to use the associated text as a guide for exploring the book's contents.

THE EXPERIENCED BRYCE USER AND COMPUTER ANIMATOR

If you are an experienced Bryce 2 user and also have invested a good amount of time mastering your computer animation skills in other applications, you will find Bryce 3D easy to understand. Because Bryce 3D has tools and options not contained in other 3D applications, however, you should read this whole book. If you have studied the documentation, you can spend less time on Section I of this book, and most of Section II will be an easy read. Section III will probably be your main focus, since it explores new ways to apply Bryce 3D to specific projects. You should look at all of the animations and associated project files on this book's CD-ROM and customize them to your liking before re-rendering them.

THE BRYCE USER WITH LITTLE OR NO ANIMATION EXPERIENCE

If you are an experienced Bryce 2 user, but have no animation experience, then here is how you might benefit best from this book. Skim Section I, except where the new Bryce 3D tools and options are covered. Spend most of your initial time reading through and working from section II (after you have, of course, worked through the Bryce 3D animation documentation thoroughly). Since you are new to computer animation, save your study of Sections III until later, after you feel comfortable creating basic animations in Bryce 3D. After you have reached that comfort level, you can study and customize the animations and associated Bryce 3D projects contained on the book's CD-ROM.

THE EXPERIENCED COMPUTER ANIMATOR WITH NO PREVIOUS BRYCE EXPERIENCE

If you feel that this user category describes you best, then you can use this book to your best advantage by doing the following. Spend time learning Bryce 3D first, both from its documentation and from Section I of this book. When you have a good feel for how the general tools and options work, move on to Bryce 3D's animation capabilities. Remember that although your previous experience as a computer animator may have already given you a good understanding of the necessary vocabulary of the trade, Bryce 3D does some things differently than other 3D applications. Spend time learning about Bryce 3D Linking, and especially about the unique Bryce 3D Ribbon Paths. Compare Bryce 3D's animation options and methods with those you are already familiar with, and if necessary, jot down the differences and similarities for continued study.

THE EXPERIENCED COMPUTER 2D ARTIST WITH NO BRYCE OR 3D ANIMATION BACKGROUND

The great thing about Bryce 3D for 2D artists ready to move into 3D is that you can use the Bryce 3D presets to create astounding pictures with ease. For the 2D artist, creating (and printing out) Bryce pictures is the best way to familiarize yourself with the interface design and the tools. This is suggested before you move on to various 3D and animation options. In terms of your best way to work with this book, spend time with Section I. Reread it several times, and with the Bryce 3D documentation at your side, create a series of single images. When you feel ready to move into 3D and animation, do so slowly, so you can appreciate the options and power of each succeeding step along the way. You should also study as much animation as possible, on TV, in the movies, and on the Web. When you are ready, you can try to replicate some of the effects that you saw and found interesting. At that point, you will be ready to work through and customize the projects listed in section III of this book.

THE NOVICE USER WITH NO PREVIOUS EXPERIENCE IN COMPUTER ART OR ANIMATION

If you were attracted to the purchase of this book without knowing why, you have made a good choice. Before you can make good use of it, however, you will have to get accustomed to computer basics. This includes a familiarity with your system and its components. You may be an artist or animator whose experience includes art and/or animation with non-computer media. Bryce 3D is a great choice when moving from "traditional" to electronic media, since you can create amazing graphics with a minimum of study. More advanced projects will take deeper study and concentration, but that comes in time. When you are ready, and certainly after you have worked through the Bryce 3D documentation, work at a steady and comfortable pace through the examples presented in this book. You will be amazed at how quickly your efforts will result in beautiful images, and finally, in magical animations.

Get Ready for an Amazing Exploration

MetaCreations' Bryce 3D is an open-ended creative system. You can shape worlds that mimic the infinite variety and believability of nature with ease, taking as much time as you need to fine tune an immense and fantastic personal landscape. When completed, the results can be printed on paper for gallery presentations, sent to videotape or CD-ROMs for animated productions, or output to removable disk media for presentation to friends and associates.

Welcome to a world of your own making. Welcome to the magic realms of Bryce 3D.

Mastering the Bryce 3D Basics

CHAPTER

Preparing a Bryce 3D World

About Fractal Geometry

Bryce 3D is a member of a class of software applications known as *fractal scenery generators*, although it also contains a number of additional expanded features. Exactly what is a fractal scenery generator? To know the answer to this question, you must understand the term "fractal."

A fractal is a shape that has more than two but less than three dimensions. As opposed to two-dimensional objects whose perimeters can be finitely measured (like squares, circles, and other shapes), or three-dimensional shapes (like cubes, spheres, and other 3D volumes), fractal perimeters are infinite. That sounds very confusing, since we are accustomed to object dimensions existing only in whole numbers, making their boundaries simple to calculate. A two-dimensional object, for instance, has length and width, but no depth. By simply calculating a two-dimensional object's width and length, we can measure its boundary precisely. A 3D surface, has height, width, and depth, and its volumetric boundaries in 3D space can be precisely measured and known. Our perceptual world is filled with 3D objects, from those in nature to objects we create with our own hands and minds. Fractal dimensions, however, allow for shapes and objects that have parameters or boundaries that are new and somewhat disturbing to our understanding, boundaries that prove infinite under investigation.

The science of fractals is only a little more than a quarter of a century old. Though many investigators have contributed to the science of fractal geometry, Benoit Mandelbrot is usually credited with collecting, conceptualizing, and publicizing the language and importance of fractals. His work, done while he was a mathematician at IBM, resulted in a new language and a new paradigm of nature. This new language makes it possible to visualize basic fractal geometry, even with no prior mathematical background.

Let's do a visualization experiment that should result in your ability to understand the basic idea behind fractal geometry, why boundaries are considered to be infinite, and how fractals relate to our everyday perception of the natural world.

First, think of a coastline as observed from space, and imagine yourself looking at it while you sit in an orbiting ship. While you look at the coastline through the viewport of your spaceship, you are able to hold up a thin piece of tracing paper to the glass, and to trace the shape of the coastline with a sharp black marker.

Now pretend that you're looking at a section of the same coastline, only this time, you are standing on the edge of the sea. Your view is necessarily much "closer" than the view you had from space. In your hand is a special camera that can take a sharp picture of the area at your feet where the land meets the sea. You snap a picture and develop it. Then you look at the line traced by the camera that represents the land-sea boundary, and compare it to the line you traced of a wider expanse of the coastline from space. Incredible! There is an amazing similarity between both lines, even though the "distance" from the area to your eye is very different.

Seeking to push your observations and our example one step further, you return to the same place you were standing on the beach. In your possession is a special microscope. You lie down on the beach and focus in on a section of the land-sea boundary at 10x magnification. As the view comes into focus, you jolt backwards. Impossible! What you are seeing in miniature is a close match to the coastline you traced from space and the one you previously captured with your special camera. You crank the camera up to 100x, then 1000x, and then 100,000x. Astounded, you keep seeing close approximations to the same shape.

No matter how "close" you come to a fractal boundary in nature, you can never reach its end point. It just goes on forever, looking much the same as it did upon first observation. In a fractal scenery generator, natural phenomena are approximated and rendered through mathematical formulas that take advantage of the same "closeness" paradox just described.

A fractal scenery generator, like Bryce 3D, uses these and other special mathematical formulas (also called algorithms) to allow you to create very realistic and near-photographic natural phenomena, like clouds, water, and varied land masses. No matter how "close" you place your rendering camera to any natural form under your observation in Bryce 3D, the view always looks "real." As long as you understand and obey the conventions used in the Bryce 3D creative process (many of which are detailed in this book), detail is neither lost nor turned into blocky computer pixels in your renderings. In many respects, the natural world really seems to be a fractal world. No matter how close you get to organic objects in nature, aspects of their geometry seems to mimic the whole, to replicate it. Tree branches, for instance, look a lot like the whole tree, and in many cases, smaller branches are just smaller versions of the same tree. To be sure, all of this loses meaning at the atomic and sub-atomic level, but unless you are Superman or Superwoman (or a scientist with the latest viewing apparatus), you won't be able to appreciate that deeper environment anyway.

Bryce 3D is not the first fractal scenery generator to become available to computer artists and animators, but it is by far the easiest to understand and the most variable (as we shall prove by example). Bryce 3D does even more than allowing you to create images and animations that look photographically real, it also allows you to craft worlds that are purely imagination oriented, places that obey your own laws of physics and geometry; places where reality is obeys laws found nowhere else in the universe. These can be surrealistic places, where "real" elements (rocks, trees, mountains, water, and skies) do things that our Earth-bound laws of physics do not allow. You can integrate your own sculpted 3D objects into these worlds, from solid habitats to more organic-looking forms. This, as we will explore, is where your own unique abilities and visions push the edge.

Before You Begin

This chapter is devoted to optimizing your work in Bryce 3D. Although we touch upon every tool and menu item in the Bryce 3D interface, we do so with the intent to communicate new information on how you can work faster and better and do not attempt to explain the basic parameters of each tool. That is left to your reading and exploration of the Bryce 3D documentation, which absolutely has to take place before you start to work through this book. Without a prior reading of the Bryce 3D documentation, your ability to gather knowledge and meaning from this book will be severely limited. Our aim is to tell you what tools and menu items are especially important to your work in Bryce 3D, why they are important, and how to optimize their use.

NOTE

Remember: Reading and understanding the Bryce 3D documentation is absolutely vital to your work in this book. As a suggestion, it is best to devote a week to exploring the documentation and working through all of the tutorials. That way, you can use this book for its intended purpose, which is to take you beyond the basics into unexplored and exciting creative territory.

The Document Setup Screen

Configuring the options listed in the setup screen (Document Setup in the File menu, or the downward-pointing arrow at the bottom of the left-hand toolbar) is a necessary first step when entering the Bryce 3D environment. See Figure 1.1.

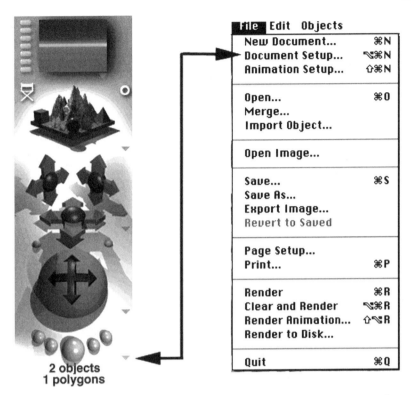

FILE Edit Objects

New Document...   ⌘N
Document Setup...   ⌥⌘N
Animation Setup...   ⇧⌘N

Open...   ⌘O
Merge...
Import Object...

Open Image...

Save...   ⌘S
Save As...
Export Image...
Revert to Saved

Page Setup...
Print...   ⌘P

Render   ⌘R
Clear and Render   ⌥⌘R
Render Animation...   ⇧⌥R
Render to Disk...

Quit   ⌘Q

2 objects
1 polygons

FIGURE *You may access the Document Setup screen from two places in Bryce 3D. Either*
1.1 *from the File menu (File/Document Setup), or by left-mouse clicking (clicking and holding on the Mac) on the bottom-most downward-pointing arrow in the left-hand Toolbar.*

NOTE

Note that on a Mac with less than an 800 × 600 screen size, the only way to access the Document Setup screen may be from the File menu and the bottom arrow in the left-hand toolbar may not show all of the options.

The layout of the Document Setup screen's dialog is easier to navigate when it is accessed from the File menu, although accessing the listing from the arrow in the toolbar is a little quicker. Either way, the options listed are the same. When you access the dialog from the File menu, either on a Mac or Windows system, the appearance of the dialog is as shown in Figure 1.2.

Document Setup

Default ◯
Max Recommended ◯
Small ◯
Square ◯
Standard ◯
Panorama ◯
QTVR Panorama ◯
Letter ◯
Legal ◯
A4 ◯
Photo ◯
35mm Slide ◯
Super 8mm ◯
16mm ◯
Super 16mm ◯
Cine 35mm ◯
Cinemascope ◯
VistaVision ◯
65mm ◯
IMAX ◯
70mm ◯
Techniscope ◯

Untitled

Document Resolution   480 X 360

Document Aspect Ratio   4 : 3
✓ *Constrain Proportions*

✓ **AntiAliasing** ● *Normal* ◯ *Superfine*
◯ *Report Render Time*

Render Resolution
1 : 0.25   120 x 90
1 : 0.50   240 x 180
1 : 1.00   480 x 360
1 : 1.50   720 x 540
1 : 2.00   960 x 720
1 : 3.00   1440 x 1080
1 : 4.00   1920 x 1440

✗ ✓

FIGURE **1.2** *The Documentation Setup Screen as it appears when accessed from the File menu, showing the selectable options.*

Document Resolution / Aspect Ratio versus Render Resolution

The most important decision in the Document Setup screen dialog is how you configure the Document Resolution and the associated Aspect Ratio. The Document Resolution sets up your Bryce 3D scene as it appears on your monitor. If your monitor cannot display this resolution because of its own limitations, the setting will not take place on the Bryce 3D screen. Along the right-hand side of this dialog is a listing of common sizes for a variety of output options, ranging from standard settings to multimedia to a number of film sizes. Clicking on any one of these options changes your Document Setting to match that choice. For instance, selecting the 35mm Slide option changes the Document Resolution to 480 × 320 pixels, and the Aspect Ratio to 3 × 2. In the Render Resolution list that follows, various multiples of that resolution are given. At a Render Resolution of 1, the rendering will be the same as the Document Resolution, or 480 × 320 pixels. At a Render Resolution of 4 (four times larger than the Document Resolution), the setting is for 1920 × 1280 pixels. Explained further, this means that you are working on the Document Resolution Screen at 480 × 320, but that your rendering will be four times as fine as the working screen. Larger renderings take more time, but allow for much clearer output. Your selections here depend on where your Bryce 3D renderings are to be displayed.

COMMON DISPLAY CONVENTIONS

Unless you are using Bryce 3D for high-end film work, you will probably select to output to multimedia (CD-ROM), videotape (NTSC or PAL, with a coming tendency to select digital TV formats as well), or print media. Table 1.1 shows you which Bryce 3D formats to select for various output mediums.

RENDERING LARGER SIZES VERSUS ANTIALIASING

In the Document setup screen dialog is an Antialiasing option. Antialiasing gets rid of the jaggies in a rendering, places where the angles of a rendered element are too severe to allow for a smooth look. But antialiasing comes at a time cost in any 3D application. There are three options here: no antialiasing, "normal" antialiasing, and superfine antialiasing. Normal antialiasing can add anywhere from a few minutes to double the total rendering time to a Bryce 3D animation or rendered picture. Superfine antialiasing, except for very high-end film or print work, should be avoided at all costs. It can easily quadruple the rendering time needed for a picture, or for each frame in an animation.

In many cases, however, there is another option for making your output look clearer and more crisp: doubling the size of your rendered image or animation frame beyond what is required, and then reducing the size later in a suitable editing application. This is really an old trick, used by print media artists since the turn of the century. It may have first come into practice by the Sunday comics artists, who usually worked at four to ten times the needed output size, allowing the camera to reduce the size of their work prior to printing. In the case of digital work, all you need is a post-production application that will do the reduction for you.

The most common applications used for post-production applications are: Adobe Premier (Mac and Windows), Adobe After Effects (Mac and Windows), Strata Videoshop (Mac and Windows), and Ulead's Media Studio version 5 (Windows). You may find other suitable commercial or shareware applications that also allow for these post-production operations. See Appendix G at the end of the book for more details.

TABLE 1.1   Bryce 3D Settings for Output Options

Output Purpose	Bryce 3D Setting	Constrained Ratio	Rendering Suggestions
Multimedia (CD-ROM)	Standard	4×3	Render at 320×240, or 1/2 of the standard 640×480 setting. Antialiasing can be set to none.
Video and Television	Photo	3×2 (Note that digital TV sizes are still in debate, with a likelihood that 4×3 or even 5×3 may be the best fit)	Render at a ratio of 1:1 or 768×512. This will result in some necessary bleed at the borders of your renders, about 25 pixels on each side and top-bottom, places where the image will not be shown on-screen. Make allowances for this when designing the scene and animating. Antialiasing should be set to normal.
Web Display	Standard Another option is either Panorama or QTVR (Quicktime VR) Panorama, for interactive virtual reality sites.	4×3 Panorama is 8×3 and QTVR Panorama is 13×4 ratios	Render at 1:0.25, or 160×120 pixels. If your intended browsers are QuickTime enabled, render as a QuickTime movie. If you are going to need a GIF animation, render as single frames, and translate to a GIF movie in a suitable translation application. Antialiasing should be set to none
Print Media	Selection is determined by the maximum output of the printer or printing press being addressed, with common choices including square, letter, legal, and A4.	Determined by Bryce 3D settings at left	Render at the highest resolution needed by the medium you are addressing. Antialiasing should be set to normal or superfine.
Photographic Slide (Output to a suitable film recorder)	35mm Slide	3×2	Render at the 4X setting as a bare minimum for clarity: 1920×1280. Antialiasing should be set to normal.
High-end Recorder (for motion picture film)	Selection is determined by the needs of the display medium being addressed, with common choices including Super 8mm, 16mm, Super 16mm, Cine 35mm, Cinemascope, VistaVision, 65mm, IMAX, 70mm, and Techniscope.	Determined by Bryce 3D settings at left	Render at the highest resolution needed by the medium you are addressing. Antialiasing should be set to superfine.

Always work at the maximum screen size possible, even when the output rendering is set for 1/2 or 1/4 of that size. This allows you to see what you are doing better so your "actors" (models and other elements) can be manipulated clearly, especially when the scene becomes very complex.

CONSTRAIN PROPORTIONS

Usually you will leave this option checked (on), since it allows you to put in one dimension while the computer automatically configures the other dimension according to the aspect ratio that is set. There are times, however, when you want direct control over both the width and height of the screen and the rendering, perhaps for a special print size for a calendar or a graphic in a magazine. If that happens, turn the Constrain off (uncheck it) and enter the exact dimension (in pixels) by hand.

REPORT RENDER TIME

This option is useful for first test renderings, but after that, it can be turned off. There is no need to get a report on render times with each test render you do, since you will do many test renders in an involved scene to get lights and camera angles the way you want them. If necessary, you can toggle this item on again at various points in the scene development process. Unless you start to apply a lot of transparent textures in your scene or make other radical changes, the render time first reported will remain about the same. Rendering times start to differ from one frame to the next when the camera moves to encompass an entirely new perspective, one that might involve new rendering challenges. Other than that, render time reports are only approximate at best. See Figure 1.3.

Render Report

Untitled		
Total Render Time:		Per Pixel
01:20		
Pixels Rendered:	172800	
Pixels AntiAliased:	0	
Primary Rays:	172800	1.00
Shadow Rays:	90511	0.52
Total Rays:	263311	1.52
Ray Hits:	147282	0.85
Ray Misses:	257503	1.49
Total Intersect Attempts:	404785	2.34

FIGURE **1.3** *The Render Report lists the rendered pixels in the scene and all the information you might wish to know concerning the raytracing used in the rendering.*

Edit/Preferences

The Preferences item under the Edit menu brings up a small dialog with a few very valuable options that help you optimize Bryce 3D further, shaping it to the way you work. Four options are listed in this dialog (Figure 1.4).

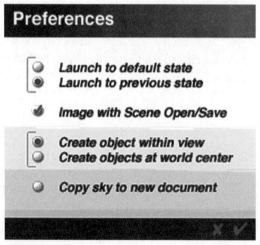

Preferences

- Launch to default state
- Launch to previous state

✓ Image with Scene Open/Save

- Create object within view
- Create objects at world center

- Copy sky to new document

FIGURE **1.4** *The Preferences dialog under the Edit menu lists four options that can optimize your work.*

LAUNCH TO DEFAULT OR PREVIOUS STATE

If you have a favorite resolution, **Launch to previous state**. Each time Bryce 3D opens a new file, your resolution preferences from the last session will be applied. If you would rather set the resolution each time, click the **Launch to default state**.

IMAGE WITH SCENE OPEN/SAVE

It is suggested that you leave this item checked. When checked, each time you save a Bryce 3D file, the last rendering you did is saved as a PICT (Mac) or BMP (Windows) graphic.

When saving a Bryce 3D project file on the Mac, include the Bryce 3D extension required by Bryce 3D on Windows. That way, you can always port your creations back and forth from either platform. Bryce 3D on Windows adds this extension automatically, while the Mac does not normally require any extension to be added to file names.

CREATE OBJECT WITHIN VIEW OR AT WORLD CENTER

This is a very important option. I suggest that you select to create new objects **Within the View** rather than at the **World Center**. This allows you to see the object on-screen immediately, no matter where the camera is pointing at the moment, and to place new objects very close to where you want them with less movement required. When a scene gets very complex, as can happen fairly quickly in Bryce 3D, you can move to an empty part of the scene, far from any other objects. Having selected the **Within View** option, you can create and texture your object in a space free of the confusion from other objects. If necessary to move it into the more cluttered part of a scene, this can be accomplished afterwards.

COPY SKY TO NEW DOCUMENT

Turn this option on when the new document will be woven together with the one you just completed. Skies can be time-consuming to configure. Though they can be saved, this option can be used to make the flow of your work run more smoothly. It is usually left off, since new Bryce 3D scenes are usually not connected to each other. Every situation is different however, and it's nice to have this option when needed.

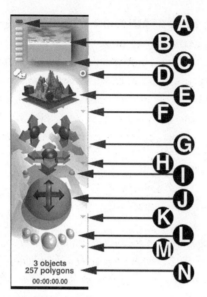

FIGURE   *The configuration of the left-hand toolbar.*
1.5

The Left-hand Toolbar

Figure 1.5 shows the tools you will access most in Bryce 3D as you build your scene.

We are not going to repeat the basic information on the left-hand toolbar usage here. You should read the Bryce 3D documentation as far as learning the basics are concerned. What we will do is to point out options and suggestions not found in the documentation or not emphasized enough.

A. MEMORY DOTS

Exactly how you use the memory dots depends upon your work habits. I suggest that you definitely make use of them, since they can speed up the process of switching from one view to the next. I noticed, for instance, that when I design a Bryce 3D scene, I am constantly switching to different views in the following prioritized order: Camera, Top, Right, and Front. I use the other options far less frequently. These four views then become the views I place in the top four memory dot spaces, exactly in that order. That way, I can click on a memory dot and be transported instantly to that view, rather than selecting the view from the view list.

A second use of memory dots is to store alternate camera placement when your scene gets large. You can, for instance, easily design a Bryce 3D world that covers hundreds or even thousands of virtual acres. Perhaps you have a city, flanked by outlying townships or other points of interest. It is a chore to move the camera manually each time you want to visit another area in your world. So, set up alternate cameras beforehand. Each click on an associated memory dot will instantly present that view through the camera, allowing you to edit just that area of your world quickly.

B. NANO PREVIEW

Though you can turn Auto Update on in the Nano Preview list, I would suggest that you leave it off. As the Nano Preview is rendering, other operations come to a halt. This prevents you from continuing your creative pursuits. I would suggest that the best way to use the Nano Editor is to click inside it when you need to see a rendered version of your world. It's also advisable to remember that clicking anywhere on a blank portion of the screen halts the Nano Preview. This is helpful when you have seen enough, even though the edit is only partially complete. The Nano Editor is especially helpful when adjusting the lights and general contrast of a scene.

C. NANO OPTIONS LIST

The most useful items in the Nano Options list, other than the view selections already covered, are the three choices you have for Nano Rendering: Sky Only, Full Scene, and Wireframe. Click on Sky Only when you are designing a sky and don't need to preview anything else in the scene. Full Scene should be chosen 99% of the time. Selecting Wireframe is fairly useless, as the view is far too small to do you any good.

D. FLYAROUND

At first glance, you might think that this feature is nothing but eye candy, a way of getting a cheap thrill by watching your scene spin in 3D space. You can, however, make use of this feature by noticing what global camera angles might prove to be interesting when it comes time to render the scene as you see it from different angles.

E. VIEW CONTROL TOOL

It's usually far better and more efficient to use the memory dots whenever possible to change views, rather than this tool icon. Clicking on it marches you through the view options in sequential order, but holding the mouse down while dragging on it flips through the various views. For Bryce 3D users who feel comfortable in visual interactions only and experienced game players who enjoy the interactive magic this tool provides, it might be a better choice than either memory dots or using the verbal view list. In presenting the user with many ways to get the same result, Bryce 3D can accommodate any designer's personality.

F. VIEW CONTROL LIST

It's far better to use the memory dots whenever possible to change views, rather than the listings presented here. Use this list, or the View Control tool, only when a memory dot does not yet hold your selected view, or when the memory dots are full.

G. CAMERA CROSS CONTROLS

These controls represent Bryce 3D's virtual joystick and can be used to fine tune your needed camera view. Remember that they can't be used when you are in anything but the Camera View or the Director's View. Practice before using them in a project, though users who are familiar with interactive games may get the hang of their use quicker.

NOTE

*A Note about the Director's View: This option is new to Bryce 3D. It allows you to work in perspective with more options than the Camera View. The most important item in the View Options list (which follows) are those marked **Camera >> Director's** and **Director's >> Camera**, as far as the Director's View is concerned. These options allow you to snap the Director's view to the camera view, and vice versa, so that whatever manipulations you carry out while in the Director's View can be forced to be the same as the Camera View. This is important because it allows you to move the camera into place with the additional freedom offered while working in the Director's View. You can think of the Director's View as an exploratory perspective window. Until you commit your alterations to the Camera View (by selecting **Camera >> Director's**), nothing you do will affect the scene. The Director's view can always be reset to the present Camera default position by selecting **Director's >> Camera**.*

Remember that the Director's and Camera Views can be alternated by simply clicking on the camera or Director's icons below the Memory Dots.

H. CAMERA CROSS CONTROL OPTION

It's easy to get lost in a Bryce 3D world when scenes become overly complex. You may want to get a specific object in view but find it time consuming to zoom and move the scene to the correct position. When this happens, use one of the following:

- **Center Scene.** Use this command to reset the scene's center to the center of your working screen. It's a great option when you have been working far off in the distance and want to get back to ground zero.
- **Center Selection.** Use this command to center your working screen on any selected object or object group. This is a vital command when you want to do additional editing on an object or its material.
- **Eye Level Camera.** Use this setting to drop the camera to the ground, especially when you need to bring it back to a default location.

*When you select the **Eye Level Camera** command, the camera drops to eye level, and maintains the keyframe setting already allocated to it. Attempting to set a new keyframe has no effect on the camera. If you rotate it in space, it uses the preset keyframe point as the camera center. Section II in this book. This is because the keyframe point for the camera is its Origin Point. You must reset the camera's Origin Point (numerically or manually) to the new eye level position to have the camera rotate around this adjusted point.*

Editing the Current Camera

With the Camera View selected, the Edit Current Camera command brings up a dialog with three tabs: General, Linking, and Animation. We will cover Linking and Animation later in this section, so let's dwell on a few points related to the information in the General tab. See Figure 1.6.

The Bryce 3D documentation explains the basic operations listed under the General tab in the Edit Current Camera dialog quite thoroughly, so make sure you read and understand what it says, because the complete details are not repeated here.

You can tell if you are in Camera View if the only Camera Mode option available to you in the left column is **Free.** You should always leave two

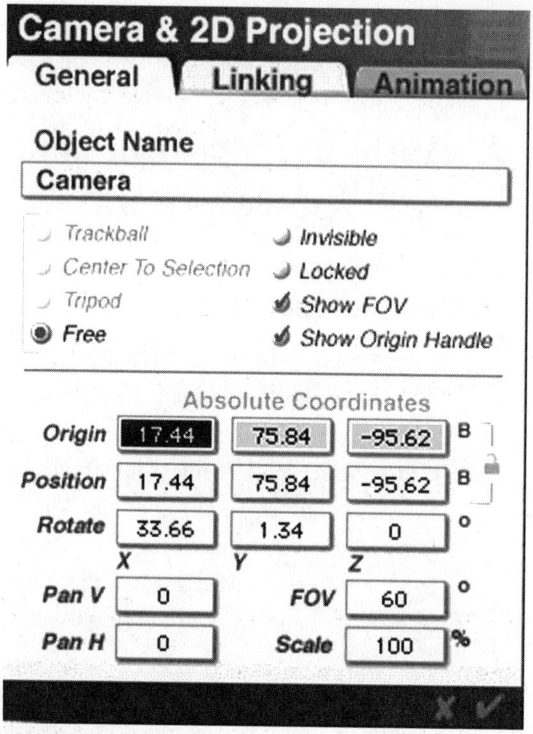

Camera & 2D Projection

General | Linking | Animation

Object Name

Camera

- Trackball
- Center To Selection
- Tripod
- ● Free

- Invisible
- Locked
- ✓ Show FOV
- ✓ Show Origin Handle

Absolute Coordinates

	X	Y	Z	
Origin	17.44	75.84	-95.62	B
Position	17.44	75.84	-95.62	B
Rotate	33.66	1.34	0	°

Pan V | 0 | FOV | 60 | °
Pan H | 0 | Scale | 100 | %

FIGURE 1.6 *The General tab in the Current Camera Edit dialog, with the camera View selected.*

items in the right-hand column checked: **Show FOV** and **Show Origin Handle**. FOV, Field of Vision, must be checked so you can manipulate this camera attribute in an animation (see Section II, Chapter 18 in this book). The Origin Handle determines the point that acts as a fulcrum for camera rotations and so should be made visible at all times.

I. BANK AND ZOOM

Just under and to either side of the XZ Cross Control are two small buttons, which are not mentioned much in the Bryce 3D documentation, but they are extremely important to your animation work. The one on the left is a banking control, while the one on the right controls the camera zoom. These controls work by dragging the mouse over them (left and right), and they are only accessible in either the Director's or Camera View. Both controls affect the animation only when accessed by the Camera View, so if you use them in the Director's View, you will have to use the command **Camera >> Director** to apply them to the camera.

Bank is very important for simulating flight, because banking an aircraft as it turns creates a far more realistic feeling of flying. Zooming in on an element of interest can create an entire animation, since zooming in also accentuates the zoomed detail of an object.

J. CAMERA TRACKBALL

Gamers will have an easy time adjusting to the use of this tool. See the **Trackball** option in the Camera Modes list that follows.

K. CAMERA MODES LIST

Only in the Director's View mode is it possible to access all of the Camera Modes, emphasizing the importance of the Director's View. The only option allowed in Camera View is Free Camera; working in the Director's View allows three more important options for optimizing your work and creating specific types of animations:

- **Trackball.** This is the item to choose when you want to create an animation that is similar to the Flyaround option. It locates the camera so that it is focused on the global center of the scene, allowing you to orbit the scene by using the Trackball. Set this option while in the Director's View and set the keyframes (if this term is new to you, reread the documentation and see Section II in this book). After setting each keyframe, select **Camera >> Director's**, then set the next keyframe in the Director's View.

- **Center to Selection.** This is the item to choose when you want to create an animation that orbits a selected object in the scene. It locates the camera so that it is focused upon the selected object in the scene, allowing you to orbit the object by using the Trackball. You could, for instance, use this option to orbit one selected building in a cityscape. Set this option while in the Director's View and set the keyframes. After setting each keyframe, select **Camera >> Director's**, then set the next keyframe in the Director's View.

- **Tripod.** This is the item to choose when you want to create an animation that simulates a camera attached to a tripod. It locates the camera so that it is securely fastened to a tripod, allowing you to view the scene from that vantage point by using the Trackball to rotate (but not move) the camera in 3D space. The **Tripod** option is best used in conjunction with the **Eye Level camera** selection in the camera Cross Control options list.

L. RENDER CONTROLS

This grouped array of five buttons controls single picture rendering (rendering an animation is controlled by selecting the **Render Animation** command from the File menu). From left to right, they are: Texture toggle, Fast Preview toggle, Render, Resume Render, and Clear and Render. Some considerations for their use follows.

- Use the first button to turn textures off when you need to see how light placement is affecting the objects in your scene. The rendering takes place faster, and you can see how shadow and light cones overlap much more clearly.
- If you have complex textures in your scene and need a preview render, selecting the Fast Preview button doesn't make much sense. It gives you a poorer idea of what the textures look like, and still takes its time to show you the results. If you need to preview the look of textures, use the middle Render button.
- Use Resume Render when you have partially rendered a scene and have decided to move or add an object without moving the camera. This can be a real time saver.
- Clear and Render is of dubious use. It's just as good to hit the Center Render button when a complete rerender is called for.

Plop Rendering

Plop Rendering is available only in Bryce, and it is without question one of the most valuable rendering tools you have if you are rendering a single picture. The Bryce 3D Plop Renderer has its own Render and Resume Render controls. Here's how Plop Rendering works.

1. Make sure a rendered or partially rendered picture is showing on your screen.
2. With the mouse, click and drag (left mouse button for Windows users) a rectangle over a section of the picture. A rectangular frame will become evident, with two buttons attached.

FIGURE *Here is a sample of the Plop Rendering operation, with the new rendering frame*
1.7 *in place over a prerendered picture.*

3. Select new settings options (usually antialiasing). Click the top button to rerender the content in the frame.
4. Click on the downward pointing triangle below the Plop Render buttons, and select **Hide Selection**. Your rerendered frame borders become invisible, and the section becomes a part of the original picture. See Figure 1.7.

Why Is Plop Rendering Important?

Plop Rendering is important for three reasons.

1. To render an antialiased section of a picture that you want to preview without rendering the whole picture.
2. To rerender sections of a picture that could benefit by antialiasing, when the rest of the picture looks fine without antialiasing.
3. To render a new object placed in the scene, after the scene has been rendered (antialiasing should remain the same, and the camera should not have been moved).

There is a caution to observe when applying Plop Renders to a picture with different antialiasing settings involved. The Plop Renderer works within rectangular borders, so whatever appears inside has to blend completely with the part of the picture the Plop Rendering is placed over. Doing a Plop Render on something sitting on a cloudy sky and turning on antialiasing, when the rest of the cloudy sky was not antialiased, will result in a distinct and observable difference between the Plop Rendered section and the rest of the picture. So look closely at the section of the image you are Plop Rendering and pay attention to that portion where the Plop Render borders meet the rest of the image.

A Brand New Way to Use Plop Rendering

A true artist learns the rules thoroughly and then explores what can result when the rules are broken or stretched. Be careful to NEVER move the camera or change the basic background accidentally when doing a Plop Render over a prerendered picture, but moving the camera on purpose can actually lead to some interesting composite montages. Here's what to do:

1. Render a scene with no objects, but with a interesting sky and ground involved, with antialiasing set to the Normal option.
2. Place a Plop Render frame over part of the background, making sure that a section of sky and ground are included. Go to the Sky Presets, and select a different sky. Rerender the Plop Render section.
3. Repeat step two as many times as you like, each time on a different section of the image, changing the material of the ground plane and the sky preset. Add an image to the scene if you like, and render part of it over other prerendered sections with the Plop Renderer.
4. When you are satisfied with the montage, save the finished graphic to disk (Export the image).

With this method, and the infinite ways you can customize it, you can use Bryce 3D as a superlative image compositing application. See Figures 1.8 and 1.9.

Another exploration of this method would be to render a scene in daylight, and then Plop Render half of the scene at night, or perhaps half in summer and half in winter.

FIGURE   *Using the methods described above, this composited montage was created by*
1.8   *altering the sky and ground looks and then Plop Rendering the sections.*
         Materials on the spheres were also changed between renders.

Attention! Undocumented Feature

Plop Rendering is only referenced in the documentation for pictures, not animations. But guess what? It also works with animated renderings. If you thought the montage feature mentioned previously was neat, wait till you explore Plop Animations. Here's how:

1. Create and render a scene, with any elements you wish. As a first exploration, try a simple scene with basic textures so it renders quickly.
2. After the scene has rendered, create a 30-frame animation. Move one of the elements in the scene, so that it changes location from frame 1 to frame 30.
3. Place a Plop Render frame over the section of the scene that shows the animated object. DO NOT hit the Render button on the Plop Render frame.
4. Go to the **Save Animation** command in the File menu and select a name and file destination. Render the animation.
5. The Plop Render frame's contents will render as an animation, and the rest of the image will remain as it was previously rendered as a still frame.

A

B

FIGURE 1.9 *A. The scene is rendered with the objects in place and a mirrored sphere reflecting the whole environment. B. The same scene is Plop Rendered. This time, the objects have been removed, but the mirrored sphere still shows them. Only the bottom half of the image has been Plop Rendered, so the tops of the objects look like they have been placed on the horizon, which is an effect impossible to achieve in any other way.*

TIP

*See the Ploperz1 project and the Ploperz1 movie on the book's CD-ROM as an
example of this effect.*

M. DOCUMENT SETUP LIST

We have covered this item previously. Document Setup is best accessed here
as opposed to the File menu since it is quicker. Remember that a Mac with
less than a monitor setting of 600 × 800 may effectively disable your ability
to use this list. In that case, simply bring up the Setup options from the File
menu (File/Setup Document).

N. DATA AREA

In most cases you will find the data display area to be of little use, except as
a diversion to watch while an image or animation is rendering. It can, however, provide important information concerning the difference of rendering
times involved when antialiasing is set to none or normal.

The Top Toolbars

There are three toolbars that you can toggle among at the top of the Bryce
3D interface. Though their general use and purpose is well documented in
the Bryce 3D manual, here are some additional items about each of them
that you will want to take notice of.

CREATE TOOLBAR NOTES

See Figure 1.10.

FIGURE *The Create toolbar allows you instant access to Bryce 3D object creation. From*
1.10 *left to right: Water, Sky, and Ground Planes; Terrain, Rock, Mirrored Terrain;
Sphere, Elongated Sphere, Torus, Cylinder, Cubic, Tetrahedron, Cone, Flat
Plane; Lights.*

Here are some things to explore and keep in mind concerning the Create Toolbar items:

- Be careful about building animated objects with Bryce 3D primitive objects. They tend to skew when rotated and can add hours of frustration to your endeavors. It's best to use the Bryce 3D primitives for stable objects in a scene and imported Wavefront (OBJ) or DXF objects for animation purposes.

- The documentation makes no mention that the infinite planar objects (the Water, Cloud, and Ground planes) can be rotated in space. You can also stack any number of these planes, making some transparent to others farther away from the camera. To create a riverbed, for example, stack a Water plane on top of a Ground plane. Texture the Water and Ground planes as you like and add a 60% or more transparency to the water plane. At various camera angles your riverbed will show through.

- Another effect not mentioned in the documentation is that you can apply Boolean operations on infinite planes. This is covered by example in Chapter 2.

- Use the same Terrain object for background mountain ranges. Just duplicate, and rotate, and possibly resize the original. You'll be surprised how different a single terrain object can appear when rotated just a few degrees.

See Chapter 3 of this book for a detailed look at Terrain modeling.

NOTE

- If you need to build a cityscape from these primitive objects, make sure it contains more than just rectangular or cubic objects. This is especially true if your urban environment is supposed to emulate a future city. Use hemispheres sunk in the ground and stack nonlinear elements on top of cubic ones. Bryce 3D primitives can offer you a myriad optional looks if you spend some time exploring the possibilities.

- Use a flat disk in the distant sky to emulate a sun or planet. Although Bryce 3D allows you to configure the sun and moon (see Chapter 7 on Environmental Effects), these sky objects are confined to earth parameters and laws. It's much quicker to use a flat disk most of the time, and you can customize the texture easily.

- As an alternative to Boolean models (see Chapter 2), think about using the flat rectangular plane to build a box with a hinged (linked) top.

You'll be able to see the exact shape of the box and its inside. This is not possible when using Boolean modeling to configure a similar object.

- Although designing with Lights is covered thoroughly in Chapter 6, remember that lights can be grouped and linked. This leads to all manner of effects, especially using lights as part of vehicles in an animation.

The Object Libraries in the Create Toolbar

As you are aware from a reading of the Bryce 3D documentation and your own explorations, the downward pointing arrow next to the word "Create" allows you to access the object libraries. See Figure 1.11.

When working with the Object Libraries, here are some important tips:

- Import Boolean objects sparingly. They are impossible to see in Bryce 3D, appearing as the grouped primitives from which they were constructed.
- Terrain objects can be used vertically as well as horizontally in a Bryce scene, and this library collection has many novel examples. Terrain objects also contain a lot of polygons, so if you are working with a limited amount of memory, try not to import too many.
- The Rock objects can be used as much as you like, with the same memory cautions as Terrain objects. Be wary of the Tree Objects, however, since they are constructed by using materials with various transparency settings. This costs you in rendering time. Many of the Tree objects are also Boolean constructs. See Appendix C of this book for a look at Tree Professional from Onyx Software. With Tree Pro, you can design and import far more realistic trees into Bryce 3D.
- The Path library items can be used for animation paths and also (as we show in Chapter 2) for object creation. There are some wonderful Path examples here, and with Bryce 3D's capability of treating Paths like objects, an infinite number of worlds are just a click away.
- There are a number of primitive forms in Bryce 3D's Imported Objects library. They render quickly, take textures without a hitch, and can be used to extend your composite creations. Use them as often as necessary.
- Get used to saving your models regularly. You can save them to your Bryce 3D folder, in one of the included libraries, or (recommended) save them to an external source. In no time, you will have amassed your own customized model libraries.

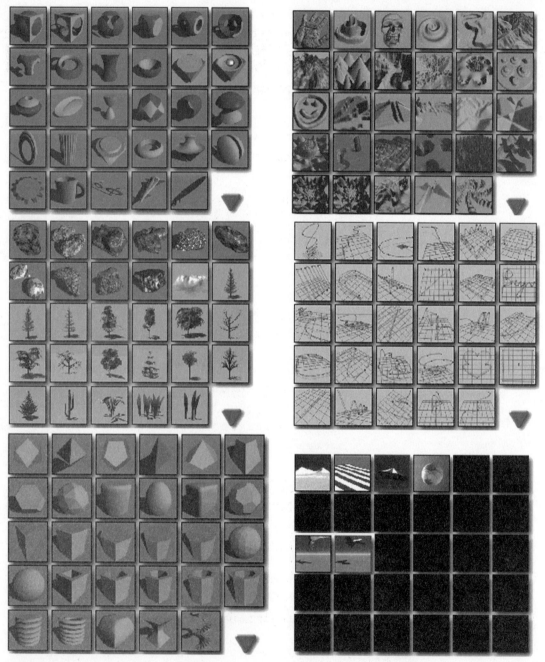

FIGURE   *The Object libraries contain a number of diverse object resources, and you can always add your own. Bryce 3D*
1.11   *ships with hundreds of objects to start your world creating tasks. Included are Booleans, Mountains, Rocks and*
          Trees, Paths, Imported Objects, and spaces for your own creations (though you can also add objects to any library).

FIGURE   *The Edit toolbar has seven icons: Materials Lab, Resize, Rotate, Reposition,*
1.12   *Align, Disperse, and the Terrain Editor. The almost invisible double arrows at*
the top right access object substitution.

EDIT TOOLBAR NOTES

See Figure 1.12.

Here are some things to explore and keep in mind concerning the Edit toolbar items.

Materials Lab

- Use the list, accessed by the arrow at the bottom of this icon, to quickly choose either 2D or 3D materials editing.

Note that the Materials Editor is detailed in Chapter 5 of this book.

NOTE

Resize

- The quickest way to resize an object that needs customized resizing is to resize it globally first, followed by shortening or elongating the needed axis.
- Resize primitive objects before you rotate them, or skewing may result. Skewing may be prevented in many cases by selecting **Object Space** instead of **Global Space** from the list that can be accessed from the downward-pointing arrow beneath the icon.
- Remember that global resizing is a great animation tool. Something that appears smaller in an animation seems to be farther in the distance from the camera. You can often place objects fairly close to the camera and, by making them smaller, create the illusion of distance. See Section II on animation.

Rotate

- There is a big difference between selecting multiple objects (Shift-selecting them) and selecting multiple objects that have been grouped when it comes to rotating them. Shift-selected multiple objects rotate individually, while grouped objects rotate around a common axis. This leads to very different animation effects.

- It is advisable to stick to one rotation mode whenever possible, accessed from the arrow beneath the Rotation icon (**Object Space, World Space,** or **Camera Space**). This is because each of the Rotation handles in this icon work very differently in each space, and confusion is the mother of frustration, especially in a complex animation. If you have to alternate between rotation spaces, attend to the following:

Object Space centers the rotation axis upon the object's original rotation parameters. If the object is an imported object, the object's rotation axis can differ from Bryce 3D primitive objects. **Object Space** is a good alternative when you notice an object skewing under World Space, and is usually a better choice when the object is to be animated.

World Space is the best choice for aligning objects to their global environment, as when placing Terrain objects on the ground plane. In general, use **World Space** to rotate objects that will remain stable in an animation.

Camera Space can be used after you have explored camera banking. Selecting **Camera Space** moves all selected objects in relation to whatever the altered camera angles have become. This is the trickiest of all three options.

Reposition

- Use the Reposition options when the selected object is either or both small and/or it is in the midst of a confusing array of other objects. The Repositioning options are best used to move objects out of the way so they can be edited or moved to a clearer space. Whenever repositioning an object with the mouse leads to the constant selection of the wrong object, use the Repositioning tool as a needed aid.

Align

- The biggest confusion in the use of this tool is the difference between "ground" and "land." Ground is defined as the ever-present and invisible ground boundary, while land is an infinite plane. Snapping a selected object to the ground will bypass any intervening objects.
- **Snapping to Land** can be used to move an object to any layer of a stack of objects beneath that object. Using **Snap to Land** after you have reached the bottom-most object will snap the object to the invisible

Ground plane. **Snapping to Land**, when a plane or object is beneath this invisible boundary, will not work.

Disperse

The Disperse tool is one of the most useful animation tools in Bryce 3D. The Disperse tool is not dwelled on heavily enough in the Bryce 3D documentation. The Disperse tool works by first selecting a dispersion mode from the list (accessed from the triangle below the tool), and then by clicking and dragging the small spherical button at the top of the Dispersion icon. The effect is applied to any multiple selection of objects in your scene. Here are some general tips on the ways to explore the use of dispersions.

- Use **3D Disperse Size** to make it look as if multiple selected objects are moving into different distances from the camera's eye.
- Use **3D Dispersions** to emulate particle systems, objects being moved by an unseen force. This works especially well with **Disperse Size** and **Rotate**.
- Use Dispersion effects to create unique members of a clone group, like fish in a swimming school.

Terrain Editor

The Terrain Editor is a deep subject in its own right, so we have devoted Chapter 3 to its use.

Object Substitution

This is a special modeling feature of Bryce 3D, activated by bringing up the Substitution menu by clicking on the double arrows at the top right of the Edit toolbar. See the Object Substitution modeling information in Chapter 2.

MATERIALS PRESETS

To the right of the word "Edit" is a downward-pointing triangle that accesses the materials Presets libraries. There are notable additions to this collection of materials in Bryce 3D. Important among these are Glasses, Metals, and Volumes, though the other libraries have been expanded as well. See Figure 1-13 and 1-14.

NOTE

See chapter 4 for details on the use of the Materials Lab and associated dialogs.

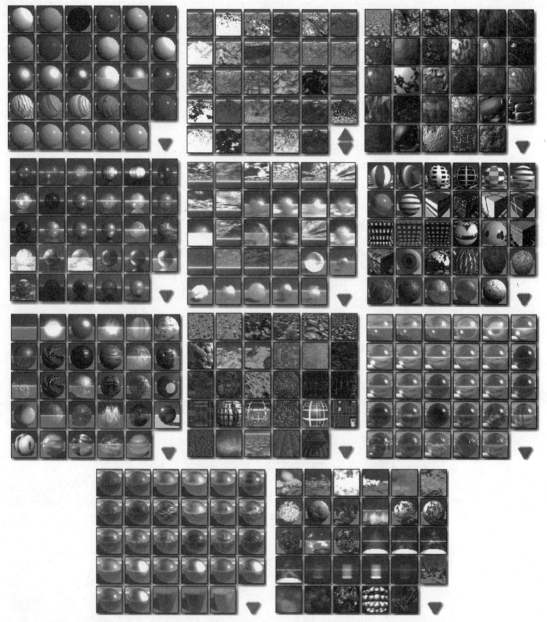

FIGURE *The Bryce 3D Materials Presets can be used as is to texture objects or infinitely customized.*

1.13

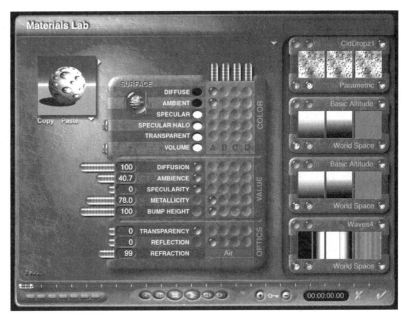

FIGURE   *Materials can be customized in the new Bryce 3D Materials Lab.*
1.14

Notes on the Use of Materials

The Bryce 3D novice will find basic materials intuitive to apply, while the Bryce 3D professional will find that materials are infinitely customizable. Applying materials to an object gives the object personality. A glass ball has a different personality and different expectations on its performance in a scene than does a ball made of stone or metal. A great deal of the allure of computer graphics has to do with creating objects seemingly made of different materials.

Bryce 3D makes a distinction between "materials" and "textures", although the two terms are used interchangeably in the industry at large. Materials, in Bryce 3D, are generally based upon algorithmic (mathematical) formulas, while Textures are bitmap graphics wrapped on the object. There is an ambiguous middle ground however, since materials can also be created by layering algorithmic materials and bitmaps together in numerous ways. In this book, unless otherwise noted, the word "textures" is used to denote both algorithmic materials and bitmaps. When a distinction is called for (as in details of the use of the Materials Lab), it will be presented.

A few important tips concerning the use of Bryce 3D materials and textures include:

- Never be afraid of assigning an "unreal" material to an object. A mountain can look interesting when made of glass, and an apple can take on a unique personality when seemingly constructed of wood. See chapter 11, "Assigning the Wrong Materials on Purpose" for more on this subject.
- Often, the only difference between one material look and the next is decided by one simple control. Metals have high secularity, for instance, while the same material with no secularity takes on the look of plastic. Tweak the materials controls one attribute at a time.
- Presets can be used as is, or layered in a four-stack sandwich. As long as the stacks on top are transparent to the ones below, you will get a composited result. In this way, nonexistent materials (such as a metalicized wood) can be created.
- Make sure you explore and understand the mapping options when assigning a material. Parametric mapping creates a far different look than the same material applied spherically. In this way, "common" materials can take on uncommon looks. See Chapter 4 for more details on this and other materials specific ideas and uses.

SKY & FOG TOOLBAR NOTES
See Figure 1.15.

Though the documentation describes each of these Sky and Fog options in detail, here are a few additional items to take note of.

Sky Modes
Soft and darker skies, two of the four available settings, are self-explanatory. Use the **Atmosphere Off** setting when you need to render objects against a

FIGURE **1.15** *The Sky and Fog toolbar contains icons for Sky Modes, Shadows, Fog, Haze, Cloud Height, Cloud Cover, Cloud Frequency and Amplitude, and the Sun Control Trackball, and the Sky Memory Dots stack.*

solid color. Just select the color from the palette attached to this option. **Custom Sky** is the option to choose when you have the clouds you want, but the colors aren't satisfactory. Alter the sky colors with any of the three palettes provided.

Shadows

Altering shadows in a scene can be a subtle animation effect. When a meteor lands, for instance, shadows may go from off to full at the explosion, and then fade to off again.

Fog

Usually, fog settings shift minimally in an animation. You can, however, use fog settings to emulate movement. A 90% fog setting, for example, means that movement cannot be appreciated, as far as seeing objects whiz by. You could take a high fog setting, and just animate an object (car, plane...) swaying from side to side. For all the viewer knows, it is moving at 1000 miles an hour in thick fog. At the end of the animation, you might animate the fog dissipating, and the object can then be truly animated receding into the background. This is a great way to save rendering time, since in the fog no objects need be rendered. The best fog effects are those that show objects only partially viewable, allowing the viewer the mystery of figuring out their exact proportions. Monster movies make great use of fog, with unpleasant beings suddenly appearing and disappearing into it.

Haze

Haze is related to fog, but it's not as thick or secret. Haze can be the thickness associated with a humid afternoon, or the poisonous smoggy aftereffects of an atmosphere gone astray. Haze in Bryce 3D has another major purpose, which is to mask the horizon line where the land (or water) meets the sky. The most important thing to remember when using haze to mask this blatant edge is the color that is used. If you select a color that is not related to either the sky or the ground (or water plane), the hazed edge will look as disquieting as a hard edge with no haze. Use a color that blends the two planes into one, most commonly a color from the sky at the point where it touches the horizon. Cloud heights of around 25 look nice with a haze applied. Lower clouds mask the full effect, and higher clouds cause too much haze. A haze setting of 100 (maximum) causes an effect much like fog. But haze cannot be set for altitude coverage like fog can. Haze colorizes the whole scene when high settings are used.

For ships disappearing into a fog bank, substitute a haze setting of 100, and set the fog to zero. Color the haze a light green.

Cloud Height

Explore various height settings with each new sky you design. Cloud Height is one component of sky settings, and a lot of play time is involved with each new sky. A good place to begin is around 25. Realize that altering the color in the palette attached to the Cloud Height tool (Sky Dome Color) will colorize the ground, as if there was a colorized blanket around the world. Altering Cloud Height produces interesting animation effects.

Cloud Cover

A setting of zero creates a blank sky, showing only the color set for the middle color slot in the Sky Modes/Custom palette (as long as the frequency and amplitude of the clouds is flattened). Realize that altering the color in the palette attached to the Cloud Cover will colorize the clouds and have no effect on the coloring of the rest of your world. Altering Cloud Cover produces interesting animation effects.

Cloud Frequency and Amplitude

This tool is completely intuitive, allowing you to "read" what the clouds in your sky will look like. When flattened, clouds are set to zero. Since this tool works by clicking and dragging the mouse (LMB on Windows platforms), you should experiment with its use, along with previewing the results in the Nano Preview screen. Altering Cloud Frequency and Amplitude produces interesting animation effects.

See chapter 8 for a more detailed look on animating Skies, Fog, and Haze.

Sun Control Trackball

The most important thing to remember when using this device is that the "Moon" is directly opposite the "Sun." To see either the sun or moon on the horizon, you have to place them just on the very edge of the trackball's perimeter, which takes some practice. Also remember that colorizing the Sun affects the colors in the whole scene, so opt for subtle pastels rather than primary colors, unless a truly alien look is your desire.

See chapter 6 on Environmental Effects for a detailed look at the use of the Sun trackball and other related material.

Sky Memory Dots

At the very right hand of the Sky and Fog toolbar is a stack of Memory Dots meant to store your favorite sky designs. You can also store them in the Sky Presets library (accessed from the small triangle at the bottom right of the Sky and Fog toolbar title). The difference is that the skies stored in the Memory Dots are saved for the present work session only. Once your computer is shut off, the Memory Dots are emptied. If you save your skies in the Sky Presets library, they are available (unless deleted) every time you use Bryce 3D.

Randomize Buttons

No matter how much creativity you were born with, everyone runs low on ideas once in a while. When that occurs during a Bryce 3D world building session, and you can't seem to find a sky that looks unique enough, try clicking on one of the Randomize buttons just to the left of the Sun icon in this toolbar. These buttons work the same way as similar options offered in other MetaCreations graphics applications—by allowing the computer to suggest new possibilities.

Unless you have all the time in the world, leave the Auto Update item in the Sky and Fog list set to OFF (uncheck it). It can be very annoying to get an automatic render each time you change a sky setting.

The Sky Presets Library

See Figure 1.16.

The sky listings in the Presets library are meant to be jumping off places for your work, not copy art. The moment you alter the colorization, frequency and amplitude, or any other parameter, and you are enthralled by the results, save your creations here. The best ways to save your own creations are to a separate library on your hard drive or on removable media. That way,

Sky&Fog   Psychedelic Sunset

Add   Delete   Import Export   ✗ ✔

FIGURE   *The Sky Presets library in Bryce 3D contains a number of added choices. Save*
1.16 *your own customized skies here for further use.*

you can share your customized library creations with friends and associates. Here's how:

1. Create a new sky.
2. Bring up the Sky Presets library and click on Export.
3. Select a destination, preferably in a folder with a name that relates to the new contents.
4. Save your customized sky.

Later, if you want to use it again, just click on the **Import** command in the Sky Presets library. Locate the saved preset and load it in.

The Right-hand Toolbar

Sliding your mouse to the left, across the border of your Bryce 3D editing screen, makes the icons in the right-hand toolbar visible. See Figure 1.17.

FIGURE *(Left) The toolbar on the right side of the screen contains icons for (top to bottom): Demo Marker, Display Max/Min, Background Paper, Nano Editor On/Off, Plop Renderer On/Off, Wireframe Depth Cue On/Off, Wireframe Shadows On/Off, Wireframe Underground On/Off, Wireframe Resolution On/Off, Display Modes, Zoom In/Out, Pan, and the Time/Selection Palette toggle.*

TIPS ON THE USE OF RIGHT-HAND TOOLBAR OPTIONS

Although you have already read the documentation and have probably explored some or all of these tools, here are some further tips to guide your workflow.

Demo Marker

This tool is meant for production houses, where a creative team may be working on a Bryce 3D project. The marker leaves a bright red trail, useful to production managers and art directors for calling attention to needed details in a Bryce 3D scene. It works on any part of the Bryce 3D interface, so it can be used to call attention to tools as well as elements in a scene.

Display Max/Min

This is probably one of the more useful tools in this toolbar. One click, and your display is either maximized or minimized. It's the fastest way to get more elbow room in Bryce 3D.

Background Paper

Except as an interesting option, this tool has little professional use. The exception might be that by selecting White from the attached list, your edits can be seen against a contrasted white backdrop.

Nano Editor On/Off

This is a small edit screen window, useful when quick editing is needed. It appears as an overlay on top of the camera controls. It is interesting, but saves little time when using the camera controls.

Plop Renderer On/Off

Use this control to turn the Plop Render frame off after a render is completed, so you can see the newly rendered section against its backdrop.

Wireframe Depth Cue On/Off

It's best to leave the Wireframe Depth Cue on, so you can get a better idea of where objects are placed in a scene.

Wireframe Shadows On/Off

Shadows are best left on, so you can appreciate where an object is placed on the Y (height) World axis.

Wireframe Underground On/Off

Except when you are designing a scene that has no ground plane (a space scene, for example), leave the Wireframe Underground set to ON.

Wireframe Resolution

There are three Wireframe resolutions involved here: Motion, Static, and Selected.

- *Motion* Motion Resolution refers to the on-screen resolution of objects in motion. Explore setting this as high as possible (depending on the speed of your system), so you can get the best idea of exactly how objects will appear in an animation. On slower systems, setting this too high will affect preview playback speed adversely.
- *Static* Static resolution refers to the on-screen resolution of unselected objects at rest in your scene. This is usually set to medium, and you can choose to heighten the resolution of your Selected items.
- *Selected* Selected Resolution is the on-screen resolution of selected objects. This should be set as high as possible in order to allow you to see object elements more clearly for editing purposes.

Display Modes

You will use this control often during the design phase of a Bryce 3D world. Of its three options (Wireframe, Wireframe/Render composite, and Render), the Wireframe/Render composite is extremely useful in the design phase of your project. It allows you to work as you would in the edit screen with wireframe proxies of objects, except that you see the wireframes against the last-rendered picture. This is very useful when placing objects in relation to others.

NOTE

Important: When working in the Wireframe/Render composite, do not change your camera position from when the Render was done, or the Wireframe and Render screens will not register (match up). Also, work in the same view as the Render screen references.

Zoom In/Out and Pan

Zooms will always center on the presently selected object. If no object is selected, the zooms will be centered globally. The Pan tool is many times faster than it was in previous Bryce 3D editions.

Time/Selection Palette Toggle

This toggle (shaped like a wireframe globe) alternates between the Time (animation) and Selection palettes, which are detailed next.

The Time and Selection Palettes

The Time palette and Selection palette are located at the bottom of the Bryce 3D interface.

TIME PALETTE

The Time palette, also referred to as the Animation toolbar, is where all of your keyframing activities take place. See figure 1.18.

There are several unique features of the Bryce 3D Time palette that must be mastered so that you can optimize your animation work in Bryce 3D.

FIGURE *The Time palette has VCR-like tools for navigating through your animation and setting keyframes.*
1.18

Timeline

When you drag the Timeline indicator, you indicate the length (in both time and frames) of your animation. Note that even when Auto key framing is on, you have to manually hit the keyframe plus (+) button to tell Bryce 3D that this is the last frame of an animation. I prefer leaving AutoKey off during the initial stages of animation design.

Timeline Scaler

This tool is almost invisible. It is at the upper right of the Timeline, represented by a series of rectangular dots. Clicking and dragging while over this icon shortens or lengthens the amount of time represented on the Timeline. Not that time itself is not stretched, but only the room it takes on the timeline (the closeness of one tick mark to the next). When you have an animation that is too long to be represented as a whole on the timeline, use this tool to bring it all into view.

You will want to scale the Timeline in the other direction if you have to jump from one frame to the next in a long sequence, since it gets harder to move the Timeline indicator by small increments when the ticks are very close together.

Keyframe Memory Dots

Use these dots to move quickly from one frame to another on the timeline. As your animation becomes more involved, you can substitute needed frames for others already listed here.

VCR Controls

These are standard VCR editing buttons. The most useful when designing an animation are the buttons that jump to the next and previous keyframes.

Keyframe Controls

If you have Auto keyframing on, most operations automatically update the location of a keyframe as you move the Timeline indicator with an object selected on the screen. I prefer to alternate between Auto on and off, so as a precaution (even when it's on) I click on the keyframe plus button. The Delete keyframe button is very useful when you get yourself into a confusing jam and need to redo all or part of an animation.

- *The Keyframe Options Menu* When you click and hold on the keyframe plus button, the Keyframe Options menu appears (see Figure 1.19).

When Auto is off, Bryce 3D allows you to keyframe each discrete aspect of the camera, Sky, and Sun. This allows for very subtle changes in an animation. For professional broadcast and film work, the way to work is with Auto off, so that these small but important alterations can add to the realism of an animated scene.

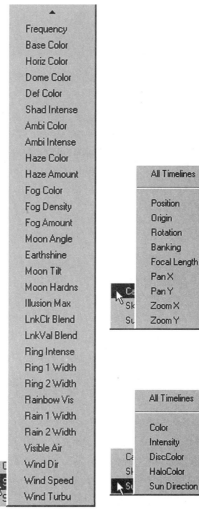

FIGURE   *There are itemized listings in the keyframe Options menu for keyframing every*
1.19   *aspect of the camera, Sky, and Sun.*

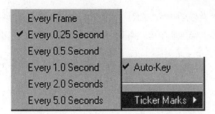

FIGURE **1.20** *Knowing when to use the Auto-Key function is the secret to worry-free animating in Bryce 3D.*

Motion Lab Activator

For detailed information and a walkthrough of this new Bryce 3D option, see Chapter 10.

Options Menu

Without a doubt, the most important command in this menu is whether Auto is turned on or off. Auto should be on at the start of your animation edits, and then set to off when it comes time to fine tune your work. The same menu allows you to set what time increments are indicated by the tick marks. See Figure 1.20.

When you want to keyframe the sky, make sure no other object in the scene is selected. Auto should be on, or you may wind up having to keyframe every sky attribute individually.

NOTE

SELECTION PALETTE

See Figure 1.21.

As opposed to other 3D art and animation applications, Bryce 3D knows what you need when it comes to locating any object in your scene. It makes no difference how complex the scene is or how hidden in the mix your specific object may be. The Selection palette is Bryce 3D's answer to every animator's dream in this respect.

FIGURE **1.21** *The Selection palette's purpose is to allow you easy access to any object in your Bryce 3D composition.*

Icons for every Bryce 3D object type are included in the selection palette, while separate options are listed in the associated Selection menu for imported objects and grouped items in the scene. For Bryce 3D objects in the scene, click and hold on any one of the specific icons that represent that object type, and a popup list appears with every member of that type in the scene. Select the specific object from the list.

Alternatively, you can use the VCR control arrows to march through the objects in the scene, either by type, or in the sequential order they were created (by making sure Alternate VCR Mode is selected in the Selection menu). See Figure 1.22.

To locate an object that appears later in an animation, do the following:

1. Move the controller on the Timeline until you see the object on the screen.
2. Select the object if possible, or use the selection arrows (or the selection menu associated with its object type) until it is highlighted.

Of course, you can also use the Pan tool (the hand in the right-hand toolbar) to move the whole scene (commonly from the top view) to locate it as well. But this method is easier and less time-consuming in most cases.

NOTE

After having read the Bryce 3D documentation, it is important to remember that individual objects embedded in a group can be selected by clicking on them while holding down the Control key (Mac and Windows). Objects hidden under layers of other objects can be highlighted by holding down the Shift key while clicking on them, and then marching through the appropriate selection arrow keys as necessary.

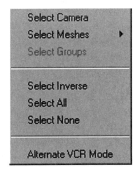

Select Camera
Select Meshes   ▶
Select Groups

Select Inverse
Select All
Select None

Alternate VCR Mode

FIGURE   *The Alternate VCR Mode option should be checked in the Selection menu when*
1.22   *you want to step through each of the objects in the scene sequentially.*

Important Menu Options for Optimizing Your Work

The top menu bar contains the File, Edit, Objects, and Help menus. The Bryce 3D documentation does a satisfactory job of describing the items involved in each menu, but it is worth pointing out several of these items (ones that do not appear in any of the toolbars) in order to remind you of their importance and use.

FILE

- Save, Save, Save! Save your work every twenty to thirty minutes, unless you enjoy seeing it all disappear in a computer crash. It's not that Bryce 3D crashes that often, but that other elements of your computer work (like not enough RAM allocated to Bryce 3D) intervene to cause a crash. Save both the Project file and any associated renderings that need to be saved separately.
- Keep merging in mind for developing large scenarios. With merge, you can prepare a scene by developing separate scenes that focus upon individual complex elements and merge them together at the end. The only caution is to make sure that you have enough RAM to handle the size of the merged final scene.
- Try to export Wavefront OBJ object files to Bryce 3D for Import, not DXFs. DXFs are very chunky, with polygon edges all over the place. This may not matter for machines and such, but it makes organic forms look false. Besides, OBJ files take parametric mapping.

EDIT

- Remember that copying and pasting materials can allow you to create scenes with cohesive elements much faster. You can load in a few terrains, followed by a number of rocks and a ground plane, and assign the same material to each element in this fashion.
- Copy/Paste Matrixes is a time-saving shortcut when you need to apply resizing/position/rotation parameters to an object. Look for further details of this in chapter 12 on Incorporating Null Objects.
- Duplicate and Replicate commands offer you new opportunities for object design alternatives. See Chapter 2 on 3D Modeling.

OBJECTS

- The **Edit Object** command, which alters the faceted look of an object and smoothes it out, does not work on imported DXFs or OBJ files. The difference is that OBJ files come in very unfaceted at the start. The solution is to stay away from DXF models whenever possible, and to work with Wavefront OBJ imports, or even 3D Studio imports (which can be smoothed with the Edit Object command). See Figure 1.23.

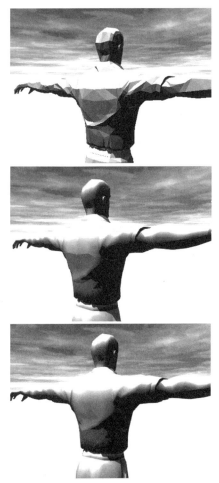

FIGURE
1.23   *Here is visual proof that various object file formats appear very different when imported into Bryce 3D. The top figure is a Poser DXF, the middle is a Poser OBJ, and the bottom figure is a Poser 3D Studio file. Though the 3D Studio file comes in just as faceted as the DXF, it does allow for smoothing in the **Edit Object** command, which has been applied here.*

If you absolutely must import a DXF model, you can sometimes hide the faceting by applying a complex material to it. Just make sure that reflections are set to zero in the Materials Lab, which hides the faceting further.

- **Create Path**, a command that lives in this menu, is one of the most important commands in Bryce 3D. It allows you to transform an ordinary animation path into a Ribbon path, which can be edited like any other object. See Ribbon Path Arrays in Chapter 2, and Chapter 7 on Animation Paths.

HELP

Always look at the topics in the Help menu when you are starting to learn an application. The material included is always more updated than the paper documentation and most times includes a number of last minute additions and help files.

Moving On

In this chapter, we have taken a look at the various tools and options in the Bryce 3D interface, with an eye toward presenting new information and valuable tips. In the next chapter, we will look at the ways that models can be created and customized in Bryce 3D.

2 3D Models

Enter, the Actors

The 3D models in your Bryce 3D world are the actors on the stage. Their movements give life to a scene, and their interactions with each other and their environment are interpreted as meaningful acts by the onlooker. Your models are alive, whether they emulate organic creatures or mechanical artifacts. The moment that an object moves, it is surmised that they have some form of intent and purpose. Even cars, planes, and rockets seem to be breathing on their own as they fly through the world on their assigned paths. The secret that all animators know is that in the animated world, everything is potentially conscious. In the animator's world, unlike the world of our everyday experience, it is possible that at any moment a tree might dance or a car sneeze.

There are two general types of objects (actors) that bring a Bryce 3D scene to life: 2D planes and 3D models. Chapter 5 covers the use of 2D planes in Bryce 3D, and Chapter 3 covers Terrain Models, a special type of 3D model. This chapter focuses upon the differences and similarities among various types of 3D models and how they are constructed and manipulated. There are many ways to create and use different model types in Bryce 3D, which is what this chapter will explore.

Primitive Modeling Elements

What does "primitive" mean in a 3D application? Simply answered, a primitive is a 3D object that can be brought into a scene by clicking on its icon or an associated button. Different 3D applications have varying numbers of primitives. The common ones shared by all are the cube, sphere, and cone. Bryce 3D goes beyond that, by adding variations of these volumes as well as other primitives. The Bryce 3D primitives can be seen and activated by clicking on their associated icons in the Create toolbar (Figure 2.1).

FIGURE
2.1
The Bryce 3D Create toolbar displays various nonterrain primitive objects. From left to right, they are the Sphere, Stretched Sphere, Squashed Sphere, Torus, Horizontal and Vertical Cylinders, Cube, Stretched and Squashed Rectangle, Tetrahedron, Stretched and Squashed Tetrahedron, Cone, and Stretched and Squashed Cones.

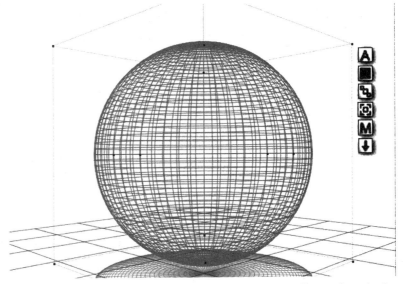

FIGURE   *An Object's transformation tools are displayed in a vertical menu alongside of*
2.2   *the object when it is selected.*

Transformation Tools

Any object that is added to a Bryce 3D scene, primitive or imported, displays its own transformation menu once it is selected. Reviewing the purpose of each tool in this menu is important before starting to create elements in a scene. Click on the Sphere in the **Create** menu, which places a Sphere in your workspace. The Sphere is selected by default, and its associated transformation menu is displayed alongside it (Figure 2.2).

From top to bottom, the icons in the transformation menu list represent **Object Attributes** dialog, **Family** color palette, **Link** icon, **Target** icon, **Materials** icon, and **Gravity** drop arrow. These should be familiar to you after having read and worked through the documentation. Special chapters in this book are devoted to expanding your knowledge on the use of these icons. Materials are covered in Chapter 4, and the use of the new Materials Lab in Chapter 5. Tips on Links and Targets are detailed throughout Section II on animation.

As far as primitive objects are concerned in this chapter, it's important that you become familiar with the use of the **Object Attributes** icon (the letter **A** in the transformation menu), and for now, with the options contained in the General tab (Figure 2.3).

Though the use of items in the General tab will be referred to at different points in the coming chapters, working with primitives in this chapter assumes you are familiar with the following items listed in this dialog:

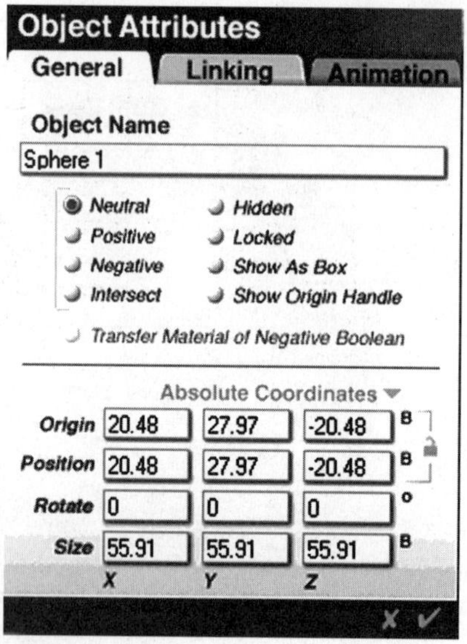

Object Attributes

General | Linking | Animation

Object Name

Sphere 1

- ● Neutral   ◡ Hidden
- ◡ Positive   ◡ Locked
- ◡ Negative   ◡ Show As Box
- ◡ Intersect   ◡ Show Origin Handle

◡ Transfer Material of Negative Boolean

Absolute Coordinates ▼

	X	Y	Z	
Origin	20.48	27.97	-20.48	B
Position	20.48	27.97	-20.48	B
Rotate	0	0	0	°
Size	55.91	55.91	55.91	B

✗ ✓

FIGURE *The General tab in the Object Attributes dialog.*
2.3

- How to change the name of a selected object in the top input area.
- How to lock/unlock a selected object.
- How the alter the numeric coordinates in the bottom half of the dialog.

If any of this is new to you, reread the documentation for that item.

The First Primitives Projects

By combining selected 3D objects in the Create toolbar (as shown in Figure 2.1), you can construct an infinite number of recognizable objects, as well as using these primitives on their own as objects in a scene. The Torus, for example, can become a bagel or a car tire, while the Sphere can be transformed into a planet, a beachball, or a dome in a cityscape. In fact, a cityscape is a good place to begin exploring the use of primitives as stand-alone objects.

PRIM CITY

We are going to use unaltered primitives to construct a futuristic cityscape as our first project. Because you have already read and worked through the tutorials in the Bryce 3D documentation, no extra time will be spent explaining the location of the tools used, or where they are located. Here's how to do it:

1. The first thing you should do is to go to the right-hand toolbar and turn on the grid in the background paper display. This gives you a way to

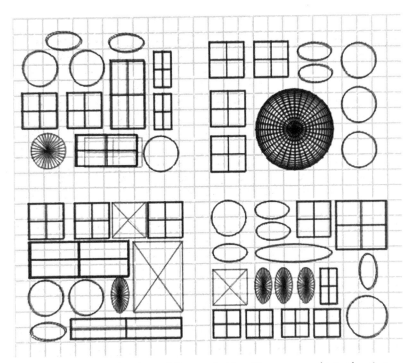

FIGURE   *As your city takes shape, different primitive objects are moved into place (top*
2.4   *view).*

place objects in a common urban pattern. remove the Ground plane for
now and start your work in the top view.

2. Click on various object primitives to place your structures in the city.
Click on them one by one and move them into place on the grid. Use
more than just rectangular primitives to give your cityscape a more interesting look. Resize some of the primitives from the top view to vary
the buildings (Figure 2.4).

*Remember that spherical primitives contain more polygons than other objects, so to
cut down on storage space for the file, use spheres sparsely.*

TIP

*In Chapter 3, we'll show you another simpler way to design a cityscape with the Ter-
rain Editor.*

TIP

3. Apply a solid color material to all of the objects (simple and fast—blue
metal), and create a ground plane mapped with Planes and Terrains: Mud
and Snow. Take a look at it from a perspective camera view (Figure 2.5).

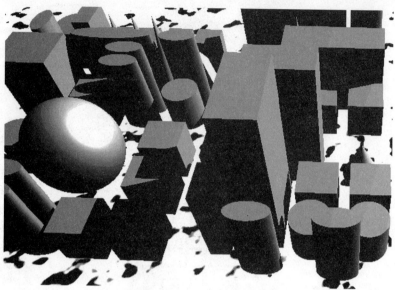

FIGURE
2.5 *When seen in perspective, the cityscape begins to take on a more believable appearance. The city so far has only 1219 polygons, and because it has simple material mapped, it renders very fast.*

4. The cityscape could stop here for rendering, or it can be tweaked a bit to make it more interesting. First, select any spheres you have in the scene and move them down so that they show only their top half, like geodesic domes.

5. Next, edit the sizes of some of your similar shapes (cubes, for instance) to give more variety to the scene. Make some taller and some shorter.

6. Then add a few more primitive shapes on top of some of the buildings. Especially effective is the addition of smaller rectangles on top of larger ones, and pyramidal shapes on top of rectangles. Experiment. Render a preview to judge your efforts thus far (see Figure 2.6).

7. After you have adjusted all of your buildings so they seem right for the scene, there's one more step. Cities have roadways. If you are going to be animating a scene close to the ground, they might even have street lamps and other details. For this project, the city is animated from a rather high flyover, so unnecessary detail is not warranted. For roads, simply add a few rectangles, squashed, so they're close to the ground and elongated beyond the city's borders, coloring the roads with a black simple and fast material (see Figure 2.7). Do it. Figure 2.8 adds some additional detail to the cityscape.

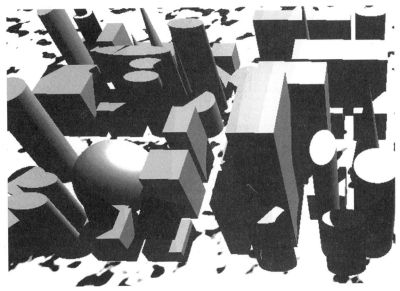

FIGURE *By varying the buildings even more, we make this scene more realistic.*
2.6

FIGURE *With the addition of roads, this simple cityscape is ready for an animated*
2.7 *flyover.*

NOTE

The cityscape pictured has only 1363 polygons and renders in less than five minutes without anti-aliasing on a 200 MHz non-accelerated system. On the same system, with normal anti-aliasing on with reflective material took twenty minutes. You can find it in the Projects folder on the CD-ROM as Chpt2_A. We will customize this same project further in Chapter 5 with the Materials Lab.

THE GREAT PYRAMID

Just to show you that creating a startling graphic in Bryce 3D is as simple as it can get, let's create a virtual view of the Great Pyramid on the planes of Giza. This project should take five minutes to design and about ten minutes to render on a 200 MHz system (with anti-aliasing off). Here's how to proceed:

1. Place three pyramids (primitive tetrahedrons) from the top view as shown in Figure 2.9.
2. Create a sky from one of the sky presets and add materials to the pyramids (investigate the Pyr_1 project on the CD-ROM for the object and ground textures chosen by the author).

Though a very simple composition, it is very effective. The completed project is shown in Figure 2.10.

FIGURE
2.8 *Rendering our simple cityscape against a cloudy sky from a head-on view with a Haze setting of 60 gives us another rendition. In this case, the reflection was set to 40 for all buildings, causing them to mirror each other.*

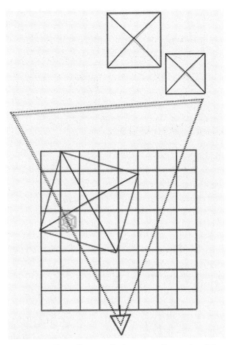

FIGURE **2.9** *Place the tetrahedrons as shown in this top view, with camera located as you see it here.*

FIGURE **2.10** *The finished Giza rendering, created from three primitive objects.*

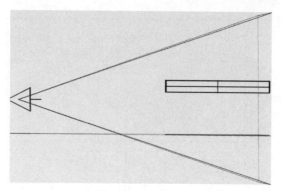

FIGURE *A resized cube is the start of the table.*
2.11

THE COMMON TABLE

You can create a million variations on this theme, but this is the general form. This table is created entirely from Bryce 3D primitive objects.

1. Go to the right view and place a cube in the scene. Place it as indicated above the ground and adjust its height so that it looks similar to Figure 2.11.

2. Place an elongated cube and a tetrahedron in the scene. Resize them as shown in Figure 2.12 and place them as shown in this right view. Group them together.

3. From the top view, copy/paste or duplicate the table leg to generate the other three legs. Refer to Figure 2.13.

4. Texture with whatever materials you prefer and save to disk. The finished table is shown in Figure 2.14.

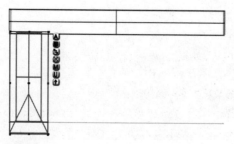

FIGURE *The first leg is added to the table and placed in position in the right view.*
2.12

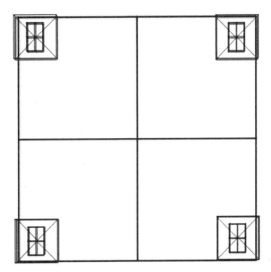

FIGURE   *The legs are cloned and placed in position in the top view.*
2.13

FIGURE   *The finished and rendered table, made with primitive objects.*
2.14

NOTE

See the Table1 project on the CD-ROM.

A BASIC ARCHWAY

Archways are great to move through in an animation. They can be used outside as part of a garden scene, inside a domicile between rooms, or enlarged to bridge a river. However you use them, basic archway objects can be constructed using primitive objects. Here's one example:

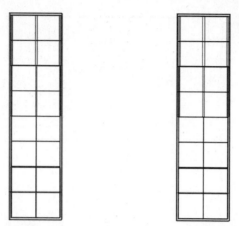

FIGURE *Two columns constructed from four cubes each begin the archway.*
2.15

1. Create two columns with four cubes in each, similar to the illustration in Figure 2.15.
2. Create a Torus primitive and place it so that its outer radius touches the outer edges of the columns as shown in Figure 2.16. We will use this as a template and erase it when our task is accomplished.

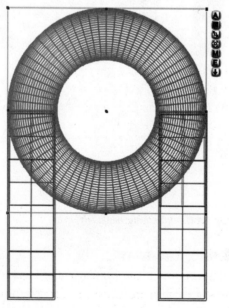

FIGURE *The torus is created, resized, and placed as shown.*
2.16

FIGURE *The arch blocks are placed using the Torus as a template.*
2.17

3. Place seven cubic blocks, using the Torus as a template. When finished, delete the Torus. Your archway should look similar to the one in Figure 2.17.
4. Apply any material you desire, or even a mix of materials. The reason smaller blocks were used is so that the materials would look mapped individually and not to the whole form at once. The completed archway is shown in Figure 2.18.

We could have used a Boolean method for a more elegant archway, as we will demonstrate later in this chapter.

TIP

See the Arch1 project on the CD-ROM.

HOUSE

NOTE

Remember the houses you used to draw in second grade? They were probably created by placing a triangle on top of a square, with perhaps a chimney added. The same thing can be done by using a cube and a tetrahedron in Bryce 3D, but try pushing your creative efforts a little farther than that. Here's how:

FIGURE **2.18**   *The archway is textured for a finished look. This example uses a Pitted Concrete material from the Rocks and Stones library, with three duplicate archways placed for effect and a 60% haze applied.*

1. Go to the Front view. Just for fun, start with the basic second grade form, placing a red squashed tetrahedron on top of a cube. Group the cube and tetrahedron. Duplicate the group and move the duplicated element away from the original (Figure 2.19).

2. Next, we'll add some resized cubes colored black for a series of windows and a door. You're free to experiment here. Refer to Figure 2.20.

3. Now add the main house, simply by adding another cube-tetrahedron group to the scene. Populate it with cubic windows and doors. If you like, add a porch with columns made from primitive cylinders. Add the ground and sky and render for preview. Refer to Figure 2.21.

FIGURE **2.19**   *The first step is to create these two duplicate forms, made from a grouped cube and squashed tetrahedron.*

FIGURE
2.20
Windows and the door are simple cubes colored black.

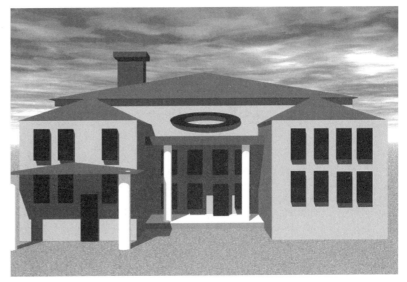

FIGURE
2.21
By adding more primitive elements, the house can become a veritable mansion in a matter of seconds.

NOTE

See the House1 project on the CD-ROM.

ROBOX8

Though creating organic forms with primitive objects presents a problem when it comes to curved shapes, we can do the next best thing and build a robotic figure. Though Links won't be covered until Chapter 9 (Animation Paths, Links, and Targets), you may want to link the parts of this figure together on your own. This section will just be looking at the primitive objects used in its construction.

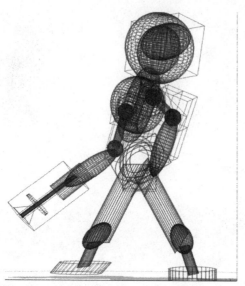

FIGURE *Investigate the RoboX8 figure from the RoboX8 project on the CD-ROM. Notice*
2.22 *that it is entirely constructed from primitive objects.*

*See the full RoboX8 project on the CD-ROM, which includes the linked parts (see
Figure 2.22).*

The primitives used in the construction of this robot are mostly spheres and
distorted spheres. This gives a more humanoid robot than if it were constructed from cubic forms. There's no doubt that it's still a robot, but we are
made to feel that we might be able to reason with it if push comes to shove. Another version of RoboX8 is shown in Figure 2.23.

**Imported
Modeling
Elements**

As we have already seen, Bryce 3D allows us to import objects in the DXF, OBJ
(WaveFront), and 3DS (3D Studio) formats. In addition to this, Bryce 3D can
import 3DMF object formats (QuickDraw 3D Metafile). 3DMF files are
cross-platform, though more common on the Mac. DXF objects come in
faceted and cannot be smoothed. OBJ objects come in smoothed and cannot
be smoothed or faceted in Bryce 3D. 3DS objects come in faceted, but can be
both smoothed and faceted in Bryce 3D. The obvious choice is to import OBJ
and 3DS objects whenever possible. Import and use DXFs when faceting presents no problem, or is in fact a look you want.

FIGURE *Here's a rendering of RoboX8, from side and front.*
2.23

With some exceptions, as indicated in this chapter, Bryce 3D has a minimum of modeling tools and options. Professional modeling applications offer much more choice for creating objects of every description, including human, animal, and other organic forms. If you are a professional computer artist and animator, you already have an advanced degree of familiarity with 3D applications more suitable for creating 3D objects. The only question that remains is "Does the application I use export objects in a format compatible with Bryce 3D?" If the answer is yes, then you have all you need to create infinite object content to place in Bryce 3D worlds.

There is another reason for selecting imported objects over Bryce 3D primitives. Bryce 3D primitives tend to distort when animated, which can be a big problem. Imported objects and object elements are much less prone to this anomaly, and animations look cleaner and more professional as a result.

The general rule is to use primitive objects to construct background elements in Bryce 3D, or composite objects whose parts are grouped and not linked.

TIP

There are dozens of CD-ROM libraries with a variety of 3D objects in a number formats available for purchase. Many of these libraries contain objects suitable for your Bryce 3D work (see some examples in Figure 2.24 and 2.25).

If an imported 3DS object will not accept smoothing in Bryce 3D, there's a good bet that it is a DXF object incompletely saved in the 3DS format. In that case, use an object translator application to import it (see Appendix E), and save it again as a real 3DS object.

TIP

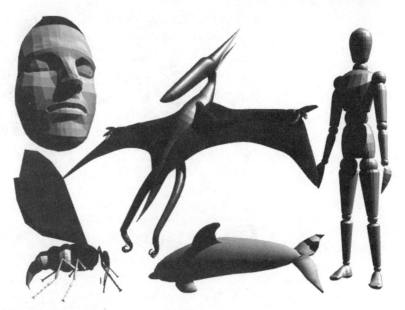

FIGURE **2.24** *Here is a selection of 3DS and DXF objects from the Light ROM 5 Collection on CD-ROM, imported and rendered in Bryce 3D. See Appendix G for contact information.*

FIGURE **2.25** *This 3DS object, also found on the Light ROM 5 Collection CD-ROM, was very faceted when imported. By applying maximum smoothing, it is transformed into an object that can be used to create some spectacular Bryce 3D worlds. The object and image are contained in the Phar1 project on the CD-ROM.*

MIX AND MATCH IMPORTS

This is a very interesting way to customize imported objects to create fantastic characters. It is based upon the fact that all complex imported objects are saved as a Group and can be Ungrouped in Bryce 3D. Once an imported object is Ungrouped, you can delete any unwanted parts. You could import a bird, for instance, and delete everything but the wings. In this way, you can wind up with a diverse number of character parts on screen. Parts can be moved into position and recombined to form new characters for your Bryce 3D world, characters that exist in no other object collection.

When you form new recombinant characters, don't forget to save them to your object library, either inside Bryce 3D or in your own folder.

THE NEFERSAUR

You will have to resize and often rotate one or all object parts in order to get a believable fit when you mix and match them. You will also have to copy the material of one and paste it to the other, or invent a new material for all of the parts. Even ungrouping may not give you the movable parts you need, in which case you will have to edit and regroup the parts in a separate application (see Appendix E). Figure 2.26 shows an example of mix and match.

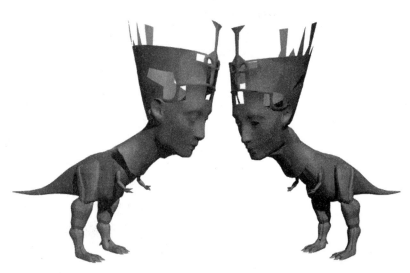

FIGURE *One example of the imported object mix and match procedure is this model, a*
2.26 *combination of Nefertiti and a tyrannosaurus. The elements were taken from the Light ROM 5 Collection CD-ROM in 3DS format.*

Multi-Replicate

Quantity 1   ○ Scale Translation

Relative Coordinates

Offset   0   0   0   B

Rotate   0   0   0   °

Size   100   100   100   %
         X   Y   Z

FIGURE *The Multi-Replicate dialog in the Edit menu allows you to apply offsets, resizes,*
2.27 *and rotations to each succeeding object in an array.*

Multiple Replication Array Modeling

One of the best modeling tools in the **Edit** menu is the Multi-Replicate tool. With this tool, you can create as many clones of an object as you like (as long as you have enough RAM). You can determine how each object in the array is separated from other objects by offset on the XYZ axis, as well as rotation and sizing. Each object in the array will continue the progression of offsets, resizing, and rotations. All of the members of the array can be grouped as one object, or acted upon separately. Figure 2.27 shows the Multi-Replicate dialog box. Figures 2.28 and 2.29 show examples of stairway objects. Figure 2.30 and 2.31 show other objects.

FIGURE *This stairway object was created by selecting an elongated cube and applying an*
2.28 *offset of 20 on both the Y and the Z axis, with a quantity of 12.*

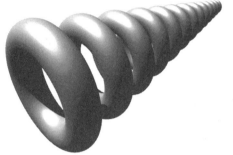

FIGURE
2.29
These spiral stairs were create by multi-replicating an elongated and squashed cube with an offset of 12 on the Y axis, and a rotation of 12 degrees on the Y axis. The Origin Handle was moved to the end of the initial shape so the stairs would rotate around an end point.

FIGURE
2.30
This Toroid tunnel was created by multi-replicating a front facing Torus. Offsets were 0, −26, 0, and resize was 85, 85, 85, causing each succeeding Torus to be 85% of the last one. Standing on the large Torus makes a great futuristic building in the background (3328 polygons).

FIGURE
2.31
This object is based upon a multi-replicated group of squashed cylinders. Quantity was set to 12, Offset to 0, 7, 0, and rotation to 0, 30, 0. Size was set to 90 on all axes. It was grouped and multi-replicated again four times, with an offset of 40 on the Y axis. The result was a denuded tree-like structure (6240 polygons). The object was then duplicated and rendered in a Bryce 3D scene.

THE CUBIC GAUNTLET

This array is a cubic structure that consists of separate cubic elements. It can be used to create a mesmerizing animation, with almost illusionary results, as the camera flies through the rows of cubes. Here's how to create the array:

1. Place one Cube in your workspace. Select the Multi-Replicate command and enter the following in the Offset row: 0, 0, 35. Set the quantity to 6. Click on the checkmark. An array of seven cubes now stretches into the Z direction.

2. Group all of the cubes. Select Multi-Replicate again, and this time enter the following in the Offset row: 0, 35, 0. Set the quantity to six. Click on the checkmark. Now you have a wall of 49 cubes, with 7 rows and 7 columns. Group everything.

3. Repeat the multi-replicate operation one more time. This time, enter the following in the Offset row: 35, 0, 0. Set the quantity to 6. Click on the checkmark. Now you have a cubic array with 7 × 7 × 7 cubes (343 cubes). Group all of the cubes as one object. Save the object to disk as a possible animation project (see Figure 2.32).

Create a similar array with spheres or Toruses, or perhaps do it with an imported object that doesn't contain too many polygons (since you'll be multiplying the polygons by 343!).

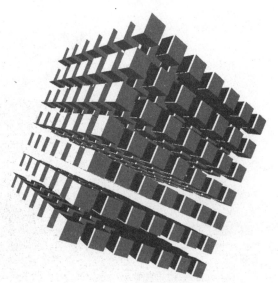

FIGURE *The Cubic array rendered and ready to fly through.*
2.32

A cubic array is a prime target for dispersion animations. See the movie Cubikz2A on the CD-ROM.

A FLEET OF SHIPS, A FLOCK OF BIRDS

Use Multi-Replicate whenever you have a single object in Bryce 3D that is to be the archetype for a group or a flock (see Figure 2.33). The only thing you have to watch out for is the complexity of the model, since you will be multiplying its polygons by whatever quantity of clones are produced. Just select the original model and look at the polygon data reported for it at the bottom of the left-hand toolbar.

If the master object you select has too many polygons for a multi-replication operation and it accepts object editing, you can sometimes reduce its polygons in Bryce 3D. If that fails, you can import it into your 3D modeling application, reduce the polygons, and save it out under another name.

You can always leave the offset and rotation settings at zero in the Multi-Replicate dialog, so that the clones are drawn in the same place as the original model. That way, you can simply select the model, and the top clone will be highlighted for movement. Do this when the group or flock has to be moved in complicated relationships that the Multi-Replicate dialog does not allow. The only caution is that you will have to spend time moving each clone separately.

CIRCULAR ARRAYS

Using the Multi-Replicate command, you can arrange objects in a circle. Doing this manually can be a time-consuming task, but using the Multi-Replicate option makes it easy. Here's how to create a circle of standing stones.

FIGURE *Multi-Replicate generates flocks and fleets from one selected object master.*
2.33

1. Place a Stone primitive on your workspace. Stand it up vertically and elongate its height until it has the appearance of a standing stone (like those found at Stonehenge). Its size should be 85, 20, 42, or close to these dimensions.

2. Select Object Space. Go to the Multi-Replicate dialog while the stone is selected. We will need a total of 12 stones, so the number in the dialog should read 11 replications. Input the following data: Offsets of 0, 50, 50: Rotations of 0, 30, 0. Click on the checkmark.

3. After the stones are replicated, select all of them. Go to the Rotation tool in the Edit toolbar, and rotate until they are all facing towards the center of the circle. With the group selected, apply a material globally. Render and save (see Figure 2.34).

See the Stonez1 project on the CD-ROM.

RIBBON PATH ARRAYS

Ribbon paths are new in Bryce 3D. A ribbon path is a selected path transformed into an object. Ribbon paths are commonly used for Bryce 3D animation purposes, which we cover in Chapter 9. Here, we will look at ribbon paths for another purpose altogether—as a way to create special array objects. This subject is not covered in the Bryce 3D documentation.

The idea for creating arrays with the help of ribbon paths is straightforward and simple to understand, as long as you understand the basics about ribbon paths first. You can apply this method to any ribbon path in your scene, but for

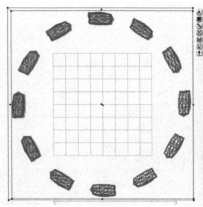

FIGURE **2.34** *The top view of the stones, and the finished standing stones example after rendering.*

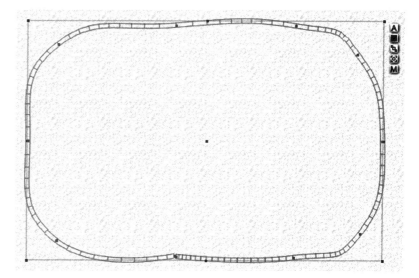

FIGURE   *The top view of the Oval Racetrack ribbon path.*
2.35

a basic understanding, we will import sample ribbon paths from the Bryce 3D library. Go to the Create toolbar, and bring up the **Objects** menu. Select the Path library (all the paths here are ribbon paths), and load in the Oval Racetrack Path. Clicking on the checkmark loads the Oval Racetrack ribbon path to your scene (see Figure 2.35).

If you want to explore this technique with your own paths, just make sure you translate them to ribbon paths first, by selecting them and choosing Create Path from the Objects menu.

TIP

The Wild Ribbon Bridge

1. With the Oval Racetrack ribbon path loaded, create a bridge object. With primitive objects, create a 3D form similar to the one displayed in Figure 2.36.
2. Link the grouped bridge section to the ribbon path. It will snap to the path. Now, with the bridge section selected, use the Replicate (not Multi-Replicate) command seven times. This will clone the bridge section seven times on top of the original section.

You can also use the Duplicate command to do this. The difference between the two is that Replicate will create the clones with their original orientation. Duplicate will create the clones in whatever orientation the object has been rotated to.

TIP

FIGURE *This is the start of our bridge object, a 3D form made from two cylinder and*
2.36 *two cube primitives.*

3. All of the sections are linked to the path, so they can bc moved anywhere
   on the path. From the top view, move the sections so they touch one another in a line, and rotate as necessary (Y rotation in Object Space). You
   should have a composite object that looks like the one in Figure 2.37. Do
   not delete the Ribbon Path unless you unlink every section, or you will
   delete the sections along with it. Group the sections and the Path. Pick

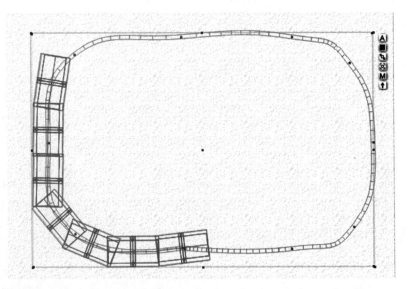

FIGURE *This is a top view of the replicated sections placed in position on the ribbon*
2.37 *path.*

FIGURE   *A completed bridge rendering.*
2.38

an interesting camera angle, render and save to disk (see Figure 2.38 for the completed bridge).

See the BridgeZ1 project on the CD-ROM.

Complexity Multiplied

It is logical to assume that complex modeling takes more time than creating simpler 3D forms, but this is not always the case. Having already introduced the idea of using ribbon paths to create arrays of cloned object elements, it's worth investigating some additional steps that can aid you in the production of even more unique alternatives. All of these options are based upon two facts:

- Ribbon paths can be treated like any other object in a scene when it comes to transformations.
- Objects assigned (linked) to a ribbon path stay attached to that path.

Using these two concepts as a base, it's time to suggest the development of more complex 3D forms. Proceed as follows:

1. Import the Simply Square Ribbon Path from the Objects/Path library.
2. Create a sphere and link it to the path. Assign any material you like to the sphere. Duplicate the sphere three times, giving you a total of four spheres. Move them so there is one in every corner of the square path.

FIGURE *Your final object should look like this, a complex arrangement of spheres.*
2.39

3. Select the Ribbon Path. Remember that any object linked to a path is duplicated when the path is duplicated. Duplicate the path twice and move each path and its spheres on top of each other. Rotate the middle path 45 degrees. You should wind up with an object similar to the one pictured in Figure 2.39.

Object Substitution Modeling

Here's another modeling tool that is unique to Bryce 3D. We might even call this modeling technique a "post modeling" alternative, since it works on models already positioned in your scene. Follow this exercise:

1. Place an imported model in your scene. It should be a model that has multiple grouped parts, like a Poser figure. Select the model if it is not already selected.

2. Go to the **Replace Object** menu in the Edit toolbar (activated by clicking and holding on the double arrow icon at the top right of the toolbar). With the grouped figure selected, go to the Cylinder icon. Each part of the Poser figure is replaced with a cylinder (see Figure 2.40).

This is a fast way to generate a robot from an imported Poser figure.

TIP

FIGURE *The original imported figure is on the left, and the Cylinder object substitution*
2.40 *figure is in the middle. At the right is an object substitution accomplished with*
Toruses.

Boolean Modeling

There are two steps to remember when executing Boolean modeling operations:

1. Determine whether a selected object is positive, negative, or intersecting, and check the appropriate item in the object's (or group's) Attributes dialog (see Figure 2.41).
2. Group the target (positive) object or group with the cutter (negative) object or group.

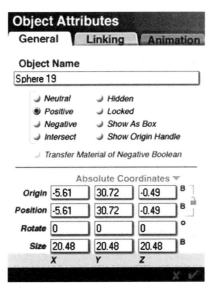

FIGURE *Check the appropriate item in the object's or group's Attributes dialog prior to*
2.41 *grouping the selected target and cutter together.*

FIGURE *Sample Boolean objects included in the Boolean collection in the object library.*
2.42 *A careful study of the construction of these objects will help you in the design of*
your own Boolean models.

At the start, you may wish to investigate some of the Boolean models included in the Bryce 3D object library. See Figure 2.42 for some sample objects.

NOTE

At first, the fact that Boolean models are represented on-screen with the cutters displayed instead of hidden may be confusing and seen as a liability in Bryce 3D. Later, when you animate Boolean models, you'll appreciate this attribute. See Chapter 15 on Boolean Animations.

Here are a few ideas for constructing interesting Boolean models.

Wine Glass

1. Create an elongated sphere for the body of the glass, and map it with a Standard Glass material. Use a light blue color in the Diffusion channel to tint it. Make the elongated sphere Positive in the Attributes dialog.
2. Create a cube that intersects the elongated sphere about halfway down. Make the cube Negative and group it with the elongated sphere. Your object should resemble the one on the left in Figure 2.43.
3. Duplicate the object, and make the duplicate 10% smaller. Place the duplicate inside the original object and apply a red glass material to it. This is the liquid, as illustrated in the middle of Figure 2.43.
4. Create the glass stem and the base. The stem is a cylinder, and the base a squashed sphere. Use their Attributes dialogs to check Boolean Inter-

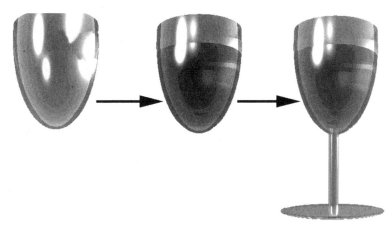

FIGURE   *The Wine Glass object, from start to finish.*
2.43

secting and group both together. Place them in position and group the whole glass. The result should be similar to the right illustration in Figure 2.43.

TIP

Be aware that glass exacts a severe rendering time penalty, because Bryce 3D has to trace all of the lights that interact with the object's refraction and reflection. Glass objects can cause a scene to render five to ten times slower, depending how large they are and if anti-aliasing is on or off. One solution is to render the scene without the glass objects, and then Plop Render only the glass objects on top of the background.

BOOLEAN CHAIR

1. Start by placing a cube in your workspace. Resize it to twice as high as it is wide and deep. Apply a wood material to it in Object Space. In its Attributes dialog, make it positive. Refer to the left illustration in Figure 2.44.

2. Create three elongated rectangular blocks to be used to cut away spaces for the legs and top from the right view. Give each block of the three a negative Boolean attribute. Place the blocks so they cut away unwanted parts of the positive block and group all together. Render a preview. Refer to the middle of Figure 2.44.

3. Ungroup everything. Create two more blocks to cut away unwanted parts of the chair from the front to back and make them negative Booleans. Create cut-aways for the back of the chairs' slats and make each

FIGURE *The progressive construction of the Boolean chair.*
2.44

a negative Boolean. For the last negative Boolean, create a cube that cuts
away the excess from the bottom of the chair. Place a shiny red cushion
on the chair by adding another cube resized to fit. Now, group everything together for the final render. Refer to the right-hand illustration in
Figure 2.44.

TIP

*If any part of this tutorial is not clear to you, load the ChairX1 project from the CD-
ROM, and study the object.*

BOOLEAN ARCHWAY

Remember the archway we created earlier in this chapter? Well, using Booleans
on archways produces more complex models than simply gluing primitives together. Using the same techniques as those used to create the chair in the previous example, you can cut away primitive objects (and imported ones) in
seconds to produce extremely complicated models. See Figure 2.45, and if the
illustration intrigues you, load the ArchZ2 project from the CD-ROM.

INTERGALACTIC SHIP

Space ships go hand in hand with computer graphics, and using Boolean techniques, you can create mega vehicles in Bryce 3D. It's one thing to create a
small planetary ship, but an intergalactic ship requires enhanced levels of believability. A ship of this kind must be perceived as massive, something strong
enough to weather the star storms and spiraling time tornadoes that whip
through the void. We have included a model of just such a ship on the CD-
ROM. Look for it in the project folder, as Galact1. Open the project and study
the way it was put together. Booleans are used throughout the construction (see
Figure 2.46).

FIGURE   *Another variation of the archway, this time created with Boolean operations.*
2.45

FIGURE   *The Galact1 star cruiser is a force to be reckoned with, and it's no wonder it*
2.46   *can stand the tremendous forces that a jump to lightspeed entails.*

Moving On   In this chapter, we have concentrated upon a number of ways that you can create and modify models in Bryce 3D. The next chapter will take a look at a special type of Bryce 3D model—Terrain—and the ways you can customize it.

CHAPTER

Terrain

Getting Grounded

When the word "Terrain" is used in a Bryce 3D world, it generally refers to a specific object type. A Terrain object has depth, or what is known as extrusion on the Y World Space coordinate system. Common Terrain objects include hills and mountains, but the possibilities do not end there. True Terrain objects can be edited in the Bryce 3D Terrain Editor. Four items that are associated with Terrain are represented by icons in the Create toolbar: Ground Plane, Terrain, Stone, and the Symmetrical Lattice (see Figure 3.1). Of these four items, only two can be edited in the Terrain Editor: Terrain and the Symmetrical Lattice.

Real Bryce 3D Terrain objects, as we have said, can be customized and modified in the Terrain Editor. Only the Terrain and Symmetrical Lattice fit this description. But what about the Ground Plane and the Stone objects? In common parlance, a terrain is a part of the ground, so the Ground Plane and Stone objects fit the general description of terrain as an descriptive object class. That being the case, the next two sections will look at the Ground Plane and Stone objects.

The Ground Plane

Bryce 3D has three planar objects, each of which can accept material mapping: Cloud, Water, and Ground Plane. There are only slight differences among these three planes. First, they each load onto the workspace at different heights. Second, they attain their personalities by the materials mapped to their surfaces. Each of these three planes can accept any materials, and each can be moved to any height desired. You can easily map a cloud material, for instance, to a Ground plane, or water to a Cloud plane. So although they have separate icons, any one will suffice for the others. Most of the difference lies in their material settings, which distinguish them from their counterparts. Keep this in mind during the discussion of the Ground Plane, since what is said can apply equally to the other two planes.

Each of these three objects is an infinite plane, meaning that although they are represented on the workspace by a rectangular surface, they have no boundary as a horizontal limit. This in itself makes for some interesting visual magic.

FIGURE
3.1 *The four items in the Create toolbar associated with Terrain: Ground Plane, Terrain, Stone, and the Symmetrical Lattice.*

See Chapters 10, 11, and 12 for new ways to animate infinite planes, as well as how they can be configured as interesting backdrops.

The Ground Plane, and each of the infinite planes, can be stacked, rotated, and drilled with Boolean objects. Each of these three possibilities is worthy of further investigation.

STACKED GROUND PLANES

The reason for stacking ground planes is primarily to create more complex textures. To do this effectively, the top Ground Plane(s) must be either moderately transparent overall, or they must have surfaces that are wholly transparent in spots (see Figure 3.2).

FIGURE
3.2
Here is an illustration of two stacked Ground Planes. The bottom one is mapped with a stone material, while the top one is mapped with partially transparent horizontal bars with totally transparent areas in between. Notice how the object reacts when placed on the bottom plane, and the shadow cast on it by the bars on the top plane.

FIGURE
3.3
There are three stacked planes here. The top one is mapped with a water material, the middle one with the Disco Kelp material, and the bottom one with a rocky material. Notice that objects stuck in this mystical swamp show through the top layers, and that the "kelp" creates shadows on the bottom layer.

Stacked Ground Plane Project Ideas

Here are some suggestions for projects that would benefit from stacked Ground Plane techniques. See Figure 3.3 for some examples.

- Apply a ground fog to the top plane, and a normal surface to the bottom plane. You might even use several planes on top to simulate layered fog. The top plane(s) could either have a splotchy material with see-through sections, or be textured as an overall transparent with muted color.
- Create a multicolored checkered surface by stacking two Ground Planes fairly close together. Map the bottom one with a left-to-right striped material in green. Map the top plane with a front to back striped material in red, with 100% transparency between the stripes and 50% transparency for the color (see Chapter 5 for customizing materials in the Materials Lab).
- Create a swampy effect by using two or more Ground Planes stacked moderately close together. Map the top plane with the Disco Kelp material found in the Bryce 3D Complex materials library.

Be aware that the use of transparent stacked planes comes at a cost. Raytraced transparency in Bryce 3D consumes many times the amount of rendering time as compared to opaque materials.

ROTATED GROUND PLANES

Depending upon where you place your camera and how you apply materials to planes, you can create some powerful optical illusions. Using multiple planes and rotating them compounds their infinite nature. The trick is to look at them from the correct position to see what is going on. Figure 3.4 presents an example.

The Infinite Corridor

Infinity can be infuriating, because there's no way out, no end. This is another artifact of fractal geometry and of Bryce 3D infinite planes. Inexorably, infinity goes on forever, as this exercise disquietingly demonstrates. Do the following:

1. Load two Ground Planes into your scene. Rotate them so that they are each standing vertically (90 degrees on the Z axis in World Space) and facing each other with a space between. Make the camera look down this infinite corridor.

FIGURE **3.4** *These two Ground Planes were placed at a 20-degree angle to each other as seen from the camera. The right plane was mapped with a Steel Cage material, so you can see through it to the left-hand plane. Strange things happen when you double infinity. Flying at an even distance above the right-hand plane would cause the left plane to recede further below you.*

2. Now rotate each plane on its Y axis 3 degrees, so that the camera is placed at the narrow end of the corridor, and the corridor gradually opens wider at the end. Place the sun in front of the camera so that the corridor is illuminated from the front.

If you travel the camera down this corridor, you will never reach the sky at the end. What will happen however is that the sides will seem to recede slowly as the corridor widens and the planes diverge. The effect is like that of a dark curtain gradually opening to the sky. The corridor will always be there though, as a look to either the left or right will prove (see Figure 3.5).

Load the Fig3.05 project from the CD-ROM to explore how this effect is composed.

DRILLED GROUND PLANES

Another undocumented feature in Bryce 3D is that infinite planes can be treated like any other object when it comes to Boolean operations. This means that you can take any object, primitive or imported, and use it to drill holes in the plane. If the plane is a solid with another plane stacked below it, light will shine in the hole to reveal the material of the plane below. Drilling numerous holes in the top plane would multiply the effect. If you "traveled" in the space between the planes, it would be pitch dark until a hole let sky and light through.

FIGURE 3.5   *Looking down the infinite corridor at the sky beyond.*

If you placed an object (like a futuristic habitat) on the lower plane and let it rise above the upper plane through a hole, you would enhance the suspicion of the viewer that there was a whole world beneath the one they were looking at. You could then journey down into that murky world, as a virtual spelunker.

A Breath of Air

Here's an exercise that will allow you to explore one of the drilled plane effects. See Figures 3.6 and 3.7.

1. Create two Ground Planes in your world. Make sure there is space between them, and make each parallel to each other and to the Bryce 3D horizon line, as seen in the front view.
2. Apply materials (your choice) to each plane. Place the camera between them. Your preview should show a completely black scene.
3. Use a cylinder standing on its end to cut a hole in the top plane. Place another cylinder object on the bottom plane, poking up through the hole. Place the camera so it is in the space between the planes, looking up at the second cylinder and viewing the sky. If you like, you can also place a light in some part of the space between the planes, mysteriously illuminating some of the dark space in the distance.

FIGURE *A hole in the upper world reveals a spire and the mysterious terrain below.*
3.6

FIGURE *The same scene as viewed from below.*
3.7

Make sure that Haze is set to zero, or you'll get a dim horizontal line across the screen.

TIP

See the Fig3.06 project on the CD-ROM as an example of this exercise.

Ground Plane animation is covered in subtle detail in Chapter 10.

NOTE

Stones

When you need to place a cliff or other sharp escarpment in your Bryce 3D world, consider the use of a Stone rather than a Terrain object. Why? Because Stones can be resized as large as a Terrain object without the squarish base that Terrain normally has. The only detriment in using Stones for this purpose is that they can't be edited in the Terrain Editor, which may be fine if the object looks the way you want it to at the start. If you don't like the shape of the Stone that is placed in your scene, simply delete it and hit the Stone icon again. Do this until the Stone object meets your expectations. There is one more alternative, which is to use the Object library in the Create toolbar. The Object library has a special folder called "Rocks and Trees," which contains preset Stones (see Figure 3.8). Make sure you save your own favorite Stone objects to this library when you discover those that please your designer's eye.

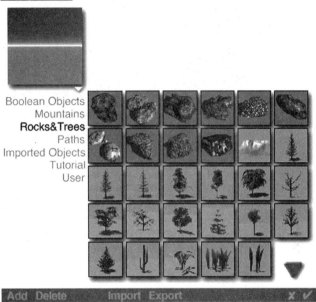

FIGURE *The Rocks and Trees section of the Create/Object library has a number of Stone*
3.8 *objects to choose from. You can save your own here as well.*

When you need a lot of different Stone shapes but want them all to exhibit the same
material texture, just Copy the material (Edit menu) and paste it to the other Stones.
Stones used as larger Terrain elements should be moved so they intersect one another.

TIP

See the Fig3.09 project on the CD-ROM for a detailed look at the stone cliffs de-
picted in Figure 3.9.

NOTE

Terrain and Symmetrical Lattice Objects

Having touched upon Ground Planes and Stones, it's time to move on to the two object types that can be edited, Terrain and Symmetrical Lattice objects.

TERRAIN OBJECTS

The Mountains folder in the Objects library is the first place to go to explore preset Terrain designs. It's also important to notice that the Terrain objects stored here give some indication that Bryce 3D Mountains can be more than mountains, but include a variety of object concepts that lie somewhere between a geological outcropping and the items they commemorate. Letters, for

FIGURE *Stone objects make great seaside cliffs.*
3.9

instance, can be translated into rocky objects that look like mountains from the side, while retaining their logo appearance from the top (see Figure 3.11 for an example). There is no reason that you can't do this with your own company or personal logo. See the section on working with the Terrain Editor later in this chapter.

NOTE

See Chapter 22 on logo animations for a closer look at Terrain logo design.

Remember the exercises that included the rotation of infinite planes? The same thing can be done with Terrain objects. You can literally turn mountains on their sides in Bryce 3D, creating surrealistic rock walls, and even using the Terrain object as a wall of a medieval house. Although Terrain objects are normally used to create awesome mountain ranges, you do not have to be constrained to this use alone (see Figure 3.12).

FIGURE *The Terrain icon in the Create toolbar.*
3.10

FIGURE **3.11** *This Bryce 3D Terrain object is included in the Mountain folder in the Objects library. It appears as a mountain from the side and is logo-like as seen from the top.*

FIGURE **3.12** *This exquisite tiled grating, through which the desert and sky can be appreciated, was created by multi-replicating the form from the Mountains folder in the Objects library.*

FIGURE *This scene was created with just one replicated Terrain object, which was*
3.13 *resized and rotated to produce the different geological looks. Even the grassy hills in the foreground were constructed from the same Terrain object. Different materials were used to map some of the clones.*

To investigate this effect further, load the Fig3.12 project from the CD-ROM.

NOTE

When you want to cover your backdrop with mountains and hills, it may not be necessary to use more than one Terrain object. Since Terrain objects can be resized on any axis and rotated, one replicated Terrain object can serve as multiple objects. Figure 3.13 presents an example.

By turning a Terrain object upside down, you have a perfect meteor crater, or even a receptacle for a crater lake, as shown in Figure 3.14.

See the Fig3.14 project on the CD-ROM.

NOTE

SYMMETRICAL LATTICE OBJECTS

Symmetrical Lattice objects are objects mirrored vertically at their center. For this reason, they can be used to create objects with balanced top/bottom or left/right symmetry. This is especially useful when you need to create mechanical objects or fantasy terrain like floating mountains. Symmetrical Lattice objects are best used in conjunction with the Terrain Editor, which is

FIGURE **3.14** *When a Terrain object is flipped vertically, it becomes a hole in the ground. Placing an object inside a hole enhances the depth effect.*

explored next. The Create toolbar icon is shown in Figure 3.15, and Figure 3.16 shows an example.

TIP

You can also use a Symmetrical Lattice object to fake a reflection, since the mirrored bottom half is always the same as the top half. If you take a journey "below" the liquid surface, you will still see the reflected lattice, an interesting optical illusion if you travel from below to above the surface in an animation. The surface doesn't have to be a common transparent surface, but can also be a surface with "holes" in it, with no reflective capabilities at all.

FIGURE **3.15** *The Symmetrical Lattice icon in the Create toolbar.*

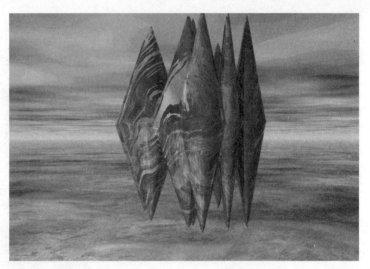

FIGURE
3.16
A conic map was applied to this Symmetrical Lattice to produce the effect seen here, which was then texture mapped with a Psychoactive Christmas Ball material.

Mastering the Terrain Editor

"Mastering" is a somewhat dubious term to use here. If by mastering, the complete coverage of all possibilities comes to mind as a definition, then it should be stated up front that you could never hope to exhaust your options in the Terrain Editor. What you can hope to accomplish is to gain a familiarity with the tools and techniques, so you are free to combine them in exciting and novel ways. The Terrain Editor is activated by selecting its icon in the Edit toolbar, shown in Figure 3.17.

NOTE

Important: It is absolutely essential that you read and work through the Bryce 3D documentation that deals with the Terrain Editor and the editing process before delving into the topic as covered here. It is assumed that you have the basic knowledge on how to navigate to different tabs in the Terrain Editor and have some basic knowledge concerning the options and operation. This section can then be used to augment your skills in terrain and symmetrical lattice editing.

FIGURE
3.17
The Terrain Editor is activated by clicking on its icon in the Edit toolbar after a Terrain object or a Symmetrical Lattice is selected.

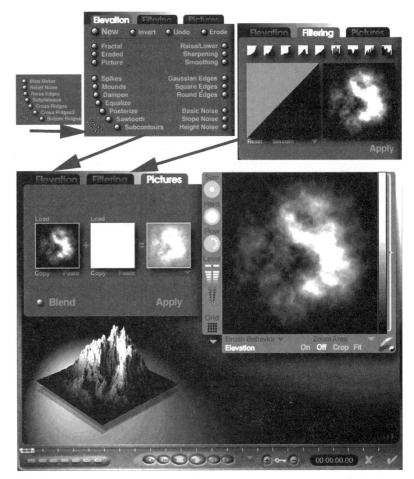

FIGURE **3.18** *In order to understand and work through these examples, you must be familiar with and know how to work all of the tools and options in the General, Filtering, and Pictures tabs of the Terrain Editor, as well as the options in the rest of the Terrain Editor dialog.*

This section will present some example object needs and show you how to achieve them using various tools and techniques in the Terrain Editor. Figure 3.18 illustrates some of the other screens and operations you should know before using Terrain Editor. The first step is always to use the Terrain icon, so that a Terrain object is placed on the screen. This object is only a proxy object, so that we can open the Terrain Editor. If you want to explore these methods on a Symmetrical Lattice instead of a Terrain object, just make sure you click on the Symmetrical Lattice icon to place its proxy on screen first.

CREATING AND CUSTOMIZING OBJECTS IN THE TERRAIN EDITOR

Look at each of the pictures that accompany these examples. The instructions that follow tell you how the object was produced with specific tools and options in the Terrain Editor. If you work through these exercises, you will be well on your way to mastering the Terrain Editor.

The Cross-sloped Cabin Roof

With a Terrain object selected in your workspace, open the Terrain Editor and click on New in the Terrain Editor General tab, so you can start with a blank 3D canvas, then do the following:

1. Click on Cross-Ridges2. A cross-ridged roof shape will be created (see Figure 3.19). This object has no sides if ported to your workspace at this point, so we have to create some.
2. Click on Erode, and then on Undo. This sets up the effects brush. With Paint Effect selected, draw your brush down the perimeter of the cross-ridged shape. You have added rough vertical faces to the object. They are somewhat random and cracked, but this will be just right for the roof we want. Place the roof on your workspace (see Figure 3.20).

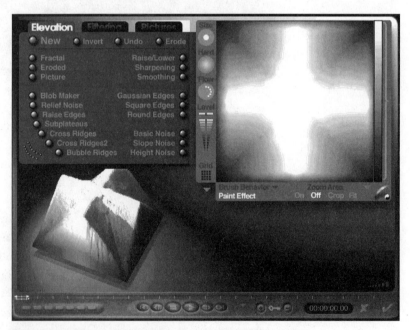

FIGURE *The Cross-Ridges2 operator creates a nice roof object.*
3.19

FIGURE *Here is the roof placed on the rest of the house.*
3.20

TIP

For smooth vertical faces, click and drag on the Square Edges operator.

How about the Rest of the Cabin?

You can investigate this scene, listed as Cabin1 in the Projects folder on the ac-companying CD-ROM. The base of the house is a cube, with windows and a door cut away by other Boolean cubes. The "tree" by the side is a Boolean ob-ject from the Bryce 3D library, and it added two hours to the rendering time. Be careful about using complex Boolean objects in a scene. A Terrain object was added as the ground, since it adds more realistic bumpiness than a flat in-finite plane. An infinite Ground Plane was added under it and mapped with the same material. This extends the horizon.

Variations Ad Infinitum

Starting with the basic Cross-Ridge operator in the Terrain Editor, you can cre-ate an almost infinite array of roof variations. This is done by exploring various other operators to be overlaid on top of the Cross-Ridge. See Figure 3.21.

TIP

Using the Replicate command on a Terrain object after it has been customized in the Terrain Editor reverts the copy back to a standard Terrain. Using the Duplicate command makes the copy the same as the original.

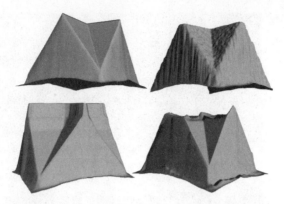

FIGURE 3.21 *Here are just a few examples of roof variations that can be created in the Terrain Editor in seconds, using the Cross-Ridge as a base.*

FOREST

With a Terrain object selected in your workspace, open the Terrain Editor and click on New in the Terrain Editor General Tab.

1. Create a group of Mounds by clicking and sliding the mouse (LM on Windows systems) to the right over the Mounds operator.
2. Create a series of SubPlateaus by sliding the mouse (LM on Windows systems) to the right over the SubPlateaus operator.
3. Write the Forest Terrain object to the scene.
4. Add some height (Y World axis) when you return to the workscreen. Use the material to add a convincing color.

This is a useful object because adding groups of trees any other way is rendering prohibitive. Used in the distance with a 50% to 60% haze (light green), and a 70–70 Fog setting (light green) this technique provides a realistic forest (see Figure 3.22). These trees can be especially effective when reflected in water across a lake. Submerge the base beneath the ground plane or underlying terrain.

VOLCANO

With a Terrain object selected in your workspace, open the Terrain Editor and click on new in the Terrain Editor General tab.

1. Create a basic Volcano cone shape by clicking on the Blob Maker operator.
2. Select a mid-level gray with the Elevation brush, and click ten times in the middle of the cone. This flattens it out.

FIGURE
3.22 *Using the Mounds and SubPlateaus operators in the Terrain Editor creates a convincing forest.*

3. Select a black Elevation brush, sized smaller than the flattening brush in step 2, and click ten times in the middle of the flattened cone. This bores a hole for the calendra.
4. Click on Erode, and then on Undo. Use a Paint Effect brush to go around the perimeter of the volcano, adding selective cracks and fissures. Paint from the inside outward in shaky uneven strokes. When satisfied with the preview model, write the object to your workspace (see Figure 3.23).

You can resize the Volcano or duplicate it as needed in your scene. Add a fire material to a plume and run for your life!

FIGURE *The Volcano lives on earthly and alien terrain.*
3.23

STANDING STONES

Creating this scene with primitive objects was covered previously. This section explains how to make it within the Terrain Editor. With a Terrain object selected in your workspace, open the Terrain Editor and click on New in the Terrain Editor General tab.

1. Use an Elevation brush to paint in 7 standing stones as seen from the top. Use a maximum white ranging to a medium white, so they all have separate heights.
2. Use the Eroded Effects brush to give the stones a little character, then click and drag right on the Smoothing function twice. Write the object to your workspace (see Figure 3.24).

This group of stones looks very nice reflected in water, so our example shows a reflective pool around the stones. A Torus is used as a border for the water. See the Stonerz2 project to investigate it fully.

HOUSE INTERIOR

With a Terrain object selected in your workspace, open the Terrain Editor and click on New in the Terrain Editor General tab.

1. Create the top view of rooms in a house, like a floor plan. Use the smallest and whitest brush possible. Draw the walls as straight as you can.

One way to get straight lines in the Terrain Editor is to slide your mouse along the edge of a ruler when drawing.

TIP

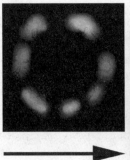

FIGURE *The standing stones look more mysterious when reflected in a pool of water.*
3.24

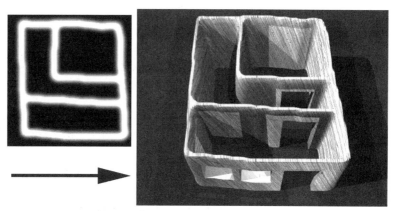

FIGURE   *You can add lights and position the camera for a walkthrough of the rooms.*
3.25   *Add furniture as needed, or live in it very frugally until you can afford to*
          furnish it.

2. Use the Smoothing operation twice, by clicking and dragging the mouse to the right over the Smoothing function. Accept the object and write it to your workscreen.

3. Use a series of resized cubes to cut windows and doorways in the walls. Figure 3.25 shows the coupleted house interior.

NOTE

See 3.25.br3 in the Projects folder on the CD-ROM, so you can customize this house further. You may want to add a roof to keep out the weather.

RIVERBED

With a Terrain object selected in your workspace, open the Terrain Editor and click on New in the Terrain Editor General tab. Then do the following to create a Terrain object with a riverbed.

1. Click on these three operators in the following order: Cross Ridges 2, Cross Ridges, and Eroded. This will produce a blocky structure.

2. Use a medium-sized solid black Elevation brush, and trace a meander from the upper left to the lower right of the object. This is the start of your riverbed.

3. With the same brush, select a medium gray color. Trace next to the meander on either side. This cuts away some of the sheerness of the cliffs next to the riverbed.

4. Click on Erode, then on Undo. Use the Effects brush to add some erosion to the sides of the cliffs that face the riverbed. Write the object to your scene.

FIGURE   *Rollin', rollin', rollin' down the river.*
3.26

5. Use a material on the Terrain object (Planes and Terrains/Grassy Peaks works well). Add a water plane to the scene, and map a material to it (the "Nice Water" material will do nicely). Nestle your camera over the river for a nice view, and render (Figure 3.26).

CASTLE FORTRESS

With a Terrain object selected in your workspace, open the Terrain Editor and click on New in the Terrain Editor General tab. Get ready for a medieval thrill.

1. Use a medium-sized Elevation Brush set to a 100% white to paint in the four towers at the corners of your Terrain Editor workspace. The best way to do this is to click the same number of times for each tower, assuring that they will have equal height.
2. Select a color two shades darker than the towers for the walls. Draw a line between towers to create the walls. Try to make them as straight as possible, but don't be concerned if they wiggle a little. The Terrain Editor will interpolate them and make them straighter.
3. Write the castle to your workspace and add Boolean cutaways as needed. If it is to be used as a distant edifice, you don't have to do much further detail work. Use a rock material to texture the object (explore the Barnacles material), and set it on a mound in your world, adding a 50% Haze. Figure 3.27 shows the finished castle.

MACHINE PANEL

With a Terrain object selected in your workspace, open the Terrain Editor and click on New in the Terrain Editor General tab.

FIGURE *The old castle sits on a misty hill, remembering its past days of glory.*
3.27

1. For this exercise, we are going to use one of the preset Terrain maps in the Bryce 3D folder. Click on Picture in the General tab and then find the Terrain Maps folder. Select the City2 map.
2. Click on Posterize and drag the mouse to the right as far as it will go. Click on the Raise/Lower function and drag the mouse to the right so that the object has its height lowered by about two-thirds. Write the object to your workspace (see Figure 3.28).

For a neat effect, stack these panels, or variations of them, and set them in place as a backdrop for a high-tech room. You can even create the bridge of a spaceship in the same manner.

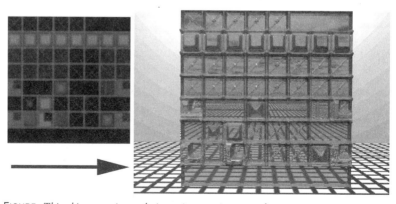

FIGURE *This object creation technique gives you instant techno props.*
3.28

CRATERS

With a Terrain object selected in your workspace, open the Terrain Editor and click on new in the Terrain Editor General tab. Then do the following:

1. Create a Solid block by clicking and dragging right as far as you can over the Raise Edges operator. This produces a solid block (colored white).
2. Lower the height of the block to about one-third of its size by selecting the Raise/Lower operator and clicking and dragging to the right while watching the 3D preview.
3. With a 70% white Elevation brush of medium size, pick the place for your first crater. Click over the area as you watch the circular area raising itself in the 3D preview. This will be the wall of the crater.
4. Now select a 70% black Elevation brush a bit smaller than the raised area. Click and watch the hole being formed. Make the hole about twice as deep as the walls of the crater are high.
5. Repeat this process to develop several craters in the block.
6. Click on the SubContours operator and then on Undo. Select the Effects brush, resize it to minimum, and paint some erosions onto each of the crater's walls. Watch the 3D preview as you are working. Repeat this process with SubPlateaus. When finished, write the object back to the workspace (see Figure 3.29).

Avoid using complex material if you want to appreciate these craters more clearly, or they may be hidden by the material. On the other hand, materials that work by altitude work well on craters, since they paint the upper parts differently and allow the crater to stand out. See Chapter 4 on Materials.

TIP

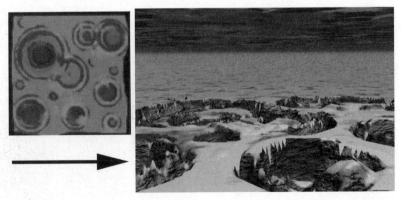

FIGURE *Cratered environments can be produced quickly and interactively in the Terrain*
3.29 *Editor.*

CITYMAP PICTURE BLEND

With a Terrain object selected in your workspace, open the Terrain Editor and click on New in the Terrain Editor General tab.

1. Load the Cones preset from the Terrain Maps folder into the first channel of the Pictures tab.
2. Load the CityMap 2 preset into the second channel.
3. With Options set to Blend, click and drag on the blend arrow until the final picture area shows about a 50% blend between the two Terrain Maps (see Figure 3.30). Use the Bladerunner material to map the terrain object.

GENERAL TERRAIN EDITOR TIPS

- To quickly black out an area of your Altitude map, select darkest color and no smoothing on brush. Click mouse once over area needing deletion. This is also how holes are cut in objects, after selecting a very dark shading.
- For stairstepping object elements, paint down your brush with smoothing off. Select the "lowest" step first, with the darkest shade. Then, move progressively brighter, painting down the next highest step. Doing this inside of the Terrain Editor creates circular or partially circular steps, since Bryce 3D has no rectangular brushes for this operation.
- Use the edge of the altitude map window as a straightedge when you need to paint a line along the perimeter of the object. This is especially useful when applying effects with the paintbrush.
- For altering the ho-hum symmetry of an object, load a different graphic into the Alpha channel in the Picture tab. Use the Blend slider to mix the original graphic and the Alpha graphic on screen. This is very useful

FIGURE   *Blending the cones with the citymap 2 gives the cityscape a much more bizarre*
3.30   *look, like something out of this world, or maybe it was something you ate.*

when creating cities whose buildings look too similar from just the altitude map. The Blend can also be used as a keyframe, so that it can change over time, creating unusual and experimental effects.

HIDING OR DELETING AN OBJECT'S SQUARE BASE

Terrain objects always have a square base, while Symmetrical Lattice objects can have theirs painted out (when they have one).

NOTE

If your Terrain objects appear with a square base and you do not want to see the base in the rendering, do one of the following:

- If the object is sitting on an opaque plane (like the Ground Plane), just move it down so that the base is hidden by the overlying plane.
- If the object is in transparent water, move the base of the object below an opaque plane that lies below the water plane.
- If the object is to float in the air (floating or inside of a cloud) or in space, then use a Symmetrical Lattice initially in the design phase instead of a Terrain object.

If the Symmetrical Lattice object displays a base, you can use the Edge tools in the General tab to paint it out, or alternatively, you can apply selective Erosion on the edge with the Effects paintbrush.

TIP

- An alternative method to all of these is to group a negative Boolean cube at the positive object's base, cutting off the visibility of the base for the viewer, or to painstakingly use negative Boolean spheres to cut away the superfluous parts of the base.

CREATING ALTITUDE MAPS

You can create altitude maps in the Terrain Editor with the paint tools provided, or you can create them in a separate paint application, and import them into the Terrain Editor afterward. It is best to use the internal painting tools for editing and touchup in most cases, and to create new altitude maps outside of Bryce 3D. The reason for this is that external bitmap painting applications give you far more painting options, and they usually have large filter plug-in libraries to alter the image further.

Internal Altitude Map Painting

Internal altitude map painting is most commonly used for editing purposes on a Terrain preset, or on an imported altitude map. This is because compared to a paint application, Bryce 3D's Terrain Editor painting tools are severely limited. There is no square tool, for instance, and no constraints for straight lines. This doesn't mean you can't paint some interesting terrains, but it does mean that you should know the limitations beforehand.

Using the painting brush to edit a Terrain preset or an imported altitude map is another story. This is where the Terrain painting process in Bryce 3D really shines. By clicking on any of the terrain creation operations (like Mounds or Erode), and then hitting Undo, the effect selected before the Undo was activated becomes the operation your brush will use in the editing process. This allows you to deftly paint erosion over selected parts of the altitude map, as opposed to targeting the whole altitude map for alterations. Let's look at some visual examples.

Tips for Using the Terrain Editor's Painting Tools and Options
These tips assume you have spent time exploring the Terrain Editor's painting options.

- Remember that you are working in the Terrain Editor and not in a standard 3D object environment. If you need to create smooth machine-like structures, it's far better to use another 3D application suited to that purpose. The Terrain Editor usually introduces some random anomalies to your objects. If you must have objects with a minimum of structural anomalies from the Terrain Editor, try making two or three passes with the Smoothing function.
- Add Erosion and Fractalization selectively with the Effects brush. This allows you much more control over your models.
- Create a negative (inverse) of your image in a paint application and store it with the positive image. In the Pictures tab, load the inverse image into the second channel. Use the Blend slider to mix the two. The result will be an object slowly reversing its geometry. At midpoint, this obliterates the object, while at either end of the spectrum, it allows either the positive or negative object to exist.
- Use the Paint Effects brush with Relief Noise to add a touch of volume to elements of the image. This process puffs out the selected elements each time you use it, so you will be able to control the shaping of the object by small amounts each time.
- With the Hard/Soft selector turned all the way to soft, the Elevation brush acts more to smooth a selected altitude than to carve holes, even with the grayscale indicator turned all the way to black. When you want to carve a hole in the top of an object, turn the selector to Hard.

- For more subtle applications of an Effect brush, try using short clicks instead of clicking and dragging the mouse.

External Altitude Map Painting

Bryce 3D can translate 24-bit, 256-color, or black-and-white bitmap art into altitude maps. Since the final operation uses a 256-color palette or smaller, it's better to work in index color modes of 256 or fewer colors in your paint application to produce the altitude map art. Bryce 3D assumes the art will be saved as a BMP (Windows) or PICT (Mac) for import. There are any number of applications to use for this purpose, including four of my personal favorites:

- **MetaCreations' Painter 5**—Painter is the most innovative bitmap painting application on the market. It has loads of diverse brushes for painting any effect you can imagine, and many you can't. Version 5 also offers f/x brushes, whose output creates innovative altitude maps in Bryce 3D. Chief among its tools is the Image Hose, allowing you to spray randomized graphics. Many of the Image Hose libraries contain brushes that translate well when used as altitude map data in Bryce 3D. Painter can utilize most Photoshop plug-ins. Multi-platform. Figure 3.31 gives an example of a Painter graphic.
- **Adobe Photoshop 4**—Though Photoshop has limited painting options compared to Painter, it is king of the hill when it comes to filters. Photoshop has its own extensive list of internal f/x filters, in addition to its invitation to developers for external plug-in filters. The Photoshop Lens Flare filter creates smoothly sculpted conic spires in Bryce 3D's Terrain Editor, as shown in Figure 3.32.

FIGURE 3.31 *A Painter 5 graphic, produced with the Hexagonal Tile effect, translated to an altitude map in Bryce 3D. The hexagons range in brightness, so they are perfect for creating skyscrapers that range in height, a classic urban skyline.*

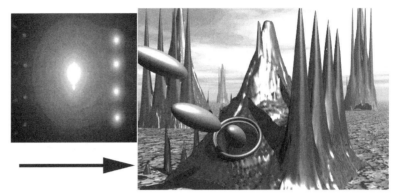

FIGURE *A Photoshop graphic, produced with Photoshop's exclusive internal Lens Flare*
3.32 *filter, translated to an altitude map in Bryce 3D. The 3D object it created is on*
the right. "Where ships of dreams amaze the eyes and golden spires touch the
skies."

- **Corel PhotoPaint 8**—Corel's PhotoPaint will access most Photoshop
  plug-in filters and also includes many of its own. Many of its filter selections are versions of separate applications that come with PhotoPaint, yet
  have to be purchased as extras for other painting software. PhotoPaint
  has one of the best 2D animation systems around for creating image sequences that can be utilized in Bryce 3D. Multi-platform. Figure 3.33
  gives an example.
- **MetaCreations TextureScape 2**—This is a Mac application, originally
  marketed by Specular International. The name says it all. TextureScape

FIGURE *A PhotoPaint graphic, produced with a Ripple Fill, translated to an altitude*
3.33 *map in Bryce 3D. The Terrain is grooved all the way around, providing a*
trough for an object to roll. Smoothed out, this would even suffice for a marble
raceway. The circular path could also lead to a temple on top. Flattened out,
this could also be a terraced rice paddy, with the right texture.

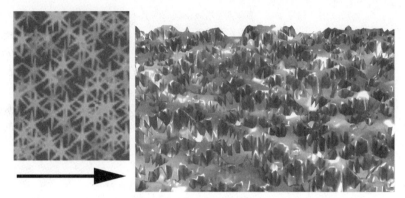

FIGURE **3.34** *A TextureScape graphic, translated to an altitude map in Bryce 3D, alongside the object created. Mapped with the Complex/Cotton Candy Mix material, this serves as great alien sludge.*

creates an infinite variety of texture maps. These not only translate well as altitude maps for the Bryce 3D terrain Editor, but work equally well as pictorial graphics for use as Materials in Bryce 3D. Figure 3.34 gives an illustration.

- **MicroFrontier's Enhance 4**—Available now for the Mac, a Windows version is promised in 1998. Mac users are familiar with this application as an expanded enhancement of "ColorIt!", a Mac favorite. Enhance offers unique capabilities when it comes to blending tiled graphics one on another. This is perfect for use as a altitude map in Bryce 3D and also valuable for creating bitmaps for materials (see Figure 3.35).

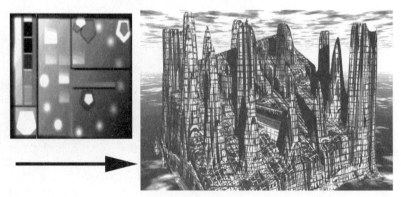

FIGURE **3.35** *An Enhance graphic, produced with its shape tools, and translated to an altitude map in Bryce 3D. A perfect map for a futuristic city in the clouds.*

TIP

For creating mountain objects in the Terrain Editor externally, use any method in your painting application that creates "cloud" graphics. Clouds translate into superlative altitude maps that then generate very realistic terrain objects. This is because clouds, like mountains, are based upon fractals.

Generating Altitude Map Data from Photos

In addition to creating altitude map images by painting them, images can be produced as altitude map data for Bryce 3D.

Digital Photography

A digital photograph is produced by any photographic method that results in data that can be read into the computer. That data can then be imported into Bryce 3D as an altitude map for Terrain object creation. There are a number of devices that can be used to generate digital photographics. These include:

- **Digital Still-Camera Input**—Until a few years ago, consumer-priced digital still cameras were capable of producing only low resolution output. Recently, this has changed dramatically, with the introduction of dozens of cameras capable of capturing very fine detail and priced to fit most computer arts budgets. You will need either the proper inputs on your computer (composite or S-VHS) to access the images ion the camera or a camera that writes images to a floppy or FlashPix disk. Figure 3.36 gives an example.
- **Scanned Photographs**—Most computer graphics art and animation studios, and many home computer workspaces, have a scanner. A scanner can generate very detailed images from original or printed photographs, as shown in Figure 3.37.

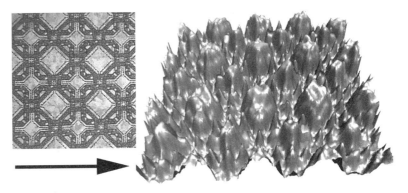

FIGURE *An original digital still-camera graphic, translated to an altitude map in Bryce*
3.36 *3D. The tiled floor is made to look like a 3D egg carton.*

FIGURE *An original scanned photograph, translated to an altitude map in Bryce 3D.*
3.37

- **CD-ROM Collections**—There are hundreds of published copyright-free collections of photography on CD-ROMs (see Figure 3.38). Most can be had for under $25 a volume, and many have images that translate into superlative altitude maps for Bryce 3D. See Appendix G for a suggested list of CD-ROM volumes to investigate.
- **Video Grabs**—If you have access to a video camera, and if your computer has an add-on card that has a video input (usually Composite and/or S-VHS), you can grab still-frames from a video (see Figure 3.39). You can also do the same thing by grabbing frames from a videotape.
- **Photocopy**—This is an option that many artists neglect, but one that can serve you well. The newer office copiers produce photographic or

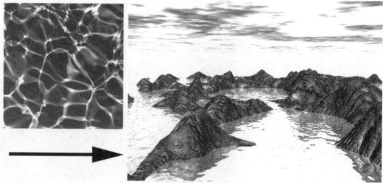

FIGURE *A copyright-free image from the Image Club Graphics Digital Vision/H2O CD-*
3.38 *ROM collection, translated to an altitude map in Bryce 3D. As it happens, this is a perfect object to use as a repository for water puddles or small islands and atolls.*

FIGURE *A frame from one of the author's videotapes, translated to an altitude map in*
3.39 *Bryce 3D. The base was cut away by a negative Boolean cube. Blur was applied*
in the paint application and smoothing in Bryce 3D.

near-photographic output, in color or grayscale (see Figure 3.40). Sometimes, however, the older office copiers that produce "poor" output create just the right look for interesting altitude maps, after the copy has
been scanned into the computer. You can even move the original artwork
on a copier while it is doing its job, creating interesting grayscale smears
that look intriguing when turned into altitude maps in Bryce 3D.

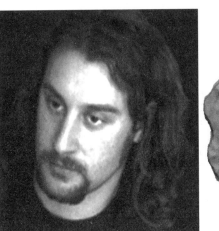

FIGURE *A photocopy of an original image, translated to an altitude map in Bryce 3D.*
3.40 *Black was used to outline the image in the paint application, and again in*
Bryce 3D's Terrain Editor.

Preparing Photos

There are several things you can do beforehand in your paint application to make photos more suitable for translation into 3D objects in Bryce 3D's Terrain Editor:

- Use a blur filter several times on the image. This tones down the areas that are prone to be translated as 3D spikes.
- Enhance the contrast of the image. This will make altitude data more obvious to Bryce 3D and make the 3D object smoother at the start.
- Change 24-bit color into grayscale. This allows you more options in the paint application, so that you can visualize what the translation might look like.
- Delete unwanted data. This can be very important. If you need to translate facial information to 3D for instance, there is no need for the background. For translation in the Terrain Editor, make the unwanted data pure black. For translation in the Material Lab (see the next chapter), make the deleted parts of the photo white. If you need both translations, create two images, one with a white backdrop and one with black. This allows you to precisely map colored image data on a 3D object later on.

TIP

It is often necessary to use a black Elevation brush on the image after you apply smoothing in the Terrain Editor, since smoothing can cause the background black level to turn gray. This may be necessary even though you have used black to outline the image in the paint application.

Copyrights

Don't neglect the copyright laws when it comes to gathering photographic art for your Bryce 3D altitude maps. The photography in most magazines and books, unless otherwise noted, is copyrighted. So are the images in most videos. Select either copyright-free imagery, or contact the publishers of commercial publications to obtain permission to use their images. Publishing copyrighted photos without permission on the Internet is especially troublesome, since so many people could potentially see your work. Be safe, and get permission or use only copyright-free material.

Plug-in Filters

Plug-in filters enhance the capabilities of the application they are folded into. There are hundreds of plug-in filters available for paint applications, each one

FIGURE *An image created with Xaos Tools Terrazzo filter, translated to an altitude map*
3.41 *in Bryce 3D. I love this object. It reminds me of rusty beetle carcasses.*

offering new and exciting image enhancement and modification capabilities.
One of my favorites is the Terrazzo plug-in from Xaos Tools. With this plug-in,
you can take any selected area of an image and use it as a basis for the creation
of a kaleidoscopic tiled graphic. Using this plug-in as a device for creating a
Bryce 3D altitude map, the resulting objects offer new 3D possibilities, as
shown in Figure 3.41.

Scanning Real-world Objects

You can scan more than 2D images on your scanner. You can also place a variety of 3D objects on the scanning platen (being careful not to scratch the glass).
Exploring and experimenting, you can wind up with a graphic that translates
into an interesting altitude map for applying to a Bryce 3D Terrain object, such
as that shown in Figure 3.42.

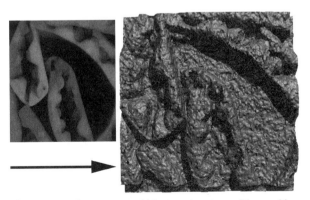

FIGURE *This object was created by scanning pieces of foam rubber on end and*
3.42 *translating the image into an altitude map in the Terrain Editor.*

Two-color Bitmaps as Altitude Maps

This is the best way to generate sharp symmetry, good for producing mechanical and architectural objects in Bryce 3D's Terrain Editor. Remember, however, that you are working in the Terrain Editor, basically changing organic objects like mountains into human-constructed artifacts when you need sharper objects, and that some anomalies will be present. There are ways to minimize them by using the smoothing operation after the bitmap has been read in, but there will usually be a few jagged anomalies left. If this bothers you, then you should not be creating objects in the Terrain Editor. Instead, you should be creating them in a more suitable application, exporting them in a format that Bryce 3D can read, and using them from there. Terrain objects will have some organic and unsymmetrical terrain attributes most of the time, no matter what the altitude map looks like.

No matter what painting application you use to create the two-color (black-and-white) original art, or even if is processed from a color or grayscale photo, it can be altered by a number of filters as well. Black-and-white art creates a Bryce 3D Terrain map that has only two altitudes, lowest and highest. Black and white art can, however, be transformed into grayscale altitude maps in Bryce 3D by using various modifications on it (such as smoothing, eroding, and combining it with other images assigned to an alpha channel). Once translated to grayscale, an image has the potential to include 256 different altitude variations. An example of this process is shown in Figure 3.43.

FIGURE **3.43** *This object began as a vector drawing in Macromedia Freehand, was ported to Photoshop and saved as a 2-color TIFF, and was then translated to an altitude map in Bryce 3D. A negative Boolean cube was used to cut away the base. This is a good technique for creating fancy wrought iron fences.*

Redundancy Altitude Maps

NOTE

Alert! This information is not mentioned in the Bryce 3D documentation, and it can help you create startling and time-saving objects in Bryce 3D.

Here's another awesome technique for creating a variety of altitude maps for Bryce 3D, one that uses Bryce 3D as the generating engine itself! Let's backtrack a bit, so you can see how and why this works. To repeat, an altitude map is composed of a series of 256 grays, with each gray standing for a separate altitude as seen from the top view. The darkest gray (or 100% black) generates the lowest altitude. The lightest gray (100% white), generates the highest altitude. The rest of the gray spectrum produces intermediate altitudes, depending upon their ranges, from black to white. The magic of it is, Bryce 3D can produce altitude maps from your 3D scenes. Here's how:

1. Using a variety of Bryce 3D primitive objects, create a customized scene. Stack some of the objects on top of one another, resize some larger and some smaller.
2. Delete the ground plane and set the sky to the pure white backdrop option. This is just for viewing, since this process never renders the sky anyway.
3. Go to the camera view. Now here's the necessary alteration. Position the objects as if you were looking down on them from the top view. The rendering will only work as a camera rendering, but in order to create a suitable altitude map, we have to configure the objects in the camera view as if they were seen from the top view.

NOTE

It doesn't matter how or where your light(s) are, since the image produced will pay no attention to lights.

4. Turn Normal Anti-aliasing on. Go to the documents presets and select the Distance Render option. Distance rendering is normally used to produce image masks for Photoshop or compatible applications. Render and save the image.

NOTE

Notice that the farther the objects are from the camera, the lighter they are. Brightness will translate into "higher" altitudes in the Terrain Editor.

5. Delete all of the objects from the scene. Create a Terrain object or a Symmetrical Lattice in your workspace. With the object selected, go to the Terrain Editor. Hit New to remove the object, and click on Picture to load in a graphic.

6. Find the Distance render you just saved and load it in as an altitude map. Click on Invert to reverse the altitudes. Use whatever other alteration methods you like to alter the object, or leave it as it is. Click on the checkmark to write it to the 3D workspace.

The more you explore this technique of object creation, the more adept you will become at foretelling the outcome. Remember that when you generate the object, the Terrain object can then become the subject of another Distance Render, which can then be translated in the Terrain Editor as another altitude map. Multi-replicating the object, and repeating the Distance Rendering over and over again, can lead to a further exploration of this process. The resulting object is textured by the one material. Since every part of it is in one glued-together grouping, rendering time and storage space is saved, as compared with the original collection of objects. It's not a complete solution, but it is a way to generate objects that can't be sculpted in any other way. Figures 3.44 and 3.45 show outcomes of this process.

Uses: Though it's impossible to predict all of the uses you may find for this technique, it can be used to create complex-looking skyscraper facades whose polygon counts are low.

A Variation on the Redundancy Method

There's more than one way to skin a carrot, and more than one way to perform this object creation option. Instead of using Distance Rendering, use normal

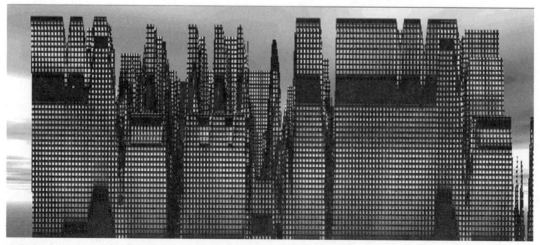

FIGURE 3.44 *A modern skyline created with the Reduction method in the Terrain Editor.*

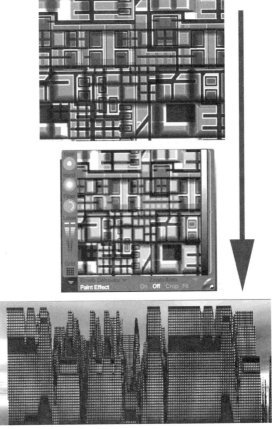

FIGURE *This figure illustrates the consecutive steps in this unique process, from creating*
3.45 *a camera view of a collection of objects, to the final resulting 3D object. There*
are infinite variations to explore.

perspective Rendering. Set the objects up so they are seen from the top view, and select the pure black sky option (delete the ground plane). When the rendering is imported as an altitude map, you won't have to invert it. Make sure that shadows are turned off on all objects, or the shadows will become object data.

Another Variation

You can also render altitude maps in Bryce 3D from the Render options. These renderings show the actual height of objects, with white being high and black low. Though Distance Renders will only work from the Camera view, Altitude Renders work in any view. To get grayscale maps from the top view, you have to move the object up or down in the World Y axis.

1. Create a row of 7 spheres. Group them and duplicate twice. Rotate the groups so that they each use the first sphere as in a stack, as seen from the top view. Move each group to a different height (Y axis), using the front and/or right views as a guide.
2. Delete the ground plane and set the sky to the pure black backdrop option. This render process does render the backdrop color.
3. Go to the top view. Use the Altitude option in the Render selections with Normal Anti-aliasing on and render the view. Export it to disk as a PICT (Mac) or BMP (Windows).

TIP

It doesn't matter how or where your light(s) are, since the image produced will pay no attention to lights, only to the comparative altitude of the objects. Notice that the closer the objects are to your eye from any view, the lighter they are. Brightness will translate into "higher" altitudes in the Terrain Editor.

4. Delete all of the objects from the scene. Create a Terrain object or a Symmetrical Lattice object in your workspace. With the object selected, go to the Terrain Editor. Hit New to remove the object, and click on Picture to load in a graphic.
5. Find the altitude render you just saved and load it in as a Terrain Editor altitude map. No need to invert the map this time, since with a black background, altitudes are in the expected places. Use whatever other alteration methods you like to alter the object, or leave it as it is. Since spheres are translated into poles by this method, you could use an Erode brush effect to give them scraggly surfaces, and use them as a tree group. Click on the Checkmark to write the object to the Bryce 3D workspace. Figure 3.46 shows an example.

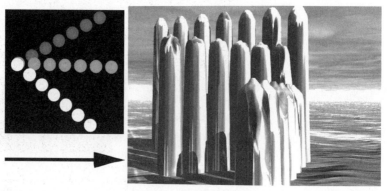

FIGURE
3.46 *From a stack of spheres to a finished group of poles, using the altitude rendering method as a precursor to Terrain mapping creates useful objects.*

EVERY MATERIAL IS AN OBJECT!

If you can turn bitmaps into objects in the Terrain Editor, then it doesn't matter what application generates the original bitmaps. Bryce 3D can generate bitmaps, so Bryce 3D itself can transform them into objects. We have already seen one example of this in the Redundancy walkthrough above, but there's another way to do it. Bryce 3D can wrap objects in Materials, and some of these materials make perfect altitude maps (see Figure 3.47). Here's how to translate a selected material into an altitude map.

1. Create a flat plane as seen from the camera view. Zoom in on it so that it fills the entire screen.
2. Go to the Materials Presets, and select the as the Miscellaneous/Urban Dwelling material for the plane.
3. With Normal Anti-aliasing on, render the camera view. Export the graphics as a PICT (Mac) or BMP (Windows).
4. Place a Terrain object on the screen, and go to the Terrain Editor. Click New to begin a new object and import the bitmap of the material wrapped plane you just saved.
5. Tweak as necessary and write the new Terrain object to your Bryce 3D World.

After importing a material as a Terrain Map, try using the elevation and effects tools on it to give it more complexity and character.

TIP

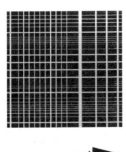 

FIGURE
3.47
Every material you use or customize in Bryce 3D can be transformed into a Terrain object. This cityscape began as a Bryce 3D material, and by importing the graphic into the Terrain Editor and painting in the domed elevations, it was transformed into a 3D object.

THE FILTER TAB

Any of the models we have developed and investigated in this chapter can be customized and explored further in the Filter tab in the Terrain Editor (see Figure 3.48). Filters are preset modification operations that apply general reshaping processes to the Terrain model. The shape of the Filter curve compares to a silhouette of the intended effect, but exactly how it reshapes the terrain depends upon the existing shape of the terrain. If there is no terrain model present, the filter process will create a stand-in model. The Elevation and Effects brushes are fully functional in the Filters environment. This method can be use to test out filters on a model.

1. After bringing in a Terrain object or creating one in the General tab from either painting tools or an imported picture, switch to the Filter tab.
2. Notice that your topography appears in two places: in a preview screen of the Filter tab and in its customary position at the right of the tab. You can continue painting on the topography in the customary view. The topography preview displays whatever Filter has been selected, and how that will affect your model if and when it is applied.

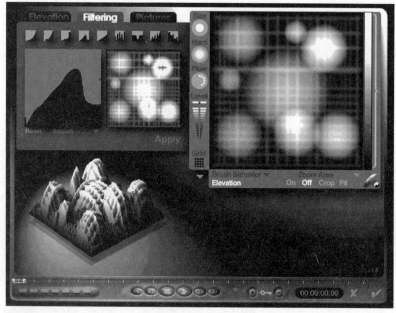

FIGURE *The Terrain Editor, showing the Filter tab at the upper left.*
3.48

If you click and hold on the Filter preview, the 3D preview model will change to what it will look like when the Filter is applied and snap back when you release the mouse button (left mouse button for Windows users). It is important to do this regularly, since it gives you a comprehensive look at the potential changes.

3. Click on one of the Filter presets, or draw your own in the left-hand Filter window. Notice that the right-hand preview of the topography changes to match the filter operation. Hit "Smoothing" as many times as need to smooth out the Filter curve a step at a time.

Hit the Reset button at any time to return the Filter preview to the same topography as your original model, as shown in the topography on the main Edit screen to the right.

4. Using the downward pointing arrow beneath the Filter window, access the Filter parameter options list to explore applying Vertical, Horizontal, Vertical Add, or Horizontal Add modifiers of the Filter shape to your model. Though these operations instantly alter your model in real time, you can always click on the Undo function in the General tab to start over again.

Important. Remember that Undo only covers one operation and that altering your model more than once in succession will mean that only the last operation can be undone. Unless you are just exploring, or know exactly where you are headed, alter your model one step at a time.

5. Apply as many filters, or customize each in the drawing window, as you like, paying attention to the preview topography as you go. When you reach a satisfactory point in your filtering process, Apply the filtering alterations to the model. See Figure 3.49 for examples that show how one model was altered in the Terrain Editor by just Filtering transformations. You must be willing to spend time exploring the filtering process to get the hang of it.

Very Important! If you have the RAM that allows you to run more than one application at a time, you can decrease the amount of time it takes to port a graphic to the Terrain Editor as a topographical map. Just copy the selected graphic to the Clipboard in the painting application and paste it in the picture slot in Bryce 3D. This allows you to preview the intended object much faster than saving it to disk and reading it in again. It also fosters a more robust exploration of image to object translation.

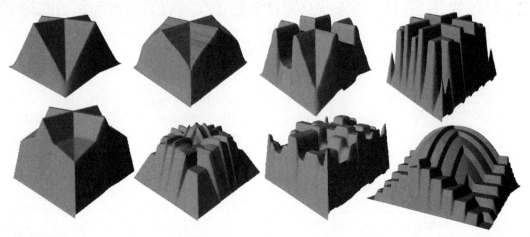

FIGURE 3.49 *The original model, our familiar Cross-Ridges2 preset, is shown at the upper left, while the rest of the models are variations created by using different types of Filters in the Terrain Editor*

Filter operations can be a vital component when animating Terrain objects. See chapter 10 for creating animated TerrainMorphs in the Terrain Editor, and the application of Filtering and painting techniques to Terrain animating.

NOTE

Moving On

If you have worked through the Bryce 3D documentation and then diligently worked through this chapter, you have an expanded and appreciative awareness of the power of the Terrain Editing process. The next chapter deals with the ways that you can give your objects personality by creating, customizing, and applying materials to them.

CHAPTER

Materials

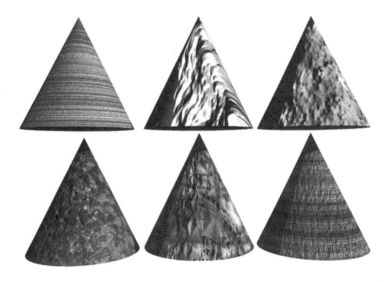

The Soul of the Matter

Objects without color or textures live in a bleak soulless void. They can be animated in complex and intriguing ways, go through maneuvers that give them breath and life, but there will be something missing. There will be nothing but their shapes to distinguish them from other actors in the scene. That will not be enough—your audience will scarcely be able to distinguish objects from backdrops and will not be enticed to observe for longer periods of time. What an object, organic or not, seems to be made of tells us more about its potential character, its motivation for action, and its perceived history than we at first realize. A space ship that's all shiny and glistens in the light of a star has a very different emotional impact than one that is rusty and looks dented in spots, and each of these choices has an effect on the substance of a story. A green tinted dinosaur is much less awesome and terrifying than one whose scales can be seen shifting as it stalks its prey. In an animation, liberties might be taken to make textures simpler because movement hides texture detail. But when the same object comes to rest, perhaps for long periods of time, the eye begins to notice textural detail. At that time, we look for definitive information so that disbelief, essential to the storytellers art, can be willingly suspended.

Adding Textures in Bryce 3D

There are two ways to add textures to objects in Bryce 3D. One is to opt for Procedural materials, and the other is to address an object with bitmap graphics. Each has its purpose, its weaknesses, and its strengths.

BRYCE 3D PROCEDURAL MATERIALS

Using procedural materials in Bryce 3D is aided by the fact that there is such a rich source of materials presets to select from. This is further enhanced by the fact that each one of the presets can be customized in infinite ways in the Materials Lab. A procedural material is a mathematical formula that contains basic texture application information. The magic of Bryce 3D is that you have simplified intuitive control over this data, without having to be a mathematician to get to it. Procedural materials are, in most cases, dependent upon fractal algorithms (or formulas). This means that no matter how "close" you get to a fractal material, there is always more detail to appreciate. Whereas procedural material in other applications tends to have a "computer" look, the procedurals in Bryce 3D have been created to emulate organic textures and other environmental f/x as much as possible. Therefore, your work in Bryce 3D will depend upon how much comfort and understanding you have concerning the application and customization of procedural materials 90% of the time, with the other 10% devoted to your awareness of how to use and modify bitmaps as textures.

The design of Bryce 3D's rich array of procedural materials did not spring up overnight. This element of Bryce 3D owes much to the experience MetaCreations gained through the work of Kai Krausse and others and can be seen in such widely used plug-in applications as Kai's PowerTools.

BRYCE 3D BITMAP TEXTURES

Bryce 3D is no slouch when it comes to addressing bitmaps.

When and Where to Use Bitmap Textures

The biggest liability of using bitmap textures as compared to procedurals is that when you zoom in on a bitmap, you are sure to see the pixels enlarge to the point that it becomes obvious that the object's texture is a bitmap and not a "real material." This can be somewhat overcome by blurring the original image, but too much blurring also adds a non-believability factor. Bitmap textures are best used when you are not going to zoom in on an object, and also when the pictorial information is vital. Portraiture, for example, must be handled through bitmapped graphics. There are no procedurals (yet) that allow you control over the design of a unique face, although who knows what the future holds. Bitmaps are also vital when you want to apply a specific facade to an object, especially useful in the texture mapping of buildings as seen from a city street. In one operation, a bitmap can be applied to an object that would require the kind of variables that a procedural cannot handle, except perhaps in stacking and manipulating procedurals in layers. But even when layered, objects in the real world need recognizable and randomized textural appearances. Though Bryce 3D procedurals can accommodate your needs in most cases, specific bitmapped graphics may be needed for that extra hint of reality.

THE BEST OF BOTH WORLDS

There are methods, detailed in this chapter, that allow you to combine both procedural and bitmap materials and bitmaps in a texture sandwich. In most cases, you will opt for one method of texturing over another, but there are situations that may arise that demand the layered approach as well. To make matters a bit more complex, some of the Bryce 3D procedural materials contain bitmap components in one or more channels. More on this later.

Look at the World Around You

The first step in valuing and evaluating texture and material appreciation is to look at the world surrounding you right now. Look at your computer. If the case were made of wood instead of metal, would that effect you or your work habits in any way? If your important other entered the room, seemingly made of water and clouds, would your surmise about who it was be altered? If the trees outside of your window took on the appearance of precious metals, would you be able to categorize the natural world the same way you do now? Computer artists and animators are always playing with the material looks of reality, sometimes to emulate those looks more closely than a photograph, and other times to shockingly alter our perception and comprehension of the world we take for granted and think we know.

How This Chapter Is Organized

In general, this chapter looks at Procedural Materials, Bitmaps, and addendum topics, in that order. This allows you to return to sections of this chapter so that the information provided there is cohesive, rather like an encyclopedia. Of course, on the first read, you should go straight through.

PROCEDURAL MATERIALS ORGANIZATION

There are a number of ways that Procedural Materials could be organized in this chapter. What we have chosen to do is to go from the surface to the depths. The surface is like a high level computer language that allows you easy access to usage without much necessary knowledge of programming. You can compare it to a visual programming language, accessible to all comers. This surface language is represented by Materials Presets in Bryce 3D, which also includes the beginning discussions and examples concerning the new Volumetric Presets. The next level down offers more customizing control over events, perhaps comparable to a computer language like Basic. Here is where you can get behind the screen to control more of what is going on. In Bryce 3D, this is represented by the Materials Lab. Included in the Materials Lab section are both the Alpha Channel and Refraction indexing, among other related topics. At the depths are controls for the controls, akin to a computer language like Assembly, where you maneuver around with some knowledge that everything you do has mega consequences at the next level up. It requires more experience and exploration than higher level languages. In Bryce 3D, this is represented by the Deep Texture Editor.

Procedural Materials topics are arranged in this chapter as follows:

- Materials Presets (including Volumetrics)
- Materials Lab
- Deep Texture Editor

BITMAP TEXTURES

Applying bitmap textures is done in the Materials Lab. In order to distinguish procedural mapping topics from bitmap topics, the bitmap focus has been separated from other procedurally targeted work in the Materials Lab and instead is presented here on its own. This is very important, because it allows us to center upon information and examples vital to understanding how to work with bitmap textures in Bryce 3D. This includes wrapping bitmaps on objects as both labels and textures and a number of tricks and tips.

NOTE

Using the Materials Lab to generate both animated procedural materials and single frame bitmap animations is covered in Chapter 10.

ADDENDUM TOPICS

The last part of this chapter focuses upon additional topics that both combine and extend useful information around both procedural materials use and bitmap applications. This includes making procedural-bitmap sandwiches and other topics.

Materials Presets

The simplest and quickest way to add a material to your selected object(s) is to access the Materials Presets libraries, click on any material represented, and check the Apply mark. To access the Materials Presets libraries, click on the downward pointing arrow next to the word "Edit" in the Edit toolbar.

ABOUT THE MATERIALS PRESETS LIBRARIES

There are thirteen libraries listed in the Material Presets list.

Simple and Fast

Don't be fooled by the title of this library. Besides assigning basic colors to objects, several of my favorite materials live here, specifically, Pale Blue Metal, Yellow Gold, Mirror, and the six Woods presets. Pale Blue Metal is a great all around material to apply to buildings in the distance, and Yellow Gold renders with absolute believable clarity. Mirror is not only great when it comes to completely reflective surfaces, but is also super when it comes to mapping water. From high up, the mirror surface makes water look very convincing, without all the time it takes to render most of the water presets. The Woods serve all of your needs for wood looks, from finished cabinet work to rough plywood (see Figure 4.1). All of these materials can be customized in the Materials Lab, as we shall see later. Render time for any of these materials is very fast.

Plains and Terrains

This library features a series of materials perfect for giving your mountains and ground planes that lived-on look. From the spring mud to the winter snow, a

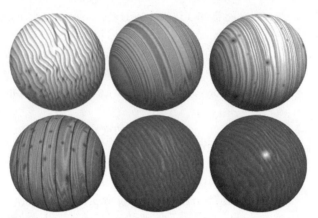

FIGURE **4.1** *Six spheres, showing the six wood materials from the Simple and Fast Materials Presets (from the top left): Warped, Light, Bleached, Plank, Walnut, and Polished Walnut.*

large number of environments are represented here (see Figure 4.2 for some samples). As we will see later in this chapter, all of the Planes and Terrains presets can be infinitely customized in the Materials Lab and Deep Texture Editor. It's advisable to remain open to all of the materials included here, so your exploration won't be hampered by attraction to any specific material over another. You will probably find yourself, however, gravitating to ones whose overall feel you especially like. Some materials seem to work better on Planes or Terrains, while some look good on both.

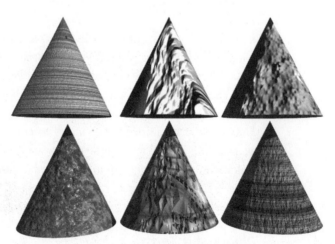

FIGURE **4.2** *Cones make excellent models for previewing materials that are to be targeted to Terrain objects. The materials on these six cones are Grassy Peaks, Iceberg, New Mexico Cliffs, Antique Pots, Etched Rock, and Grand Canyon.*

TIP

Note: When you are placing mountainous terrain in your world, consider using another lower terrain object as the base. Nothing looks less natural than a mountain sitting on a flat plane. Better to place it on a low-lying series of foothills. When you do this, the lower terrain should have the same material as a ground plane so they blend; at times, mountains, lower terrain, and the infinite plane can all have the same material.

Rocks and Stones

This library contains materials meant to be applied to Stone objects, but you will be limiting your creativity if you don't stretch their purpose to include at least planes, terrains, and any other that would look interesting if made of stone (especially stone Poser statues). Some are more "expensive" (time-consuming) to render than others, but most of these have the very convoluted and intriguing looks that you just can't resist.

Using Stone Materials

Here are some tips and hints for using Stone materials on objects. Figure 4.3 shows some samples.

- Place random stones in a scene to give it a more realistic look. Make the stones different sizes and give them different orientations, planting some deep in the ground. Use one material for most or all of them, so as not to make your scene too busy.
- Use complex materials on stones closer to the camera, and simple mate-

FIGURE   *A feast for the Bryce 3D rock collector, from the left: Riverbed, Barnacles,*
4.3   *Granite Eroded, Stone Wall, Cave Wall, and Alien Sandstone.*

rials (or even just color) on stones further in the distance. You will have a more realistic scene that will render in less time.

- Use a simple material on a stone, multi-replicate it, and use the stones to build an edifice. Examples would be a small cabin, an altar, a stone bridge, or an archway.

- Use Boolean operations on stones to build stone objects. Examples would be a bowl, ornament, or alien structure. Use a material that fits the item you are creating.

- A rock object has so many facets that having just one in your scene that is duplicated, and then rotated and resized, usually suffices for a multitude of items. Before you duplicate or multi-replicate a rock, assign a suitable material to it.

Waters and Liquids

Waters and Liquids are generally more expensive to render than most other materials, except for clouds. This is because Waters and Liquids generally include degrees of turbulence and transparency. Since raytraced light waves have to penetrate transparent surfaces and figure out the math involved in turbulence, more time has to be taken for the rendering. You will notice this most when rendering large patches of water or infinite and volumetric water planes. Water effects, however, are some of the most thrilling attributes of Bryce 3D (see Figure 4.4), so you will no doubt be waiting as they render.

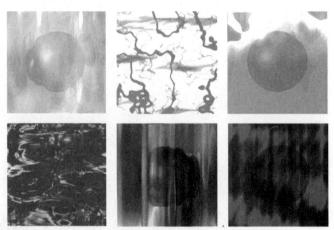

FIGURE 4.4   *Here, a series of Water and Liquid materials is mapped to a cube. The materials used (from the upper left) are: Rosewater, Foamy Seawater, Pollution Waterfall, Santraginus V, Caribbean Resort, and That Thing from Abyss. A gold sphere has been placed just below the surface on each, to give you some idea of each liquid's transparency.*

TIP

Important! Unless you already have one, it is highly advisable that you purchase an accelerator card for your PC or Mac if you are planning to be spending a lot of time doing Bryce 3D rendering. A medium level accelerator card runs somewhere in the neighborhood of $200, and it can save you hundreds of hours in rendering time a month. For Bryce 3D professional use, including animations for film (which require larger file sizes and anti-aliasing), you should consider the best accelerator card you can afford. Though Bryce 3D offers effects and options found in no other graphics or animation application on the market, it does not offer super speedy raytracing. The fastest machine and an added accelerator card will make your Bryce 3D work all the more pleasurable and will certainly handle your water material rendering with ease.

Clouds and Fogs

Clouds are moderate to highly expensive to render, dependent mostly upon their transparency and size. Anti-aliasing is also a large factor in rendering time, since a cloud can have so many edges to anti-alias. Clouds and Fogs materials should be differentiated from the Cloud Plane. The Cloud Plane is addressed by its own presets, and in general, renders very quickly. Clouds and Fogs materials are targeted to specified objects, usually a sphere or cube (see Figure 4.5 for some examples). You might consider the following as common targets for Clouds and Fogs materials:

* Ground fog in the morning or evening over the ground plane. Use a Fog material that has elevation-dependent transparency, so that it gets thicker and more impenetrable as it gets lower to the ground.

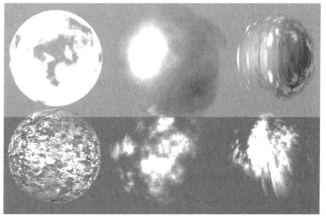

FIGURE **4.5** *Clouds and Fogs materials are shown wrapped on spheres. From upper left to lower right: Wispy Afternoon, Smokestack, Marbled Clouds, Planet Atmosphere, Bright and Bumpy, and Turbu Clouds.*

Sometimes this effect can be enhanced by using a higher Haze setting as well, so you get both vertical and horizontal fog effects. Using a high Fog setting can interfere with and negate an assigned Fog material effect.

- Clouds around a mountain summit. These can be colorized normally, taking their tint from the sun color, or colorized red for vaporous clouds around the top of a volcano.
- Flyover clouds. These are mapped to cloud planes lower than the sky plane, so that you can see through them to the ground below. It also allows you to rise above the clouds, where your sky plane might show a sunny sky.

If you need to map Cloud materials to a flyover plane, it's better to use a sandwich of three or four planes, separated from each other by an intervening clear space. Map each of the planes with a high transparency, on the order of 70% or more. This allows you to animate each plane, so the total effect looks randomized, with clear spaces suddenly appearing and disappearing as the camera aims at the ground below.

- Progressive disclosure is a term used to indicate that a targeted object in a scene is slowly brought into focus. Parting or slowly disappearing clouds mapped to an intervening plane can serve nicely in this capacity.

For more information on Cloud possibilities and animation, be sure to read Chapter 6 (Environmental Sky Effects), Chapter 8 (Earth, Water, Air, and Fire flx), and Chapter 15 (Wrong Materials for the Right Reasons).

Wild and Fun

Some of Bryce 3D's most experimental materials are included in this presets library folder. When you are seeking to attract the viewer with strange alien environments or excursions into the dream world, drop by this library of materials. The names of the materials, incorporating descriptive words like "Dali," "Tyrel" (from the movie BladeRunner), "Alien," and "Psychoactive" give you a strong hint that using these materials will tell the audience they are not in Kansas anymore (see Figure 4.6). Some possibilities for the uses these materials might be put to include:

- Use the Dali Bee material on a human head model, or even a whole Poser figure. The result will be similar to some of Salvador Dali's famous works. This material also produces surrealistic effects when targeted to fruit objects, like apples, oranges, and bananas.

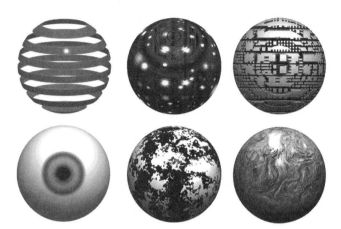

FIGURE
4.6
Dali Bee Stripes, Tyrel Building, Alien Tree Bark, What Are You Looking At?, Peeling Paint, and Psychoactive Christmas Ball.

- The Gilded Cage material makes very modernistic skyscrapers that can reflect the city they are placed in.
- The Tyrel Building material, a salute to the film BladeRunner, creates interesting effects on buildings, spaceships, and can even be used to map a ground plane for an infinite city flyover.
- One of the most awesome and effective materials to wrap on a robot is Alien Tree Bark, with Robot Fungus adding a touch of deterioration.
- The What Are You Looking At eyeball is perfect for adding eyes to any suitable object, anthropomorphic or machine.
- Peeling Paint makes an excellent ground plane material.
- Easter Egg Dye 2 and Rustic Vein are perfect when you need to create that used and worn look on a spaceship.

Complex Effects

This library of materials could just as well have been folded into the Wild and Fun folder, as far as their use in developing strange and evocative Bryce 3D worlds (see Figure 4.7). The materials with high levels of transparency and turbulence can be rather expensive to render, but they are so interesting to fold into a scene that you will mind the rendering time less. Besides, this gives you a chance to go get a sandwich. Some uses worth considering for these materials include:

- Green Lit is my favorite material for creating fake lights, from vehicle headlights to stars. Used in this manner no lighting or shadows are pro-

FIGURE *Among the materials found in the Complex Effects library are (top left to*
4.7 *bottom right) Oily Bronze, Water Puddles, Chocolate Coated Bricks, Disco Kelp, Shiny World in a Glass, and Lost Marble.*

duced, which is just perfect for illuminated far away objects. For information on how to make this material act as a real light, see Chapter 5, Lights and the Camera.

- Lit Rays is the perfect material for emulating laser beams and other light effects.
- Alien Disco Ball has the perfect shimmer for making a robot look all the more menacing and invincible.
- Copper Bump is the material to explore for shields, antique dinnerware, and sculpted Daliesque forms sitting on an infinite ground plane.
- The Retina Projector material can be used when a human eye has to be superseded by something the Terminator would be comfortable with.
- Bleeding Moon Glass is very expensive to render because of its high transparency settings, but it allows you to render near 3D alien forms that look very mysterious when sitting in layers in front of the camera.
- The two Fire materials can be used to light campfires or forests, or even for that spurt of flame from a volcano. Just wrap them to a vertically elongated sphere.

Miscellaneous

Personally, I dislike the name of this library folder. How about "Stupendous" or even "Awe Inspiring"? There are no superfluous or throw-away materials living here (see Figure 4.8), but a collection of extremely useful and novel items.

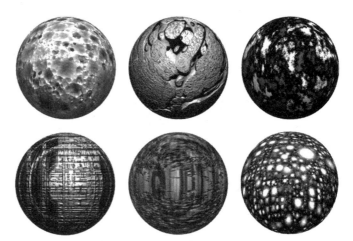

FIGURE *Moon Lava, Cracked Clay Pot, Acid Buildup, Death Star in Progress, Mud-*
4.8 *Bark Fusion, Pearl Beads.*

Some of the best ground plane materials are included here, especially when it comes to Bump Mapping. Some uses include:

- Moon Lava and Moon Lava II can be used both as a ground plane map and also to make a sphere look like a far off moon.
- Cracked Clay Pot transforms ordinary stones into artifacts from an archeological dig.
- Acid Build Up is a wonderful material for mapping the sides of an active volcano or the ground below it.
- City Lights I and II are the materials to select when the world is dark, and your tour bus is flying above populated terrain.
- Foliage I and II should be used as materials for trees and other flora that are created by Boolean operations. Be careful however, since this material can add many hours of rendering time to an unsuspecting project.
- Pearl Beads and Alien Cherries add authenticity to stone objects and collections of rusty metal respectively.

Glass

This is a new folder in the materials library collection. The most important thing to remember about glass is that it bends light. Because of this, it is very expensive to render. Your computer has to figure out what the objects behind the glass will look like when warped by the light rays being bounced around, and that takes time. If the glass is also reflective, then more calculations have to take place. It is not unusual for a glass object to add an hour to every rendered frame in a sequence, turning a five-hour rendering into days of computer tie-up. This being said however, when you need glass, you need glass.

Glass objects should always have other objects behind them, since to believe an object is glass is enhanced by how objects behind the glass object are warped by light rays and refraction. See Figure 4.9.

Glass Tips

Here are a few tips on how you can add some magic elements to your glass objects, and even make your glass objects render faster.

- When glass gets too thick, it will be impossible to see through even at 100% transparency. This is especially true of solid glass spheres. One thing you can do to thin out the sphere is to use a Boolean trick.
    1. Make a sphere and map it with a glass that has a 100% transparency (you can use the one of the three Bubble Glass preset materials). Make a duplicate of the sphere.
    2. Resize the duplicate so it is 5% smaller than the original, without moving it, and make it a negative Boolean object. The cloned sphere now rests inside the original.

FIGURE **4.9** *As light rays are traced after having been reflected and refracted by the glass sphere, the scene on the globe is warped and reconfigured. This sphere is mapped with the Standard Glass material.*

FIGURE   *Compare this picture with Figure 4.9. Here, the sphere is mapped with the*
4.10   *Bubble Glass 3 material. In this variation, transparency dominates over*
         reflection. Look closely, and you can see the thickness of the walls of the glass.

3. Make the original sphere a positive Boolean object, and group it with the duplicate inside. This creates a sphere with a hollow inside, and the glass material will react very differently to transparency levels. You can achieve a similar effect by simply mapping a single sphere with Bubble Glass, but this alternative gives the globe a little more thickness to refract the light. If you made both spheres Positive, then cut a Boolean hole in them with a negative Boolean object, the hole would show the walls where the sphere has thickness (Figure 4.10).

- To save some rendering time, render your scene first without the glass object. Create the glass object and place it when the first render is done. Now, Plop Render the glass object. Even with anti-aliasing on, this method saves time.

- Place objects that are vertically or horizontally straight lined (like chairs, poles, or window frames) behind glass objects. You will be able to see and appreciate the warping effects of the glass more clearly.

- Use a spotlight or globe light to one side of a glass object to enhance the color shadows being cast.

FIGURE *The spheres, stacked from bottom left to bottom right, use Christmas Ball 9 and*
4.11 *17, Brushed Silver, Polished Gold, Brushed Bronze, Transparent Aluminum,*
        and Eroded Gold materials. All have highly reflective surfaces, a characteristic
        of metal.

Metals

This is another new folder in the Materials library. Every metal you can think
of is either represented here as a preset or made possible by tweaking any item
here in the Materials Lab (Figure 4.11 shows some examples). Use the pitted
and eroded metallics when you want a spaceship, robot, or household item to
have more character. Use more than one metal in a scene so that the viewer is
drawn into reflections in reflections.

Transparent metals in this folder seem to render a bit quicker than transparent glass,
and in some cases may be a valuable substitute that saves you rendering time.

TIP

To view the graphic in Figure 4.11 in detailed color, open the 4-11 project on the
CD-ROM.

NOTE

Tutorial and User Folders

These folders are mainly for your use when saving (Adding) your own customized materials. After working through the Bryce 3D documentation, you
can delete the few materials in the Tutorials folder, leaving room for more materials of your own design. However, as suggested previously, if you design a material that falls within one of the categories already covered by another folder in

the library (rocks, glass, metal, etc.), think about saving it to that existing folder instead of the User or Tutorial folders. It'll be easier to locate and use later.

Volumetrics

Though Volume materials is just another preset folder in the Materials library, it deserves very special attention. Volumetric materials and the concept of Volumetrics in general are not only new to Bryce 3D, but they are a new way of thinking about models and materials across the board. What is a volumetric object? A volumetric object is any object that is constructed of mass throughout. Most imported models are not volumetrics, since they display a hollow inside when they are ungrouped or cut away. Some are volumetric, because they look solid when you turn their elements in space. Bit volumetrics in Bryce 3D have to do with infinite planes, and specifically with the Water and Cloud planes. These planes are normally wrapped with 2D textures. You can fly through them, but your journey to the other side is instantaneous. In the real world, flying through clouds or swimming through water is a volumetric experience. Depending how thick the clouds are or how deep the water is, it will take you a certain amount of time to break through or touch bottom. Until you do pass through, you are presented with a constant vision of the material that the element is made of. This is the exciting new magic of working with volumetric infinite planes, and also with the materials that address them.

In addition to flying through volumetrics is the appreciation and realism of what an object looks like when it is partially immersed in a volumetric material. It slowly disappears, just as you would expect. Water plane volumetrics are especially beautiful this way, treating the poles of a pier or a partially submerged boat as real objects.

Volumetric materials deform the objects they address by a process known as deformation mapping. Bump mapping makes it look like an object has bumps and dents, while deformation mapping actually produces bumps and dents. This allows lights to play very differently, and more realistically, on objects mapped with volumetric materials. Bump mapping is just another surface mapping type, while volumetrics soak the object to the core with the material being applied.

TIP

It is extremely expensive to render volumetrics, because the computer has to calculate all of the possibilities for the transparent layering going on. Anti-aliasing is especially expensive, because volumetric materials have a lot of edges to smooth out. Unless your project demands very high-end output (animation for TV or the movies), do not use anti-aliasing when working on a volumetric sequence. What we have said previously about the need to use a fast machine and an accelerator card bears re-peating here. Without the right hardware configuration, using volumetrics for graphics or animations projects is prohibitive.

USING VOLUMETRIC MATERIALS

The first target of a Volumetric material is an infinite volumetric plane. If you click and hold the mouse on any of the three infinite plane icons (Water, Cloud, or Ground), you can select either a Volumetric or a 2D plane. The default is a 2D infinite plane.

The magic of Volumetric substances is that you can move through them with the camera. Most times, attempting to move through a non-volumetric object with the camera will cause Bryce 3D to crash, especially during an animation. Since Volumetric planes are infinite, you could move around in one forever. Volumetric substances other than the infinite planes are not infinite, so you can fly through them and see what's on the other side. Dimensional travel, dream sequences, and moving from one environment to another—all of this and much more is possible when you use volumetric materials on an object or infinite volumetric plane.

The Volumetric materials in the Materials library represent a number of new materials specifically designed to work with volumetric objects, but that's

FIGURE
4.12
These three spheres were set at different distances from the camera inside of an infinite volumetric cloud plane. Notice how different layers of the material reveal and hide the objects.

not the end of it at all. Any of the water or cloud/fog materials can also address any volumetric object, including volumetric infinite planes. You are free then to set up an underwater scene. Just make sure that the material has some transparency. Better yet, it should have an active Alpha channel so that there are patches in the substance where no material exists.

Like any object that accepts a volumetric material, a volumetric infinite plane has volume. On an infinite plane, this volume is expressed (and can be altered) in the Y axis or height direction. Remember, as we have discussed previously, that any infinite plane can also be rotated, so infinite planes rotated on their X axis 90 degrees become infinite walls, and then make it possible to have something else waiting on the other side. The effects that can be imagined and designed with infinite planes and volumetric materials has no end. Here are some ideas:

- Fly a craft through volumetric clouds, with the camera following close behind. What you will see are the clouds breaking over the craft as it enters thicker and thinner patches of volumetric material.
- Use the Volumetric @@@ material preset, with the camera buried deep in the object. It's like being on the other end of a cosmic microscope.
- Create a Volumetric infinite plane (choose any of the three infinite planes), and map it with a volumetric fire material. It is left to your imagination what this environment emulates, but you probably don't want to go there.
- Create a world with two volumetric infinite planes, one above the other with a space between. Make the top plane a volumetric cloud material, and map the bottom volumetric plane with a water material (use a high transparency of 60% or more). Create an animation that allows the camera to dive from a starting position on top of the cloud plane through the cloud plane and down under the water. Bury a treasure object at the bottom of the volumetric water plane as a final target.
- Create a volumetric infinite water plane. Make it 80% transparent with a simple aqua color material. At different levels inside the volume, place a series of objects. Place rocks at the bottom of the water volume, and a very low but bumpy terrain map with a sandy material. Look at the scene from above with the camera and render either graphics or an animation. If you decide on doing an animation, move a visible light through the water so its path includes different depths. You can muddy the water up by using the Polluted waterfall material.
- Create a cube and map the Dented Planet volumetric material to it. Move the camera so that one face of the cube fills the screen. Render an anima-

THE BRYCE 3D HANDBOOK

FIGURE **4.13** *The volumetric material Dented Planet was mapped to this sphere. A negative Boolean cylinder, with the transfer materials option off, was then grouped with the positive sphere forming a hole. The volumetric material is a fractal, so that more detail is always available the closer you get.*

tion that allows the camera to slowly move closer to the cube. The dented planet material is a deep fractal, so that no matter how close you get (as long as you don't actually touch the object), the more detail you will see.

TIP

Use Volumetric materials prudently and rarely. Most of the elements in a Bryce 3D scene can be mapped quite effective through normal material mapping. When volumetrics are called for, try and minimize their use to objects that absolutely require them.

BOOLEANS AND VOLUMETRICS

You can use Boolean objects to cut volumetric objects, including the volumetric materials used to map them. The "transfer materials from the negative object" option should be turned off in the negative object's Attributes list. Figure 4.13 shows an example.

Adding/Deleting and Importing/ Exporting Materials

When you are performing these operations, here are some things to keep in mind:

- Instead of deleting a material preset, consider exporting it out to a separate folder for later use. Export similar presets to the same folder for later import. Then you can safely delete the item in the library.

- When you add (save) your own material creations, don't save them automatically to the User library. Instead, see if they fit under one of the other preset categories. If you have developed a nice Rock material for instance, Add it to the existing Rocks and Stones library. It will be a lot easier to find and use later.
- If you are saving an object with a customized material wrapped on it, there may be no need to save the material separately. Remember that objects are saved with materials attached, so importing the model imports the material, too. You could save a group of objects with similar materials, perhaps a group of wine glasses with materials customized for each. Loading that object to the scene would then allow you to copy its material and paste it on other needed objects. It might be easier to classify materials according to the object class they belong to, especially if that object class is not represented in the Material Presets library (like lizard skins, fabrics, or other material classifications). Lizard Skins could be added to a lizard model, fabrics to a rug model, and so on. This would give you the instant ability to load in the representative object as well as the material.
- If you have developed a series of interesting materials, think about sharing them with other Bryce 3D users. This can be done by uploading them to a specific Bryce 3D web site (search the web for a potential site), or by contacting MetaCreations directly.

The Materials Lab

When the presets in the materials library no longer seem adequate or exciting, it's time to learn how to create and customize your own materials. This is accomplished in the Materials Lab. The Materials Lab can be accessed in four ways: by selecting Edit Material in the Objects menu, by using the hot-key combination Control-M (Mac and Windows), by clicking on the Material icon in the Edit toolbar, or by clicking on the "M" in the selected object's Attributes List. All of these methods bring up the Materials Lab. Figure 4.14 shows the screen for the Materials Lab.

COMPONENTS

Refer to the Figure 4.14 callouts.

1. The Materials Nano Preview window presents a picture of the material as it looks when placed on an object. Be aware that these renders may take time, especially if you have chosen complex materials or volumetrics. It's important to remember that placing your mouse cursor in this

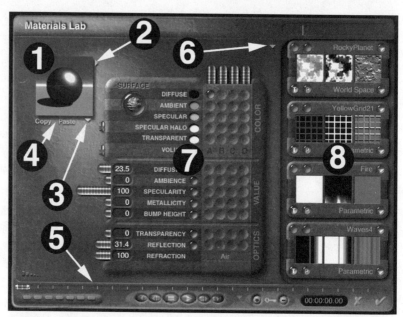

FIGURE 4.14 *The tools and components of the Materials Lab, detailed in the text.*

window and holding down the Left Mouse Button (Windows) will allow you to interactively turn the object to view the material from different vantage points.

2. This is the switch for bringing up the Materials Presets, which are very handy when you are designing your own materials. The presets act as category selections, so if you are designing a Wood Material, you may want to base it on an already existing Wood preset. After designing your own material, you would activate the presets in order to add and/or export it through this dialog.

3. Activating this switch allows you to select a basic 3D form on which the Materials Nano Preview will display your material. If you are working on a selected imported object in your world (DXF, OBJ, 3DMF, 3DS), the view in the Nano Preview will default to a sphere to display the material. If you are working on a Terrain object, you can show the actual Terrain object mapped with your material by selecting Current Selection from this list. Use the Up Close option when you want to add (save) a new material, since the preview will show it more clearly.

4. The Copy/Paste functions become extremely important to remember when you are animating a material (see Section II of this book), because

they allow you to paste the same material to the beginning and end frames in an animation (or anywhere else the material is supposed to return to its original look). Other than that, these switches work the same way as the Copy/Paste Materials commands in the Edit menu.

5. This is the animation toolbar. See Section II of this book for details of its use.

6. This switch gives you access to items that effect the Material Shading Modes and options. Details to consider when using the items in this list follow in the next section.

Material Shading Modes

You can select from among Normal, Blend Transparency, Fuzzy, and Light. Figure 4.15 shows some examples.

- Use the Normal mode to write the material to the object so it renders in a standard manner, with the expected hard edges and material details. No modifications are made to the material.

- Use the Blend Transparency mode when you want the black areas of an image's Alpha Channel to drop out, in accordance with the channel that is selected (A, B, C, or D). The Transparency Slider is normally set to a value of zero, so that the non-white elements of the Material show as opaque. Use this setting to show an object as if it were constructed from a skeleton.

- In Fuzzy mode, the apparent density of the object is read. More dense areas remain opaque, while less dense areas are rendered as more transparent. A sphere facing the camera, for example, is interpreted as having less density at the edges, so these become fuzzed out. A perfect way to use this mode is to emulate LOD (level of detail). Object farther from the camera in a 3D scene should not be as sharp as objects closer to the camera. Use fuzziness to add vagueness to objects in the distance, and your

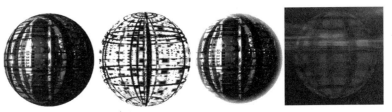

FIGURE *From left to right, the same material wrapped to a figure in Normal, Blend*
4.15 *Transparency, Fuzzy, and Light modes. The Light mode example has a material assigned in the Diffuse row.*

depth perception of the scene will be enhanced. The only caution is not to fly closer to the fuzzy objects, because they will remain fuzzy and cause perceptual confusion for the viewer.

- Use the Light mode when you want to transform an object into a pseudo-light. The color of the light is a combination of the Diffuse and Volume color settings, and the amount of transparency is set by the Transparency Optics slider. When given a material texture, the resulting object looks rather ghostly and can be used to evoke feelings of mystery in a Bryce 3D world. See Chapter 5 for details and options on this task.

Objects assigned the Light mode need not be devoid of material textures. If they derive their color and/or value from a Diffuse row, then they will show that material in accordance with the Diffuse slider setting. See the example in Figure 4.15 at the right.

NOTE

Additional Material Options

In addition to the Shading mode selections contained in this list, there are other attributes of the selected object that can be controlled from here. Each performs an important function in how your object looks and behaves on screen.

Additive

Normally set to off, click it on when you want to add all of the material settings to the area behind the object as opposed to the object's surface. Psychedelic illusions and solarization effects are many times the result, though each instance has to be explored on its own.

Cast/Receive Shadows

This setting gives you ultimate control over how an object behaves in the light in your scene. Normally, you will want to leave these settings defaulted to on. In creating storyboards, however, or flatter illustrations for print output, they can be switched off. This produces a scene that shows no obliteration of material on the objects targeted for no shadowing. There are also ways to create special effects, shadows cast from objects that are invisible. See Chapter 18 on the uses of Null objects. These options have no effect if you have selected Light mode for the object.

Distance Blur

It is advisable to always check this item when you are writing materials to an infinite plane. Blurring the distance enhances depth perception, making foreground elements appear sharper.

Volume Blend Altitude/Distance

These options have a direct relationship with the color the Volume attribute is set to. Volume Blend Altitude will gradually blend the selected Volume color from 100% to 0% along the vertical distance (altitude) of the object. Volume Blend Distance will blend the Volume and Diffuse colors from background (farthest distance from the camera) to the foreground (closest distance to the camera). This is another way of emphasizing depth and enhancing the LOD (level of detail), since object farther from the camera will be darkened out as compared with foreground objects. This is definitely an option to apply when your foreground actors are begging to be distinguished in a busy scene from more distant elements. Think about using it whenever your scene shows a deep panorama. As the camera moves into the scene farther, closer objects lighten and become more defined, so it's also an excellent animation device.

The Color, Value, and Optics Controls

These controls are number 7 in Figure 4.14 and are shown in more detail in Figure 4.16.

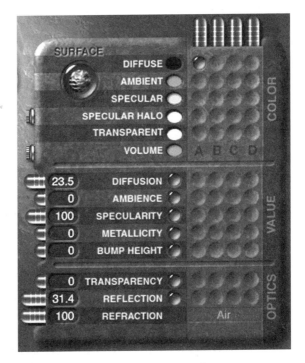

FIGURE *The Color, Value, and Optics palette.*
4.16

You may notice in the Bryce 3D documentation that materials are called both materials and textures, and the act of applying a material is called texturing.

There are three distinct parts to this palette: Color, Value, and Optics. Color deals with how colors are applied to the selected object, and where they are accessed from. The value section of the palette deals with how Value (light) is interpreted, and where this information comes from. The third section of the palette deals with assigning discrete optical properties to the object that affect its density and ability to alter light.

The two buttons at the left of the palette, Randomize (top) and Reset (bottom), are useful for creating initial materials that can then be customized. In order to get a better understanding of how the Materials Lab works, it is advisable to click on the Randomize button a few times, and watch how the screen and the Nano Preview of the material change.

COLOR CONTROLS

Figure 4.17 shows more detail of the Color Controls screen.

The Color settings occupy the top third of the Color/Value/Optics palette. Like the Value and Optics settings, they can take their data from either a palette color or from one or more of the four texture channels.

See the AB and ABC Channel Mixing information later in this chapter.

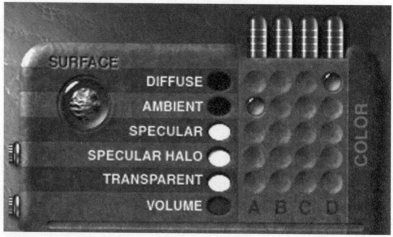

FIGURE *The Color Controls section of the Color/Value/Optics palette.*
4.17

There are six associated color sources that you can manipulate in order to apply color to your selected object: Diffuse, Ambient, Specular, Specular Halo, Transparent, and Volume. Using the sliders at the left and top of each color option, you can control the amount and extent, as well as the resource (where the color is being taken from), of each of these components. The left-hand sliders determine how much, while the sliders at the top determine from where and to what extent. This will become clearer as you read on and explore by doing.

Diffuse Color

Diffuse color is the color of the light that emanates from the material from all directions. Assigning a basic blue color as the material, for example, would show a bright blue when the Diffuse color slider is moved to 100, and black if the Diffuse color slider is set to zero. If a texture is set to be the place the Diffuse color is being taken from instead of a palette color, then the overall color of the texture would be brightest when the Diffuse color slider was set to 100%, and very dark when the Diffuse color slider was set to zero. For different material effects, both palette and texture based, adjusting the Diffuse color slider is usually the first thing you do. To test out its effect, assign the Pale cyan material to an object. You'll notice that the Diffuse color slider is set to 100%. Render the object to see what it looks like. Now, go back and set Diffuse color to 50% and render the object again. Not only is the object darker, but its 3D definition is weaker. Diffuse color can take its hue from a palette color, or from the Alpha channel of one or a combination of up to three of the four materials channels.

You can set the Diffuse color of an object to zero in order to turn it into a silhouette against a light backdrop. Set Ambient color to zero as well.

TIP

Ambient Color

Ambient color is the trickiest to apply, because it can easily throw the color in a scene off balance. In other applications, this is called a "Glow" color. It sets the color of an object to be displayed no matter what, in light or in darkness. If used consciously, it can create effects like streetlights and lit windows. If used haphazardly, it can destroy the ability of an object to receive the right shadowing and throw off the balance of a scene, giving the object a washed-out, overexposed appearance. The best advice? Use Ambient color with care and alter it subtly.

A nice effect is to set Ambient color high enough, which varies with each material, so that when the object is in the dark, part of it is still light. This can happen when Ambient color is taken from a texture separate from the Diffuse texture, and not

TIP

from a palette color. In the light, both textures will contribute to the object, while in the dark, only the Ambient texture will be visible. This allows you to see window lights on a cabin as the sunlight disappears.

Specular Color

Objects that are shiny have specularity, or a hot spot that appears when a light shines on them. Specular color is the color of the hot spot. The amount of a set color applied to the hot spot is determined by the slider next to Specular color. Try using a complementary color as a specular color, that is, for a red object use green Specular (or vice versa), for a yellow object use violet Specular (and vice versa), and for a blue object use yellow Specular (or vice versa), This is a painter's trick to make objects seem more light sensitive. The same thing works well with the color of shadows.

Specular Halo Color

The Specular halo is the blurred edge around the Specular hot spot. Try to use complementary colors here too. Remember that the Specular halo indicates the finish of the material. A hard shiny metal material has a small hot spot with not a lot of halo. A buffed metal, or a plastic, has a larger halo. Some substances have more halo and little or no hot spot, like buffed wood. Other materials, like fabrics, have neither.

Transparent Color

What happens to an object with a color assigned to its Transparency color attribute depends on either Normal or Blend Transparency is selected in the materials option list. If Normal is selected, a color assigned to the Transparency control, and 100% Transparency evoked with the slider, the object will "hold" that color as a glow.

The Normal setting is very useful when you need to show a treasure chest full of jewels. Assign a Transparency color to the selected object(s), and move the slider to 100%. Diffuse and other color settings should be set to zero.

TIP

However, if Blend Transparency is selected, at 100% Transparency the object will vanish. If the Blend Transparency color assigned to Transparency is drawn from a texture, then the material will be transparent where the texture's Alpha channel is black at 0% transparency. As the transparency amount increases, the portion of the material identified in the Alpha channel as white will also start to become invisible (see Figure 4.18). At 100%, the material (and the object it is assigned to) will disappear.

FIGURE
4.18
This example shows how an object disappears as its Transparency color setting is increased from zero to 30% to 60%. The Color in this case is being drawn from a texture channel pattern. Diffusion color is set to the same texture pattern at 100%.

Volume Color

Volume color is the color an object is filled with. It acts in concert with the Transparency color. For example, if the Volume color is yellow and the Transparency color is blue, the object (in Normal mode) will look green at 100% transparency. That's because light shines through both the Transparency color and the Volume color. Altering just one of these colors over time creates interesting internal light effects on the object.

TIP

Although you can assign a Volume Color to a material, the object that the material is targeted to will not display that Volume Color when you cut it with a Boolean object.

VALUE CONTROLS

The Value settings occupy the middle third of the Color/Value/Optics palette (see Figure 4.19). Like the Color and Optics settings, they can take their data from either a palette color or from one or more of the four texture channels. The five Value settings include Diffusion, Ambiance, Specularity, Metallicity, and Bump Height. Value controls deal with how much of that element will be applied to the material, also known as its intensity.

NOTE

See the AB and ABC Channel Mixing information later in this chapter.

Diffusion Value

How much of the Diffusion component should be applied to your material? If the Diffuse element is based upon either a color palette assignment or a texture in one or more of the ABCD texture channels, the Diffusion Value slider will

FIGURE
4.19 *The Value Controls section of the Color/Value/Optics palette*

determine how strong its presence will be in the material. In most cases, Diffusion value is set to 100%, but you can always explore what other amounts produce by looking at the Materials Nano Preview window.

Ambience Value

How much of the Ambience component should be applied to your material? If the Ambience element is based upon either a color palette assignment or a texture in one or more of the ABCD texture channels, the Ambience Value slider will determine how strong its presence will be in the material. In most cases, you should be wary of setting the Ambience value too high, or you will wash out the texture. An exception might be a material that suddenly suffers a blast effect from a cosmic or nuclear device.

Specularity Value

How much of the Specularity component should be applied to your material? If the Specularity element is based upon either a color palette assignment or a texture in one or more of the ABCD texture channels, the Specularity Value slider will determine how strong its presence will be in the material. You should adjust the Specularity value based upon the material you want the assigned object to be made of. Turn it up for metals and plastics, medium up for woods and metallic liquids, and off for softer materials like fabrics.

Metallicity Value

This value is one you will probably use less than the others. It works in conjunction with the Specularity controls to filter light for metallic material. The best suggestion for its use is to explore various settings in concert with a range of Specular settings. If you left it alone, you would probably never notice the difference in your productions.

Bump Height Value

Computer artists and animators love bump mapping. Bump mapping applies what looks like height values to parts of a material, though no real distortion of the underlying geometry of the object ever occurs. There are two types of computer artists, those who apply bump mapping gingerly and with care and those that apply it with abandon everywhere. Bump mapping looks best when applied with the object in mind. Mountains close up look great with a lot of bump mapped materials, while mountains in the distance need no bump maps. Stones and rocky cliffs usually benefit, while smooth surfaces couldn't care less. The Bump Mapping value slider is one that has both positive and negative settings, ranging from −100 to +100 (see Figure 4.20). Negative values reverse the look of the bump map, so what looks raised with a positive setting will look depressed with a negative one. Bizarre animation effect can be generated by reversing the two over time.

OPTICS

Optics occupies the bottom third of the Color/Value/Optics palette. Like the Color and Value settings, Optics elements can take their data from either a palette color or from one or more of the four texture channels. The Optics controls address Transparency, Reflection, and Refraction (see Figure 4.21).

See the AB and ABC Channel Mixing information later in this chapter.

NOTE

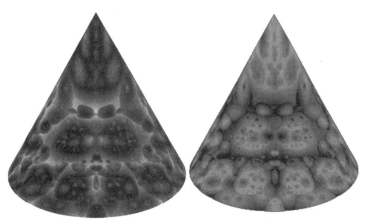

FIGURE
4.20 *Here are two bump mapped cones. The one on the left has a +100 bump map, while the one on the right displays a −100 value. The same material was used on both. Can you see the difference? The Alien Rock texture with symmetric tiling was used.*

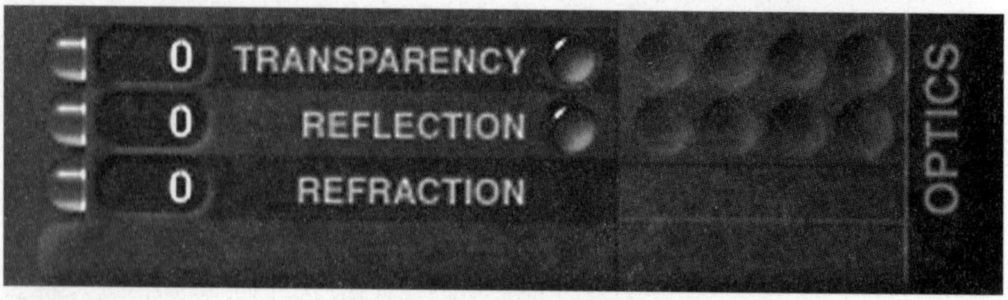

FIGURE **4.21** *The Optics Controls section of the Color/Value/Optics palette, with controls for Transparency, Reflection, and Refraction.*

Transparency

We have already referenced the ways that the Transparency gets its referenced data, from either the color palette or texture channels. This slider in the Optics channel controls how much transparency is to be used, ranging from zero to 100%. Depending upon where the transparent data is coming from and what you want your object to look like, you will have to alter the settings until you achieve what you want. Refer to the Color and Value sections covered previously.

Reflection

A completely Reflective object is a mirror, while an object with no reflection bears no witness to the world around it. Most metals are at least partially reflective, and metals like chrome are almost mirrors. Polished wood can be very reflective, ranging up to a maximum of 75%. Still water can also be reflective as a mirror, which is why in some cases you can use a mirror as a water substitute for water in a scene. This slider controls the amount of reflectivity an object possesses. Examples are shown in Figure 4.22.

Refraction Indexing

A Refraction Index indicates the mass of a material as compared to that of a vacuum. The Refraction Index of a vacuum is 1.0000, so all other materials have a higher Refraction Index than 1.0. The more massive a substance is, or dense, the higher its Refraction Index number. Clear clean air has a refraction Index number close to 1.0, but the more hazing and particulate the air gets, the more its Refraction Index number rises. Clean water, on Earth, has a Refraction Index of 1.33 at 20 degrees Celsius. At different temperatures, however, and with various pollutants added, the Refraction Index of water increases. The Bryce 3D Refraction Index numbers range on a scale from zero to 300 and

FIGURE *These three spheres illustrate a 25% reflectivity, a 55% reflectivity, and a*
4.22 *100% reflectivity. The object was placed in the foreground to give the spheres*
          something to reflect.

compare with standard Refraction Index numbers by moving the decimal point two places to the right. For example, a standard Refraction Index of 1.00 is represented by a Bryce 3D number of 100. All research texts that deal with optics, and many that deal with physics, list Refraction Indexes for hundreds and even thousands of materials. Working in Bryce 3D, only the purist will explore the use of Refraction Indexing when designing a material. In the service of the individuals to whom Refraction Indexing is both important and useful, we have prepared a partial Refraction Index table (Table 4.1) that lists the more common materials.

The refraction controls in Bryce 3D go from 0 to 300. 100 is air and 150 is water. This effectively moves the decimal point over two positions from the standard calculations, so the Bryce 3D column lists the materials in Bryce 3D equivalents that you can use in the Materials Lab.

AB and ABC Channel Mixing

Bryce 3D offers you two magical ways to combine more than one channel to create composite mixed materials. Each of these is unique to Bryce 3D. Because the four channels are referred to as ABCD, these techniques are named according to the channels they address: AB and ABC. In general, AB mixing allows a

TABLE 4.1   Using the Refraction Index Control in Bryce 3D

Material Component	Standard Measurement	Bryce 3D Equivalent
Air	1.00029	100+
Acetone	1.36	136
Alcohol	.329	33
Calspar	1.486 to 1.66	149 to 166
Crown Glass	1.52	152
Crystal	2.00	200
Diamond	2.417	242
Emerald	1.57	157
Ethyl Alcohol	1.36	136
Fluorite	1.434	144
Quartz	1.46	146
Glass	1.5 to 1.9	150 to 190
Ice	1.309	131
Lapis Lazuli	1.61	161
Liquid Carbon Dioxide	1.20	120
Polystyrene	1.55	155
Quartz	1.553 to 1.65	155 to 165
Ruby	1.77	177
Sapphire	1.77	177
Salt	1.55 to 1.65	155 to 165
Topaz	1.61	161
Vacuum	1.000000	100
Water (Clear, 20 C)	1.333	133

blend of the A and B channel so that the information in each is composited on the selected object in an altitude sensitive manner. The data in the A channel is written to the bottom half of the object, while the B channel data is written to the top half. ABC mixes are a little different. The data is written so that there is a mix of the data from A and B, mixed through the Alpha channel data of C. Let's look at some examples so you can see these mixing effects in action.

The top sphere on the left in Figure 4.23 shows a Diffuse color map in channel A, while the bottom figure displays Diffuse color in channel B. The composite material contains the A channel data at the bottom, and the B channel data at the top, both blended seamlessly in the middle.

Figure 4.24 displays an ABC mix of Diffuse color channel patterns. The Alpha channel of C allows a mix of the A and B channel data. The light areas of the Alpha channel show the B color data, and the dark Alpha areas show the A data.

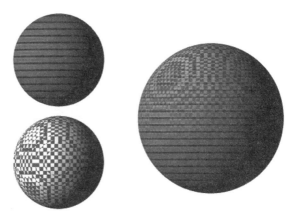

FIGURE   *This is an AB material with data taken from the A and B Diffuse color*
4.23   *channels.*

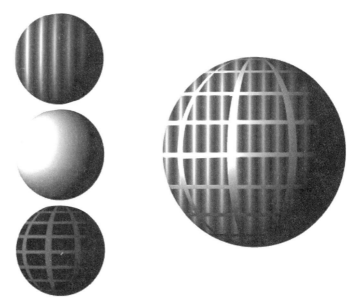

FIGURE   *This is an example of an ABC material mix.*
4.24

In Figure 4.25, Ambience channel data was used in an AB mix. Though similar to Figure 4.23, the characteristics of Ambient light would create a very different object in the scene than Diffuse color channel data. This object would literally glow in the dark, whereas the Diffuse AB mix object would vanish if no light were shown in the scene.

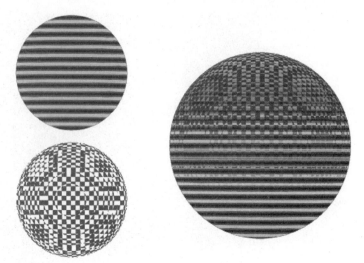

FIGURE **4.25** *This is an AB mix of data from the Ambience channels. Each Ambience channel was set to 100%.*

Now let's see what happens when we develop an AB mix material from the Transparency channel data. Look at Figure 4.26 for the results. Figure 4.27 combines different effects.

See the ABC_Tran project on the CD-ROM.

FIGURE **4.26** *AB channel Transparency data was used to create this AB mix material.*

FIGURE   *This figure uses the ABC channel mix method with Transparency, Diffuse, and*
4.27   *Ambient color. The result is a wicker ball whose construction lies beyond known*
           physics.

The Four CAB (Color, Alpha, Bump) Channels

These channels are number 8 in Figure 4.14 and are shown in more detail in Figure 4.28.

The four CAB channels are used to customize and create the component textures that are ingredients for a material. Refer to Figure 4.29.

Although the following information can be found in the documentation, it is not presented as clearly or concisely as it is here.

1. TRANSFORMATION OPTIONS

Clicking on this button brings up the Transformation Options dialog (Figure 4.30). You should always bring up this dialog if you want to resize, rotate, or reposition a texture component of the material, since it is activated the same way as the transformation items in the Edit toolbar, and intuitive to use. Keeping an eye on the Nano Preview of the material, you can get a very good idea of how your manipulations are affecting the material. Each of the ABCD channels offers this tool, and the tool affects only the texture or picture in that channel.

The range of the Size Transformation Options can be extended, by manually inputting numbers, to plus or minus 1000000.

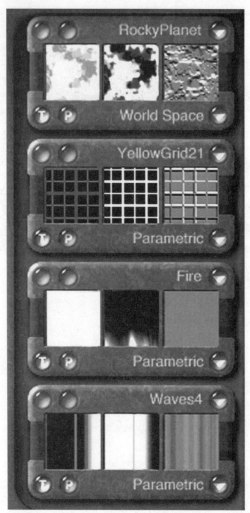

FIGURE   *The ABCD Color-Alpha-Bump channels, where textures are created and*
4.28   *customized as ingredients in a material.*

2. EDIT BUTTON

Clicking on this button brings up the Deep Texture Editor for customizing procedural textures, or the Picture Editor if you are working on a bitmap texture. See the sections devoted to these topics later in this chapter.

3. TEXTURE NAME

The name listed here is taken from the texture you are customizing, as imported from the Texture List at the right.

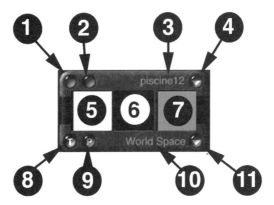

FIGURE *Each CAB (Color-Alpha-Bump) channel contains the same modification tools.*
4.29

4. TEXTURE LISTS

Clicking on this button allows you to access and import a procedural texture from the Texture Lists. There are five texture lists you can access, each with dozens of items not found or displayed in the Materials Presets library. The Lists include Basic, Bump, Clouds, Rocks, Sand, Psychedelic, and User.

Important! In designing your own procedural textures, make this your first stop. Select a texture from one of the list that sounds interesting and use it as a starting point for your own creations.

TIP

FIGURE *Bring up the Transformation Options whenever you need to resize, rotate, or*
4.30 *reposition the textures in a channel for the material you are designing or customizing.*

5. COLOR ATTRIBUTE THUMBNAIL

A thumbnail view of the Color attribute of your texture is displayed here. This is the information that is accessed when you manipulate the Color controls for that channel.

6. ALPHA ATTRIBUTE THUMBNAIL

A thumbnail view of the Alpha attribute of your texture is displayed here. This is the information that is accessed when you manipulate the Value controls for that channel.

7. BUMP ATTRIBUTE THUMBNAIL

A thumbnail view of the Bump attribute of your texture is displayed here. This is the information that is accessed when you manipulate the Bump Height controls for that channel.

8. PROCEDURAL TEXTURE TOGGLE

The four component textures can be either procedurally or bitmap based. This button selects the Procedural option. This means that editing of the texture is done in the Deep Texture Editor.

9. BITMAP PICTURE TOGGLE

The four component textures can be either procedurally or bitmap based. This button selects the Bitmap option. This means that editing of the texture is done in the Picture Editor.

Clicking on the Bitmap Picture toggle and then on the Procedural Texture button randomizes the texture for that channel.

10. MAPPING TYPE NAME

This text displays the current Mapping Type.

11. MAPPING TYPE LIST

This button brings up the Mapping Type List. Mapping Types are ways that your texture can be placed on the selected object in your scene. They include Object Space, World Space, Parametric, Parametric Scaled, World Top, Spherical, Cylindrical, Reflection Map, Random, Object Top, and Object Front (see Figure 4.31). In addition, you may select to use the Symmetric Tiling option (see Figure 4.32) with any of these choices, and Scale Pict Size can be chosen for scaling the picture to match the size of your object. Some hints about Mapping Types follow:

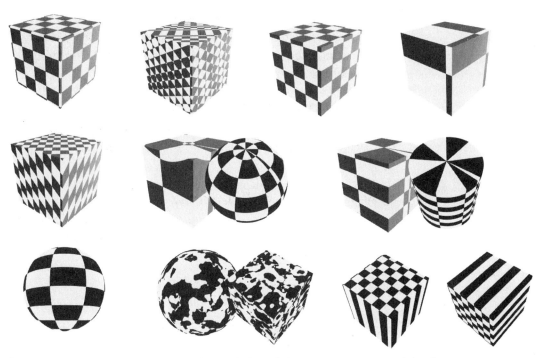

FIGURE **4.31** *The various mapping types create alternate looks with the same texture. From top left: Object Space, World Space, Parametric, Parametric Scaled, World Top, Spherical, Cylindrical, Reflection Map, Random, Object Top, and Object Front.*

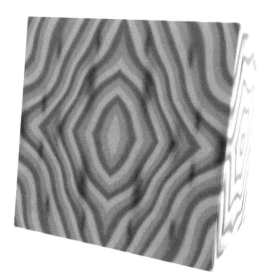

FIGURE **4.32** *Symmetric Tiling can produce interesting variations of a texture, like knots in wood or geometric floor tiles.*

- **Object Space:** This is the most common choice for mapping a material on an object, which scales the texture to the object proportionately. This is the most common texture mapping for objects that will move in a scene, since the texture realistically moves as a glued part of the object.
- **World Space:** Do not use World Space mapping if the object is in motion. World Space texture maps remain stationary, so when mapped to moving objects, the texture makes it look as if it is being projected from a stationary position, and sliding across the object.

Moving an object with a World Space mapping texture placed on it can create some interesting effects. It can substitute for a light projected image, since in a sense, the texture is being projected from the world light. Explore this possibility, and save an animation that uses it as a sample. Note that World Space mapped objects also look strange when the object is rotated on any 3D axis.

- **Parametric:** This mapping can be substituted for object mapping, but is especially vital when it comes to mapping imported WaveFront (OBJ) and 3DS objects. It allows you to remap the object with the texture map saved apart from its original application and results in perfect texture maps. DXF objects cannot use Parametric maps.
- **Parametric Scaled:** Scaled Parametric maps address every part of an object with a separate map. This can be very useful for mapping reptiles with textures that look a little different for each body part, but confusing on primitives. See the Scaled Parametric cube in Figure 4.31.
- **World Top:** This is worth exploring when mapping infinite planes. It comes out a bit differently than a standard World Space map. If the selected object has a vertical dimension, World Top is not a good choice, since it will streak the sides of an object.
- **Spherical:** Though useful on spherical objects, the polar region of the texture shows a crunched together mapping, which is not very pretty.
- **Cylindrical:** Cylindrical mapping is best used to emulate labels on cans or bottles.
- **Reflection Map:** Reflection Maps are projected on your objects as if from a spherical projector surrounding the scene. Use them on spherical or terrain objects. Reflection Maps do not work well on cubes.
- **Random:** This is the mapping type to select when you want to create splotchy surfaces, perfect for terrains, rocks, and alien world objects. Resize the texture to accommodate the object being mapped. This is also the mapping to use when you want to create marbleized materials, camouflage, or cowhide.

- **Object Top:** The map is applied to the top of the object and streaks the sides. This is great for woods, since it produces both grain ends and streaks.
- **Object Front:** The map is applied to the front of the object and streaks the other sides and top/bottom. This works best on objects that remain with their front facing the camera. This is great for woods, since it produces both grain ends and streaks.

Clicking on the Picture button and then on the Texture button randomizes the texture for that channel.

Volumetric Materials

Volumetric materials soak the selected object with the selected texture inside and out, in effect, making the texture a full 3D participant in the construction of the object. The toggle is shown in Figure 4.33. You can only appreciate the internal existence of the material if the object has degrees of transparency assigned to it however, or if a Boolean cutter slices part of the object away.

VOLUMETRIC SHADING MODES

Three shading modes make an appearance in the Shading Modes list when you select the Volumetric material type. They are Flat Shading, Full Shading, and Light Sensitive. Base Density controls the transparency of the object. Set to 100%, the object displays no internal material. Set to 0%,

Full Shading

Full Shaded Volumetric materials are displayed as 3D volumes. Circular dots become spheres. This allows you to fly through them, just as you would through any other objects in a 3D scene. The only thing to keep in mind if you want to do this is the stiff rendering cost of Volumetrics in general.

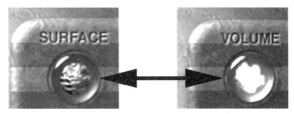

FIGURE **4.33** *The Surface/Volume toggle on the Color/Value/Optics palette switches between surface and volumetric material modes.*

FIGURE **4.34** *On the left is a cube with a Volumetric material cut by a Boolean negative sphere with a surface material. At the right is the same situation, except that the cube is also using a Volumetric material.*

Light Sensitive

Light Sensitive Volumetric materials only appear when you shine a light on them. They take on the color of the light and respond best when the light is at full intensity (though more subtle effects can be generated when the light is at lower settings). This allows you to have objects in your scene that are invisible to the eye and to make them appear as a light is turned in their direction. Figure 4.34 gives an example, and Figure 4.35 shows the Volumetric options.

TIP

Using a Volumetric material on a Boolean cutter is the same as turning transfer materials off on the cutter, except that the part of the volume material in back of the cutter is completely hidden from view.

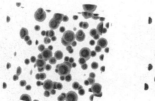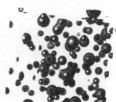

FIGURE **4.35** *A cube, shaded with a Volumetric material: Flat Shaded, Full Shaded, and Light Sensitive (with a spotlight shining in the Volume's direction).*

Very Important! Using volumetric materials with Full Shading can suffice in many instances as an animatable particle system. All you have to do is make sure that the texture channel is checked for Base Density and that you have a suitable volumetric material that gives you transparency. The best material to select for this purpose is the Ball Bearings material in the Volume folder of the Materials library.

CREATING A PARTICLE SYSTEM EFFECT

1. Create a sphere and use the Volume material Ball Bearings to map it. Tint the texture bright red. Make sure Full Shading is activated in the Shading List of the Materials Lab.
2. Make a Volcano in the Terrain Editor (refer to Chapter 3) and place the Volumetric sphere in the calendra.
3. Create an animation in which the sphere both rotates and resizes (on the World Y axis). The finished product is shown in Figure 4.36.

You can also use Light Sensitive Volumetrics for this exercise, so that the particles display only when a light is shone on them, although Full Shaded volumetric materials also take on the color of a light. This further enhances the animation effects.

FIGURE *Lava spewing from a volcano calendra is a perfect demonstration of using a Full*
4.36 *Shaded Volumetric material to emulate a particle system effect.*

If you want to explore the previous exercise in detail, load the 4_Volc project from the CD-ROM. Do not turn on Anti-aliasing when you render it, however.

VOLUME CONTROLS

When you switch to Volume instead of Surface material, the Optics section of the Materials Lab interface changes to Volume. The listings also change, because Volumetric materials must be addressed in different ways than Surface materials. The new command listings include: Base Density, Edge Softness, Fuzzy Factor, and Quality/Speed.

Base Density

This is the most important volumetric control whose use must be mastered. Using this slider, you can set the Base Density of a volumetric material from 0% to 100%. If all you are addressing is a color from the palette, then Base Density settings will have next to no effect on your material. The Base Density controls are meant to address materials with textures. Here is the best way to understand Base Density and the design of Volumetric materials in general:

1. Create a sphere in your workspace, and with it selected, open the Materials Lab. Choose the Volume mode.
2. Click in the Diffuse row on the first channel. Click in the Base Density row in the first channel. Leave all other commands set to the palette button, with no other channels selected.
3. In the first channel (A), find or create a texture that has solid black in its Alpha component.

Important! Base Density works best when the Alpha channel of the texture being incorporated has solid black in it. This is the section of the image that will drop out of the final material, leaving holes in the object the material is placed on.

4. Set Base Density to 100 with the slider. This will be drawn as your texture with holes where the Alpha component is black. Move the Base Density slider to 50%. Surprise! Instead of creating a transparency, less of the texture is seen in the material. Move the Base Density slider to 0%. No texture material is seen in the preview. See Figure 4.37.

Using Base Density operations like the one above, you can create the famous "Beam me up, Scotty" effect from Star Trek. The reverse, of course, would be "Beam me down." Everything depends upon having a good amount of black in the texture's Alpha channel: around 35% to 50%.

FIGURE
4.37
Following the above example, the Base Density settings are shown to control the density of particles in a volumetric material, not its transparency. The left object is at 100% Base Density, and moves to 10% Base density at the right.

Edge Softness

This slider adds softness to the edge of the elements that make up your material. The effect is subtle, gradually blending the material into the background. As shown in Figure 4.38, the effect is almost impossible to discern.

Fuzzy Factor

This slider adds fuzziness globally to your material, rather like a fog that blurs everything out at maximum settings.

Quality/Speed

The Quality versus Speed setting is your only chance to influence the speed that volumetric materials require for rendering. It is advisable to move the slider

FIGURE
4.38
This figure illustrates Edge Softness (top) and Fuzzy Factor (bottom) applied to a Volumetric material: Edge Softness: 20, 50, and 100; Fuzzy: 100, 200, 300.

all the way down, and to opt for maximum speed over quality. The only situation that might influence you to select more qualitative render would be an assignment to produce graphics or animations for a major print, broadcast, or movie project. Even then, you might find higher quality settings extremely prohibitive.

The Deep Texture Editor

TIP

Be sure you read and work through the Bryce 3D documentation on the use of the Deep Texture Edit. Our commentary on it has more to do with hints and tips rather than basic use. It is expected that you will understand the terminology that references the tools and processes in the Deep Texture Editor. If not, read or reread the documentation.

WHAT IS DEEP TEXTURE EDITING?

If modifying the ABCD channels in the Materials Lab is working at the molecular level, then using the Deep Texture Editor is working at the atomic and sub-atomic level. The most confusing thing about Deep Texture Editing at first is the similar nomenclature to the four channels. The use of "ABCD" to denote both attributes and components at every level of the Materials Lab throws everyone off balance at first. You just have to get used to how things work at every stage of the Materials Lab, and that means three things: practice, practice, and (oh yes), . . . practice. Neither the Bryce 3D documentation nor this book can substitute for learning by exploring and doing. That is especially true at this deeper level of materials creation.

The Deep Texture Editor is available from each of the four channels that comprise the Materials Lab component interface. These channels are called the A, B, C, and D channels. This is not to be confused with the three components that make up each channel: C (for Color), A (for Alpha), and B (for Bump map). This is the first stage of necessary understanding. The second button on the upper left of each component channel accesses that channel's Deep Texture Editor, as long as you are in Procedural texture mode, and not Bitmap Picture mode. Figure 4.39 shows the button to access the Deep Texture Editor.

Once activated, the Deep Texture Editor's interface appears (see Figure 4.40).

FIGURE **4.39** *This is the button that activates your entrance into the Deep Texture Editor for each of the four component channels in the Materials Lab.*

As we have said, the best teacher to guide you through the intricacies of the Deep Texture Editor is you. There is, however, a way that you can proceed. If you follow this method diligently, you will be able to strike out in your own direction after a few days of exploration. The Deep Texture Editor is one of the most comprehensive procedural texture creation tools offered by any applica-

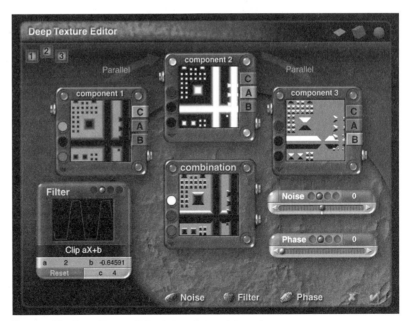

FIGURE **4.40** *The Deep Texture Editor's interface and controls.*

tion on the market. You can even use it to develop textures and materials for other 2D and 3D applications. Here is exactly what to do to start your learning curve on a gentle but thorough slope:

1. With an object selected in your workspace, open the Materials Lab. Place an activation dot in the first row (the Diffuse channel) and first column. Go to that channel's components interface on the right and activate the Deep Texture Editor.
2. Make sure that all three Component lights at the upper left are on (they will be green). This activates the three component windows (marked Component 1, Component 2, and Component 3).
3. In Component 1, make sure only the C (for Color) is selected and that A (for Alpha) and B (for Bump) are off.
4. In Component 2, make sure that only A is selected and that C and B are off.
5. In Component 3, make sure that only B is selected and that A and B are off.

You have just assigned Component 1 as your Color source, Component 2 as your Alpha source, and Component 3 as your Bump Map source. Shake your own hand for doing well.

6. Hit the Randomize button on Component 1 to load a texture. Reset the CAB buttons so only C is selected. Repeat this until you like the pattern in Component 1.
7. Repeat this same process for Component 2, making sure that only A (the Alpha channel) is selected. Repeat this until you like the pattern in Component 2.
8. Repeat this same process for Component 3, making sure that only B (the Bump channel) is selected. Repeat this until you like the pattern in Component 3.

Now you have the three parts of a texture started in all three Component channels: Color in 1, Alpha in 2, and Bump on 3. Look at the Window marked "Combination." This shows you how the three Component channels are contributing to the total texture.

9. Go to the curved arrow that connects Component 1 and Component 2. There is a word there that indicates how the data from 1 is being fed to 2. Click and hold on that word, and a list will pop up with a number of choices. Explore each choice, and watch the Combination window for a preview. Select whatever option looks good in the Combination window.

10. Repeat this same process over the curved arrow that indicates how Component 2 is passing data to Component 3. Stop when the Combination preview looks pleasing.

11. Explore the use of the Filter window on each Component and on the Combination preview by selecting the appropriate button from the top of the Filter window. By clicking and dragging in the space in which you see a mathematical curve, you can alter the way that data is filtered in the Component or Combination window you have selected. You can also hold your mouse (left MB for Windows users) over the name of the math function, and select another from the list. Explore in order to see what happens and don't rush.

12. Add or subtract noise with the Noise slider to a selected Component or the Combination preview, until the resulting Combination graphic looks like something interesting.

13. Repeat this process of exploration using the Phase slider in the Phase operator. Stop when you have something worth using as a material.

14. Return to the Materials Lab and use any of the controls to further tweak the texture you just designed for an original material. Finish by writing the material to the selected object. Render a preview. If the material is pleasing, add it to your Materials library.

It is absolutely guaranteed that if you do this exercise ten times, you will be so excited about using the Deep Texture Editor that your work in Bryce 3D will become a hundred times more interesting to you. Figure 4.41 shows some examples of texture customizing.

TIP

Remember that Deep Texture Editing works on both Surface and Volume textures.

SUBTLE ALTERATIONS

Referring to Figure 4.41, from top left to bottom right, these operations were performed one after the other. Though all of the textured materials are connected, you can see the subtle power of working in the Deep Texture Editor.

1. Original Basic Waves 5 Surface textured material.
2. Clip aX+b used as a formula in the Combination channel.
3. Procedural Blend added between Components 2 and 3.
4. Noise to –42 in Combination, and Phase to connect 1 to 2 and 2 to 3.
5. Snow Puddles formula added to Component 2 and Perturbed Noise to Component 3 with Altitude formula, Blend Max from 2 to 3, and Phase change of 770 on Component 3.

FIGURE **4.41** *Here are some examples of a material whose texture has been customized in the Deep Texture Editor.*

6. Blend random transition used between Components 1 and 2, and between 2 and 3. CAB channels switched on in all three Components.

The final result? An awesome material for creating a spectacular moon object. This material is on the CD-ROM as MyMoon1 in the Materials folder. Load it in, and explore what it looks like in the Deep Texture Editor. The process used was simply one of exploring until satisfied ("Trust in the force, Luke.").

If you use the Altitude transition between Components 2 and 3, with Color activated in each Component, the textured material you develop will be height sensitive. Color will change in relation to height. This is how the Terrain presets were built in the first place.

TIP

The Bitmap Picture Editor

Bitmaps can be assigned and modified for placement on targeted objects in the Materials Lab. Though you will probably spend most of your time in Bryce 3D using procedural materials, there are times when a specific bitmap is called for. Actually, some of the procedural materials in Bryce 3D contain one or more channels that contain bitmaps. Each of the four material channels allows you to select either a procedural or a bitmap element at any time for the creation of procedural/bitmap sandwiches in the final material.

FIGURE   *The Edit button activates the Picture Editor interface, as long as Picture (P)*
4.42   *and not Texture (T) is also selected below it.*

*Be wary of using any Bump Height mapping on imported graphics, especially pho-
tographs. Photos usually contain thousands of small defects that show up as particles
when bump mapped. The only way to minimize these artifacts is to apply Blurring
several times in a paint application.*

TIP

Bitmap pictures are configured in the Picture Editor, which is switched on
from the Edit button in one of the ABCD channels (see Figure 4.42). Figure
4.43 shows the next step.

*Attention! There is information here that is not emphasized enough in the Bryce
3D documentation. Study the following section carefully to master the use of bitmap
materials and objects in Bryce 3D.*

TIP

WORKING IN THE PICTURE EDITOR

As long as you have read the Bryce 3D documentation and are aware of a few
additional facts, it should take you all of ten minutes, if not less, to master the
creation of bitmap materials and objects in the Picture Editor. Bring up the Picture Editor now, so you can follow along.

The Picture Editor interface is very straightforward and not nearly as complicated as the Deep Texture Editor (see Figure 4.43 above, or look at it on your
own screen). There are three main windows at the top: Original Picture, Alpha
Channel, and Result. Below that are thirty visible picture thumbnail slots
(scrolling gives you access to more). Each of these slots holds one bitmap pic-

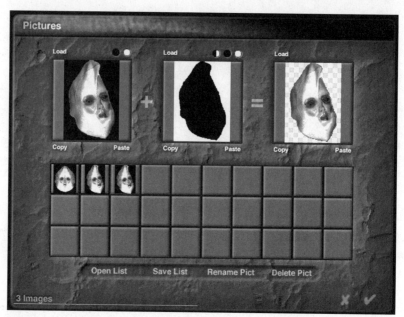

FIGURE *Once activated, the Picture Editor interface takes command of the screen.*
4.43

ture. At the bottom are four commands. The first two allow you to export and import entire Picture lists, and the second two to Rename or delete any Picture already on screen.

What you need to know about the Picture-Alpha-Result windows is something that initially will challenge your logical assumptions, but this is the way Bryce 3D has been designed to work. When you want to add Bitmapped pictures to the slots in the storage area below, you must click on the Load button in the Result window at the right, not the Picture window at the left. This is very important. Loading a Picture on the left in the Picture window will replace the current picture selected in the slot below. This is OK if that's what you want, but usually what is needed is to add a number of bitmaps in the slots all at one time. This becomes even more important knowledge when we discuss working with sequenced bitmap animation files in Chapter 13.

Here is the way to add new bitmap images in the Picture Editor:

1. Click on the Load button above the Result window on the right.
2. After the image loads, click on Copy under the Result window.
3. Click on Paste under the left-hand Picture window.
4. If you want to add the same picture as an Alpha channel, click on Paste under the Alpha window. Note that adding another bitmap on the

Alpha channel will act as a mask for the final result. Adding the same Picture as an Alpha will drop out areas of the Picture that are close to the dropout color. See the section that follows on creating an Alpha image in your paint application.

TIP

White areas of your Alpha image are normally dropped out. Hit the half moon (black/white) symbol above the Alpha window to reverse the information being dropped out. Look at the Result window to see a preview of how the Alpha is affecting the finished bitmap.

5. Finally, click on the checkmark to return to the Materials Lab, where you can use any of the controls to adjust your Picture Texture further. Set the Diffuse, Ambient, and Transparency buttons to the Picture channel. Set the Shading mode to Blend Transparency, and the mapping mode to Object Top.

CREATING AN ALPHA MASK IN A PAINT APPLICATION

You have to have an Alpha Mask in the Picture Editor that duplicates the outline of the needed image, so it can be composited correctly against a Bryce 3D scene. Here's how to create it:

1. Find the image you want and load it into your bitmap painting application (Painter, PhotoPaint, Enhance, or Photoshop will do just fine). Paint out the area you do not want to have appear with solid black.
2. Make a duplicate of the image. Make the area you *do* want solid black and the rest of the background white. Save both images to disk.
3. Load the image with the black backdrop into the Picture Editor as the Final result image. Load the Alpha mask into the Alpha window. You should now have three images that look like those in Figure 4.44.

BITMAPS AS OBJECTS

When mapped on a picture plane, Bitmaps can become objects in your scene. They are objects with no depth, so you can't orbit them. Doing so will ruin the illusion, as they will seem to get thinner and thinner and disappear, before emerging from nothing again. Kept as background elements, however, bitmapped planes make excellent elements in a Bryce 3D world. There's even a way to add Bitmap animations to a scene, something we'll look at in Chapter 13, The Human Form.

The object you should be mapping to in your world should be the 2D Picture Object from the Create toolbar.

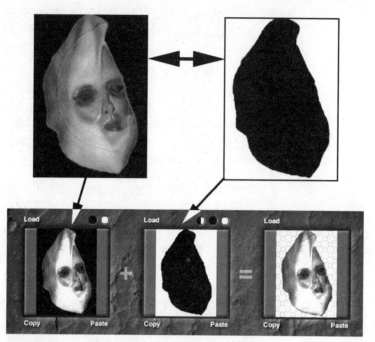

FIGURE *First, an Alpha mask is created in your Paint application. Then the original*
4.44 *image is loaded into the first window and the Alpha mask into the Alpha window. The result is a perfectly cropped image when mapped to a 2D Picture plane in Bryce 3D.*

1. Place it where you want it and make sure it is facing the camera head on. Open the Materials Lab and the Picture Editor.
2. Repeat the steps listed above ("Working in the Picture Editor") to import and adjust your bitmap. The finished picture is shown in Figure 4.45.

BITMAPS AS TEXTURES

Bitmaps can be used instead of and in addition to Procedurals as textures. We all have favorite bitmap photos and images that we have collected over time and stored away. Bryce 3D allows us to use our favorite bitmaps as textural components in a material. Everything that can be done with a procedural texture can be accomplished with a bitmap texture.

In reality, there is very little difference between a bitmap object and a bitmap texture. A bitmap object in Bryce 3D is written to a 2D Picture Plane and usually is not tiled or multiplied. A bitmap-based material, and a material that folds bitmaps in with procedural textures, use the bitmap just like a Procedural. Other than that, there are no differences in the ways that you access the bitmap data in the Picture Editor in the first place.

FIGURE   *The finished picture is composited against a Bryce 3D sky.*
4.45

The only other use for bitmaps—one we've already covered in Chapter 3—is there use as topographical maps for Terrain data. Now that you have explored the use of the Picture Editor, it's worth noting that the color information that the bitmap contains, the image, can also obviously be mapped to Terrains. This means that a bitmap that is translated into a 3D object in the Terrain Editor can be mapped with its own color image from the Materials Lab Picture Editor output. This gives the bitmap dimension as well as an image map. See Figure 4.46 for an example.

FIGURE   *Unlike Figure 4.45, the sky face picture was mapped to a 3D Terrain object of*
4.46   *the same face as topography, giving it dimension. The mountain face was*
mapped with the same material as the mountain.

**Addendum
Topics**

RANDOM PICTURE MAPS

You can apply Random Mapping to imported bitmaps as well as procedural textures. You may have to adjust the size of the image in the range of –2 to +2 to still be able to see identifiable parts of the bitmap, or simply use an abstracted version of the picture with larger or smaller sizes (see Figures 4.47 and 4.48 for examples). Colorful bitmaps provide the richest texturing possibility with this technique, especially when Symmetrical Tiling is switched on. Here's how:

1. With an object selected on screen, open the Materials Lab and activate channel one by placing buttons in Diffuse and Ambient (Color), Diffusion and Ambience (Value), and Transparency (Optics). Click on the P (Picture) button, and then on the Edit button.
2. Load in a graphic or digital photograph. No Alpha channel is need, so return to the Materials Lab.
3. Under Mapping Options, activate the Random option. This scatters your image across the object. Explore Resizing it in the Transformations palette. Explore the Symmetrical Tiling function. Keep an eye on your Materials Nano Preview to see what your manipulations are doing. When you achieve a satisfactory image, return to your Bryce 3D world. Render, and save to disk.

FIGURE **4.47** *These six spheres were mapped with a digital photo of my neighbor's tree. The first one shows the image untouched except for a small amount of rotation. The last two in the first row display Symmetrical Tiling at various size alterations. The second row of materials was developed by using the Random mapping function with various sizes involved.*

FIGURE   *This terrain is mapped from World Top with the same digital picture that was*
4.48   *used in Figure 4.47. Picture-based materials can generate intriguing and*
colorful terrain maps.

Picture textured materials mapped to Terrain objects can take a very long time to render. Consider switching anti-aliasing off, unless you absolutely have to use it. Besides, a rougher look to a terrain image often looks more real.

TIP

MULTIPLE MATERIALS ON ONE OBJECT THE BOOLEAN WAY

Except for AB and ABC mapping in Bryce 3D, you are not supposed to be able to apply more than one material to any single ungrouped object, but there is one rather convoluted way around this restriction. Figure 4.49 shows the finished product. It calls for a little knowledge of Boolean operations, which I'm sure you already possess at this point. Here's how it works:

1. Place a sphere in your Bryce 3D world. We are using a sphere as a quick example, though you can use this technique on any object, primitive or imported. Work in the Front view.
2. Duplicate the sphere in place. Name the original as sphere 1 and the copy as sphere 2.
3. Use a Boolean cube to cut off the bottom half of sphere 1, and another to cut off the top half of sphere 2.
4. In the Materials Lab, apply a different material to each hemisphere. Go back to your world, and make sure the halves line up. Link sphere 2 to sphere 1. Render and save to disk.

FIGURE
4.49 *Using the Boolean technique described, the sphere appears to be mapped with two totally different materials at the same time.*

MULTIPLE MATERIALS ON ONE OBJECT WITH TRANSPARENT LAYERS

Here is an alternate way to create object with multiple materials. The finished product is shown in Figure 4.50.

1. Duplicate the original in place, making sure it doesn't move. Name the original "1" and the duplicate "2."
2. Resize the duplicate so it is 5% larger.

FIGURE
4.50 *The cage around this inner globe was constructed by using Alpha transparency on the cage material, with the Transparent Layers technique described in the text above. The objects were created in about 30 seconds.*

3. Map a material to #2 that is 60% transparent. As yet another variation, map #2 so that it has holes in it (Alpha channel transparency). Whichever way you select, the object is to see through #2 to #1. Link the outer object to the inner one.

4. Render and save to disk.

TIP

This technique is exactly the one you would use to wrap clouds around a planet.

TIP

If both objects are transparent or Alpha transparent, there's no reason you can't place these layers over the multi-material object described in Figure 4.49. This process can be enhanced by repeating the steps as many times as desired.

ADDING BITMAP LABELS TO OBJECTS

This is a project that most computer artists and animators take on at some point, whether from their own interest or as an assignment. Every 3D application handles it somewhat differently. In Bryce 3D, with the knowledge you have gained by working in the Materials Lab, this challenge can be met quickly (Figure 4.51 shows the finished product). Here's how:

1. Develop a graphic of your label-to-be in a paint application and make an Alpha map of it as outlined previously. Save it to disk in a format that Bryce 3D can import.

FIGURE *By following the previous tutorial, you should be able to wrap your own labels*
4.51 *on a suitable Bryce 3D object*

2. Import a suitable object to wrap the label on, a bottle or glass. Use whatever materials you want on it, and give the material a 55% transparency.

3. Create a Cylinder that fits around the middle of the object, which will act as your label object. Make the cylinder about 5% larger than the object in circumference as seen from the top view (that is, enlarge the label object's X and Z scale).

4. With the label object selected, open the Materials Lab. Activate the first channel by placing the dots in the Diffuse and Ambient Color slots, Diffusion and Ambience Value slots, and in the Transparency Optics slot. Open the Picture Editor.

5. Load the label art into the first window and the Alpha map of the label into the second window. The Result window should show the label in full color.

6. Use Object Front mapping to wrap the label to the object. White areas of the label will drop out. Render the object, and save it to disk.

THE SLIDE SHOW

Place a stack of 2D Picture planes in front of the camera so they are separated by a tiny space on the Z World Axis (in and out of the screen). Each one should be the same size. Use the Picture Editor to place images on each one and make sure Transparency is activated. In an animation, make each Picture Plane go to 100% transparency to reveal the Picture Plane image underneath.

If you don't understand Bryce 3D animation, read the documentation and see Section II of this book.

Be absolutely sure to read and work through Chapter 15, Wrong Materials for the Right Reasons.

Moving On

If you have read and worked through this chapter carefully, you should know how to use materials and textures in Bryce 3D, from procedurals to bitmaps. In the next chapter, we'll take a look at Camera and Lights.

CHAPTER

5

Camera and Lights

The Camera

The Camera in Bryce 3D is your eye. Through the camera, you witness the stunning beauty of Bryce 3D landscapes and the actions of animated actors in your play. The camera is the bridge that spans the reality of two dimensions, your everyday world and the virtual world Bryce 3D creates on your computer monitor. What you do to control and manipulate the Camera reshapes the content of your Bryce 3D scenes so you can appreciate and be awed by what is taking place in the Bryce 3D worlds you create. Figure 5.1 shows the Camera iron.

The First Step

The first most important action you can take, before any elements are configured for a Bryce 3D scene, is to orient the position of the camera. This is no small matter, because it will affect everything you do on screen, your comfort in maneuvering and selecting objects, and the way that you think about light sources. Machiavelli said that a society can be brought down if you first attend to adding disquiet to the way that citizens relate to their measurement and orientation systems, and in Bryce 3D, the ease with which you set up a level of comfort and maneuverability is similarly essential.

The default position of the Camera in Bryce, the position and orientation it is placed at when you first open the program, is not suitable for art or animation work. The camera is placed so that it is looking at the scene from the northwest corner of the world. The sun, your main source of orientation (controlled by the trackball) is situated so that it looks like it functions from a bottom to top view. You can force the sun to orient itself to the camera by selecting

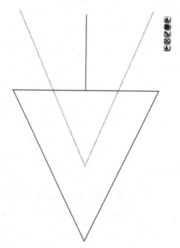

FIGURE *The Camera is represented on screen by this symbolic icon. It can be moved and*
5.1 *rotated like any other object. The Camera cannot be resized.*

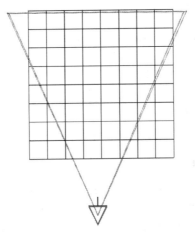

FIGURE   *This is how your initial camera position should look when seen from the top*
5.2   *view.*

the command Link Sun to View from the Sky and Fog options menu, but all
this does is to add immeasurable confusion to the issue, the same kind of confusion that Machiavelli claimed would bring down any society. In order not to
bring down your virtual society before you even start to build it, and in order to
work in a clearer and more logical fashion, here is what you should do. Go to
the top view, and orient the camera so that it is pointing from the bottom of the
screen upward towards the top of your monitor, as illustrated in Figure 5.2. To
get the camera rotated the correct amount from the top view, select the camera
icon and use the A button in its Attributes list . Set the rotation amounts to
X=0, Y=0, and Z=0.

Unfortunately, Bryce 3D has no memory of where you place your camera
when you shut the application off, so it will reboot with the camera in the same
confusing default position. So it is suggested that you save your new default to
a convenient file, best located in the Bryce 3D folder. Name the file something
like MyCam.br3, or a similar name. That way, after you boot up, all you have
to do is load this scene, and everything will be in position.

The Camera Attributes List

We've already spoken about the Attributes list for the Camera in our discussions
about changing its orientation. The Camera functions like a special object in
Bryce 3D, so it has an Attributes list of modification possibilities. There are several very important items to point out in the Camera Attributes list, though it
is assumed that your reading of the Bryce 3D documentation has already alerted

you to the Camera Attributes basics. It might be a good idea to open the Camera Attributes list now, so you can see the items we will mention. There are five associated icons involved, and important points associated with each.

ATTRIBUTES (THE "A" ICON)

Although the Camera is treated like any other object in many ways, the contents of its Attributes dialog (Figure 5.3) prove it to be a special type of object.

The General Tab

You cannot rename the camera, though this may change in future versions of Bryce 3D if multiple cameras are allowed. Free is marked by default, allowing you to move it anywhere, except if you have checked Locked. Instead of Hidden, an option given for other objects, you have the option Invisible. Hidden objects can still be seen onscreen because they can be assigned special powers. Invisible objects do not appear. Check Invisible if the camera is getting in your way, and you continue to select it by mistake. Show FOV (field of vision) should always be on, so you can see what objects in the scene are in view. Origin Handle should also always be on, since it allows you to position the Camera's center anywhere on the scene for rotations around selected objects.

Let's skip down to the FOV and Size controls, which not only determine the parameters of what the Camera sees, but are also vital in creating Camera-based animations. Decreasing FOV to 40 gives you the same initial view of the scene as increasing Camera Size to 160, but one does not really equate with the other. FOV sets the field of vision of the camera, how much of the scene the camera takes in, with 60 being the Bryce 3D norm. Taking in more of the scene widens your view and makes everything in it appear smaller at the same time. Size, on the other hand, is a zoom mechanism. You can zoom out or in, but

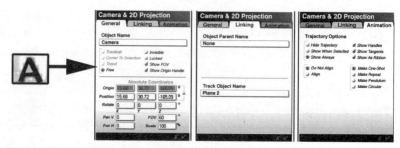

FIGURE *The Camera Attributes dialog.*
5.3

there are depth anomalies associated with pushing this tool to the extreme. Objects in your scene, especially those that move when the Camera is zoomed, seem to warp as they approach or recede from the Camera with either setting, but starting from what looks like a similar view, radical Size alterations produce more exaggerated warping effects. Try this exercise.

1. Place a sphere in front of the camera, making it about one-quarter of the screen size. Create an animation that moves the screen from in front of the camera to the right of it in 30 frames.

2. Open the Attributes dialog with the Camera selected and set the FOV to 180 for the length of the animation. Preview the animation from the Camera view. Notice that the sphere elongates in the direction of its path the closer it gets to the camera. This would be an interesting but mind-bending way to see a train moving from the distance to the right of your position. This happens because your Field of Vision is so wide, it allows you to see clearly what we normally see in a blurred fashion in our peripheral vision.

3. Set the FOV back to its defaulted position of 60 and set the Size in the Camera Attributes dialog to 20. Run a preview of the animation. The sphere still warps, but a little more evenly.

TIP

For more radical and mind-twisting space warping Camera animations, see Chapter 7. Also see the Tunnel project in Chapter 11.

TIP

See Chapter 7 for using the Pan operations, both Vertical and Horizontal, as animation engines.

The Links Tab

Be careful about Linking the camera from a distance to an object being followed, since whatever convolutions the object goes through (bouncing, sudden jolts) the camera will go through as well. Use Link when the camera is closer to an object, as, for example, when the camera is in a car looking ahead at the road. Targeting objects with the Camera require fewer cautions. Targeting the camera is the single most important procedure that shows your capabilities as a director. In general, follow these simple rules when targeting objects with the Camera:

• Try to stay away from targeting the camera from one camera position, because it's likely that intervening objects will pop into view, and it is really boring.

- Make sure to move the Origin Point on the object to an interesting location, so the object can be targeted by the Camera at a place on the object that is both interesting and central to its identification.
- Allow the camera to have its own path as it targets an object, so it can draw closer and farther at different points. The reason is viewer interest. Watch films of car chases for excellent examples of camera tracking and movement.

See all of the animations in Section III, especially Chapter 7.

The Animation Tab

Camera animation techniques, and the use of the items in this tab, are covered in Chapter 7.

FAMILY COLOR (THE COLOR BOX ICON)

Select a color for the Camera that stands out in your scene, since it is the most used object. The defaulted color (blue) is not satisfactory in my opinion, because it gets lost in other wireframe colors. Whatever color you select, do not use it for any other objects. Figure 5.4 shows the dialog box.

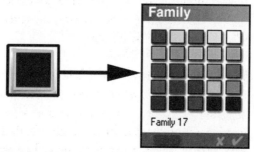

FIGURE *The family Color dialog.*
5.4

LINK (THE CHAIN ICON, FIGURE 5.5)

TARGET (THE TARGET ICON, FIGURE 5.6)

FIGURE *The Link icon. See the section on Linking under the General Tab information*
5.5 *above.*

FIGURE *The Target icon. See the section on Targeting under the General Tab*
5.6 *information.*

FIGURE *The Gravity icon.*
5.7

GRAVITY (THE ARROW ICON, FIGURE 5.7)

The Camera can get placed in positions you didn't intend in a time-consuming session, so the Gravity Arrow can be a useful aid in getting it literally "down to earth" again. As seen from the front, left, right, or back views, the camera will drop down to the next item below it when the Arrow icon is clicked on. Although Infinite Planes go on forever and are only represented by limited grids in Bryce 3D, the Camera has to be over the grid in order to notice that it exists when applying the gravity arrow.

FROM THE DIRECTOR'S VIEW

Producing a large animation project requires the use of storyboards, so the director and animators can see the scene from whatever perspective is needed for location planning and action sequences. Use the Director's View and the alternate camera modes to rotate and position the scene as needed for storyboarding and choreographic planning. The three alternate Director-only modes in the Camera Attributes dialog (accessible only when Director's View is selected) are: Trackball, Center to Selection, and Tripod. Also see Chapter 1 for a description of what these alternate modes provide.

Camera Sky Shots

There are times when you want your actors to be photographed against the sky alone. After all, sky art is one of Bryce 3D's major strong points. When you have scenes with a good number of separate objects involved, this can present a problem. Ground and Water Planes are infinite, so it is sometimes difficult to shoot your objects only against the sky unless you delete all of the infinite planes. Even when you do that, and try to shoot against the sky alone, you are presented with a banded horizon line. Here's how to proceed when you run up against this challenge:

1. Set up your scene with all of the items in place. Adjust the Camera view so that you see everything in the right frame and perspective.
2. Create or import a sky from the Sky presets and adjust the light so that the objects in your scene appear as you would like them to. Since the ground plane, or any other infinite planes, will not be needed, you may delete them.
3. Select all of the items in your scene, including the Camera (drag out a marquee around them), so that they are all included. Group them.
4. Rotate this grouped selection by going to the right or left views. make the rotation about 35 degrees tilted upward. Do a preview render to make sure you see nothing in the background but the sky. Ungroup and adjust as necessary.

The difference between this technique and simply turning the camera upward is that you can control the perspective better. Turning the camera upward enough to negate the infinite planes or the horizon line often forces you to accept perspectives that you do not want. A liability exists with this method if you plan to resize or rotate elements after they are rotated, since this may produce warping. Best to do that when they are in the initial position. Figure 5.8 gives an example of camera shots of sky.

FIGURE
5.8   *Camera shots that include only the sky are very useful for product advertisements as well as dreamlike graphics.*

Also see Figure 4.51 in Chapter 4 as an example of an interesting sky shot achieved with this method.

Creating Textures with the Camera

The Camera has a very close focus. In fact, the minimum distance that you can get to a targeted object is limited only by the material that the object is composed of. If the material is made from bitmapped components, then you may see a good amount of pixelization up close. If the material is a procedurally based, however, then the laws of fractals intervene, and closeness just reveals more detail. The only other influence that may intervene is light. You'll have to make sure the Procedurally textured material is being lit strongly enough and from the correct angle so you can see what is there to be revealed.

Why would you want to take a close-up of a Procedurally textured material anyway? The answer is, to make another material, this one bitmapped based. Here's how it works:

1. With an object selected, open the Materials Lab, and create an original material that utilizes one or more channels. Work in the Deep Texture Editor to achieve something unique. Make sure it has elements of interest that draw upon layered effects (Altitude effects are good because you get an automatic blend of the three composite ingredients). Refer to Chapter 4 if you need a refresher on this technique.

2. Leave the Materials Lab when you're done. The material is now wrapped to your selected object. Make sure the object is lit well enough so that the material can be seen.

3. Move the camera as close as you would like to the object on which the material has been placed. Make sure that the material fills your viewscreen from whatever view you select (Camera or Front views are the best to use).

Caution! Make sure Reflection and Specularity are off to prevent unwanted highlights.

4. Render the image with normal anti-aliasing on (never use fine anti-aliasing unless you are going on vacation, and don't need to see the finished render until you return, if then).

5. When the rendering is complete, export (save) the image to disk.

6. In Bryce 3D, create an object and select it. Open the Materials Lab and go to the Picture Editor after clicking "P" on one of the channels. In the

FIGURE
5.9
From the original Procedurally developed material textures created in the Materials Lab and Deep Texture Editor, the Camera is used to take a picture of the applied material.

Picture Editor, load in the graphic of the material you saved, and keep its Alpha channel solid black. Or, if you like, you might explore copying the image and pasting it into the Alpha channel. This will give you Bump mapping with the Bitmap. In the materials Lab, explore various mapping options and other controls until you achieve a bitmap material you like.

You will find that the bitmapped material acts very differently from the Procedural material when mapped to your selected object. This technique is based upon an informed use of the Camera. Figures 5.9 and 5.10 show the outcome of the process.

FIGURE
5.10
From there, a Terrain Map and bitmap material are used to construct a scene. Outrageous materials can be developed in this manner, using your knowledge of the Camera as a way to develop bitmaps from Procedurals.

The Procedural material used in this example is called gastroKelp1, and you'll find it in the MyMatl folder on the CD-ROM. The bitmapped material developed from it is called gastroKelp2, and you'll find it there as well.

Panoramic Vistas

Be sure to read pages 418 and 419 of the Bryce 3D documentation before creating Panoramic Vistas, as we are only sketching out the important points and a few tips.

You can develop panoramic Vistas in Bryce 3D that can be translated to Web panoramas for use on your home page with the display help of Apple's QuickTime VR technology or other applications. Visitors will be able to stand in the center of your Bryce 3D world and turn the Camera around to appreciate the view (see Figure 5.11). This is all made possible by understanding how to place and manipulate the Camera. Here's how:

1. Click on Default in your Document Setup dialog and on the QTVR Panorama rendering option.
2. Set up your objects with the Camera at the center.
3. Select Render to Disk and choose a folder on your hard drive.
4. Load the finished rendering into Apple's QuickTime VR or another suitable panorama application for viewing.

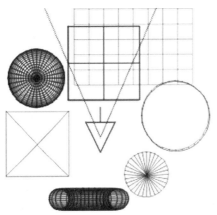

FIGURE *On the left is a view of the Camera placed in the center of the objects (Bryce 3D top view), while the*
5.11 *illustration on the right shows the resulting Panorama rendering. A panoramic image is rendered so that the left and right sides stitch together perfectly.*

For another option in the customization of your VR Panoramas, if you are serious about developing Panorama productions from Bryce 3D, check out LivePicture Inc. and its PhotoVista application. It's much more extensive than Apple's QuickTime VR software, even though it is not free. Go to the LivePicture Web site for information and purchasing data: http://www.livepicture.com.

Enhancing 3D Depth

There is a problem when looking at infinite planes through the Camera. The problem is that they are infinite. The other problem is that the computer sees too clearly. Reality is neither perceptually infinite nor clear. In the real world, I can take a plane or a car and move around the visible curve of the horizon to where not even your most powerful telescope can see me. I can also take advantage of the thickness of the atmosphere, so that as I move a certain distance from you, even though I have not moved past the horizon's curve, I will still be invisible to your eyes. Both of these problems, and their solutions, can be emulated in Bryce 3D. They are basically Camera-associated challenges because they involve optics—that is, how the Bryce 3D world is seen through the camera's eye. Here are some steps to take to help the Camera take a picture of a more "real" Bryce 3D world:

- Explore the use of a larger FOV setting in the Camera's Attributes dialog. A setting of 80 seems to enhance the depth well.
- Place an object close to the Camera that has detailed material.
- Make sure objects in the far distance are blurred as compared to foreground objects. Use the Fuzzy option in the Materials Lab when applying materials to background objects.
- Use the Resize operation to make objects smaller than they are when used in the background. This enhances the perspective.
- Color objects in the background with a bluish tint. The farther they are away, drop their complex materials in favor of a light grayish blue.
- Always use the Distance Blur option, in the Materials Lab, on infinite planes.
- Always consider a Haze setting of at least 50. Color the haze based upon the sky at the horizon.

If you consider all of these suggestions, the view through your Bryce 3D camera will look all the more believable. See Figure 5.12 for an illustration.

See the Fig5_12.br3 project on the CD-ROM to see how the picture above was created.

FIGURE **5.12**   *Helping the Camera transform computerized 3D depth into a surrealistic landscape means using every Bryce 3D function at your disposal, as suggested in the text above.*

TIP

If you were to do just one picture like Figure 5.12, not an animation, you could render a Distance Render map in addition to the color render. Then you could bring both into a suitable paint application, with the Distance Render used as an Alpha overlay. This would allow you to achieve a blurring of objects farther from the Camera just by marrying the two layers. Read the Bryce 3D documentation that deals with doing and applying Distance Renders.

Let There Be Lights

Light not only illuminates worlds, it also allows us to appreciate its opposite, darkness. To a 3D artist and animator, darkness and shadow are the defining principles of the 3D environment. It is shadow that causes us to imagine that we are seeing 3D shapes on a 2D screen. All of the information covered thus far concerning the application of Materials to objects, especially materials that look three-dimensional because of bump mapped elements, takes light and lighting into consideration. With the right lighting, materials and textures jump off the screen. With the wrong lighting, materials and textures look flat and washed out, erasing all of the long hours of effort that went into their creation.

Lighting also lends emotional content to what we see. This can be best appreciated by looking at a model of the human face with different lighting methods applied, as seen in Figure 5.13.

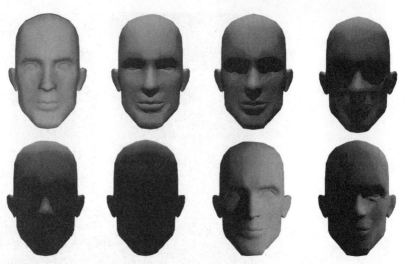

FIGURE
5.13 *For 3D interest, a face with full front lighting looks flat, when compared to lighting that casts partial shadows. Lighting also influences our perception of the actor and the story being told.*

The Bryce 3D Lighting Technician

You are given all of the tools you need to become a master lighting technician, setting and modifying light sources for your Bryce 3D worlds. Chapter 6 deals with nature oriented light sources, the Sun and the Moon, while this chapter focuses upon the other lighting tools at your disposal.

Lighting Types and Their Uses

The four Light Types in Bryce 3D are Radial, Spotlight, Square Spotlight, and Parallel Light. Each has its uses and each affects a scene in a different way (see Figure 5.14).

FIGURE
5.14 *The four Light Types are located in the Create toolbar and placed on screen by clicking on their respective icons.*

FIGURE   *The Radial Light is spherical and throws its illumination in all directions*
5.15 *equally. It's perfect for use as a light in a lamp.*

RADIAL LIGHT

The radial light is represented by the spherical light icon in the Create toolbar.
Figure 5.15 gives an illustration.

Where and When Would You Use a Radial Light?

When you need light that illuminates everything in a scene equally from a light
source, use a Radial Light. Radial Lights also throw illumination on the ground
plane, something no other light does. You might describe a Radial Light as one
that is constructed from an infinite number of Spotlights, since the illumination it throws off is represented by a circular patch on the objects that receive
the light. If you placed a Radial Light in a cubic room, you would see a circular patch of light on each wall, the ceiling, and the floor. Places to use a Radial
Light include the following:

- Drop a Radial Light in the calendra of a volcano to illuminate the calen-
  dra and anything that might be ejected out of it.
- Use a Radial Light as a placed sun in your sky. More on this in Chapter 6.
- Use a Radial Light as a Lamp. Place it inside of a Lightbulb object, and
  link it to that object. The lamp can also be a street lamp.
- Use a Radial Light, reduced in size, inside a candle flame.
- Use a Radial Light inside of any fire material, useful for campfires or
  larger conflagrations.

Create a Street Lamp

To create a street lamp that uses a Radial Light, do the following:

1. Create a series of objects in your scene that will be illuminated by the lamp. Leave room in their collective center for the lamp.
2. Create a pole from a stretched cylinder primitive and place it on the ground in the center of your objects. Place a sphere on top of the pole. Use a Gold material on the pole, and a light blue material for the globe. Make the globe 65% transparent. Move the globe to the top of the pole.
3. Place a Radial Light in the center of the globe. Make the Radial Light a Volumetric light in its Edit dialog, so you can see it.

Refer to Figure 5.30 later in this chapter for an example of a street lamp whose special bulb we will learn to create.

NOTE

SPOTLIGHT

Figure 5.16 illustrates a basic use of the Spotlight.

Where and When Would You Use a Spotlight?

Spotlights are the second most common lights that are chosen, with Radial Lights being first. Spotlights are used for two main purposes. The first is to tar-

FIGURE **5.16** *The Spotlight illuminates a scene from a specific direction, in this case, from the camera position.*

get a specific element in your scene, perhaps by moving across it to reveal it in steps. The second use for selecting the Spotlight is to emulate various light sources, listed below.

- Link Spotlights to vehicles for use as headlights.
- Use Spotlights to construct searchlights that move across the sky.
- Use Spotlights for mysterious light sources emanating from an ET ship.
- Use a group of moving Spotlights to illuminate an object of interest, perhaps a logo, in a scene.
- Use Spotlights in the eyes of a robot to add extra excitement.
- Link a Spotlight inside of the nozzle of a rocket, adding extra punch to the exhaust.

Create a Spotlight Scene

1. Use the same scene that you designed for the street lamp exercise above. Delete the lamp, globe, and Radial Light.
2. Place a Spotlight in front of the scene and aim it at the objects. Adjust the distance based upon preview renders. Render and save.

Square Spotlight

Figure 5.17 illustrates the basic use for a Square Spotlight.

FIGURE   *The Square Spotlight is the best light to choose when you need light to stream*
5.17   *through a window into a darkened room to illuminate the contents.*

Where and When Would You Use a Square Spotlight?

Square Spotlights are good for global illumination. This light casts a squarish illumination, but not as defined as Parallel Lights. The beam tends to smear and be somewhat rounded. Its best use is for general scene illumination from a specific direction. If you wanted to have light streaming through a window to light all of the objects in its direction, the square Spotlight would be a wise choice.

Load the Fig5_17.br3 project from the CD-ROM to explore this figure for the use of the Square Spotlight.

PARALLEL LIGHT

Parallel Lights are perfect for projecting Gel images onto a scene. Although you can do this with any of the four light types, Gels projected through a Parallel Light look like square-edged slides from a projector. See the section on Gels later in this chapter to explore Parallel Light projection further.

Editing Lights

Figure 5.18 shows the Edit Lights dialog box.

Here are some tips to think about when using the Edit Lights dialog:

- Keep the Light Intensity to 50 or below if you want to see the light color as long as it is anything but white (which is always visible).
- Setting the Light Intensity at 100 and the color to black produces some interesting dark light effects. Use the effects to add subtle mystery to a scene.
- Preview with the Render in Scene option if you're not sure about the parameters you're setting. Although this takes a little time, it also shows you

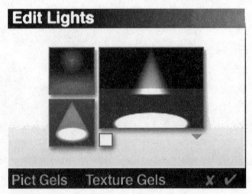

FIGURE *The Edit Lights dialog gives you access to several lighting options that can cause*
5.18 *your lights to exhibit different attributes.*

how your intensity and other changes are affecting the scene itself. Most of the time, you will use the default Render Against neutral however, especially when you get experienced enough with light settings to intuit what the results of your tweaking will be.

- Only in rare circumstances would you push the light intensity to 100%. This causes a hot spot on objects that washes out their materials. When this occurs and is opposite to your wishes, move the light back from the object(s).

- Never leave the color white when using the softened light aura. Always apply a color, usually a pastel works well.

Volumetric Lights

Volumetric Lights are new in Bryce 3D. Because they have volume as compared with surface lights, which have just a 2D presence, they appear and act uniquely in a scene. They can be made to take on 3D materials just like any other object. Normally, the materials they accept are provided by the Volume environment of the Materials Lab. But this is not a hard and fast rule or limitation. You can also explore adding textured materials to a Volumetric light, or any volumetric, within the framework of the Surface environment of the Materials Lab. When applying textured materials to Volumetric light, there are a few cautions to observe so that you can avoid overlong rendering times.

- Avoid super closeups (larger than one-quarter screen) of Volumetric lights that display a textured material.

- The alterations you make in the light's Edit dialog are always done first, before anything you do in the Materials Lab. Never return to the Edit dialog after you have customized material in the Materials Lab, or you will undo the Material Lab customization.

- The highest rendering time cost applies to transparent textured materials. You don't have to avoid them, just be aware of this fact.

See the Radial Light flx samples ahead in this chapter for a more detailed look at specific volumetric light exercises.

NOTE

Altering Light Attributes

In Bryce 3D, all lights have an Attribute dialog like any other object. There is one important setting in the Attributes dialog that has a major effect on light effects, and that is size. Whether you resize a light from its Attributes dialog or from the Resize icon in the Edit toolbar, the spread of the light cone is projected larger when the light object is larger. You can resize a light to sometimes compensate for falloff setting amounts, so that a larger light will cast its spread wider in a scene. Moving a light closer or farther from specific target objects also affects its spread and the intensity of illumination.

The Falloff attributes are listed in the light's Edit dialog. The most common is Linear. Linear Falloff is based upon distance from the intended light target. The more distance between the light and target, the less illumination. Sometimes, depending upon the lighting effect you want to create in a scene, selecting No Falloff becomes necessary. Using No Falloff will cause the light to illuminate everything in its projection beam evenly, so that objects in the far distance are illuminated the same as objects close to the light. Use No Falloff for effects like explosion flares, pseudo sun or moon elements, and surrealistic visuals.

GELS

A Gel is an image that can be projected by any light source. Bryce 3D differentiates between PICT Gels and Texture Gels. A PICT Gel is defined as any graphic that Bryce 3D can import, which can then be used as a Gel. When you access a PICT Gel, you are presented with the Picture Editor from the Materials Lab, so that you can manipulate the Alpha channel as necessary (see Chapter 4 for more on the use of the Picture Editor). Texture Gels utilize textures. These can be either presets from the Materials library, or your own customized textured materials. PICT Gels are used to project bitmap images, while Texture Gels are used for scene f/x, though there is some necessary crossover between the two. Gels are normally accessed from the light's Edit dialog. The only exception is a method of Gel access that we describe later in the section entitled "Materials and Lights: Another Method."

PICT Gels

The Gel folder in the Bryce 3D directory contains a number of ready-to-assign PICT Gels, though you can also use any of your own bitmap images from storage. The unique thing about the Gels in the Bryce 3D folder is that they are all two-color silhouettes, perfect for emulating shadows from invisible objects like trees and venetian blinds. This allows you to get the benefit of the presence of objects in a scene by their shadow, without the actual object having to be present. Figures 5.19 and 5.20 give some examples.

Texture Gels

The entire Material Presets library is at your disposal for use as Texture Gel patterns, as are your own customized textures. The benefit of using procedural textures as Gel data include the ability to resize the Gel information in the Materials Lab. Figures 5.21 and 5.22 show two examples.

FIGURE   *Here, a spotlight uses a PICT Gel to cast the Horizontal Slats pattern on*
5.19   *everything in its illumination path.*

FIGURE   *The type of light casting the PICT Gel makes a difference. In this case, a Square*
5.20   *Spotlight was used.*

FIGURE
5.21 *A Spotlight with a Object Front mapped Yellow Noise Texture Gel casts patterns on objects and ground.*

FIGURE
5.22 *The same Spotlight using the same Texture Gel as in Figure 5.21. The difference is that Spherical mapping and a higher size setting were configured in the Materials Lab.*

Very Important! PICT Gels work best on objects that have plain color materials, while Texture Gels work best on objects that have textured materials. Turn Ambience off and Diffusion down on object materials that are to receive Gel lighting.

TIP

Keep in mind that rotating the light also rotates the Gel, important for images and animations.

TIP

PARALLEL LIGHT PROJECTIONS

Parallel Lights are perfect when you need to keep the illuminated area square. This is the light type to select for projecting window lights, or for creating pseudo slide shows and movies within your scenes. Figure 5.23 shows an example.

MATERIALS AND LIGHTS: ANOTHER METHOD

You can use another method to target a light with a material texture. Simply click on the "M" in the light's Attributes list to bring up the Materials Lab, and select a material preset or design your own. This is not covered in the Bryce 3D documentation.

Important! If you use this option, do not use either Surface or Volumetric options, or your system will crash.

NOTE

FIGURE   *The Parallel Light is rectangular and throws its illumination in one set*
5.23   *direction. The edges of the illuminated area can be customized to remain completely square, perfect for projecting images like this Crosshatch Window PICT Gel from the Bryce 3D folder.*

FIGURE **5.24** *The materials used to achieve these Radial Light interference patterns were (upper left to lower right): Gilded Cage, Gilded Cage resized to 3x, Peeling Paint, Carnival Tent, Rainbow, and Volcano Heart.*

The best light to use for this option is the Radial light. The material will be transmitted to objects in the vicinity as expected. This is a way of applying a Texture Gel that is more direct than going through the Light Edit dialog. The best materials to use are those with dropout Alpha textures, since this will project symmetrical patterns on objects. If you increase the size of the texture in the Transformations dialog of the Materials Lab, you will start to see interference patterns being projected. This can be very effective for emulating energy strikes on material, like a pebble being cast into a pond, and is a great animation tool. Set the light intensity to 100, and the blur to 50. Some sample materials are shown in Figure 5.24.

 See the Water section in Chapter 8 for project ideas on using this effect.

 The color of the plane on which you map your interference patterns should not be too dark. A red color darkened to a reddish black looks good. This technique does not work with textures in the material, only color. Choose lighter colors to tint the Radial Light in its Edit dialog.

 Try using "No Falloff" in the Radial Light's Edit dialog if the projected texture is too light and moving the light closer to the material has little or no effect. Moving the Radial Light closer to the object sharpens the projected image.

Radial Light f/x Samples

Having covered a number of ways to customize lights, and especially targeting Radial Lights for texturing, let's look at a few visual examples of Radial Lights. With each graphic is a detailed description of how the effect was created. Note that the Gilded Cage material was used on all examples. You may select another preset textured material or create your own.

Work in the Edit dialog first, followed by the Materials Lab. Do not return to the Edit dialog because all of the Materials Lab settings will be undone if you do.

NOTE

TEXTURED MATERIAL, BEAM CASTING NORMAL LIGHT

To achieve the effect shown in Figure 5.25, do the following:

1. In the Edit dialog: Set Intensity and Fuzziness to 100. Make it a Volume Light with Linear Falloff.
2. In the Material Labs: Assign the Gilded Cage material. Use the channel one marker only in the Transparent Color row and the Transparency Optics row. Select the Blend Transparency type. Wrap the material to the light in Object Space.

FIGURE *This is our first example. The Radial Light has a textured material applied, but*
5.25 *the beam casts only a normal light.*

FIGURE *In this example, the Radial Light is both wrapped with the material and*
5.26 *projects the same material.*

RADIAL LIGHT WRAPPED WITH MATERIAL, PROJECTING SAME MATERIAL

To achieve the effect shown in Figure 5.26, do the following:

1. In the Edit dialog: Set Intensity and Fuzziness to 100. Make it a Surface Light and Infinite.
2. In the Materials Lab: Assign the Gilded Cage material. Use the channel one marker only in the Diffuse and Ambient Color rows (with slider settings of 80 and 30 respectively), in the Bump Height Value row, and the Transparency Optics row. Select the Blend Transparency type. Wrap the material to the light in Object Space.

RADIAL LIGHT WRAPPED WITH MATERIAL, PROJECTING SAME MATERIAL, FUZZED OUT AND SOFT

To achieve the effect shown in Figure 5.27, do the following:

1. In the Edit dialog: Set Intensity and Fuzziness to 100. Make it a Volume Light and Infinite.
2. In the Materials Lab: Go to the Volume controls and assign the Gilded

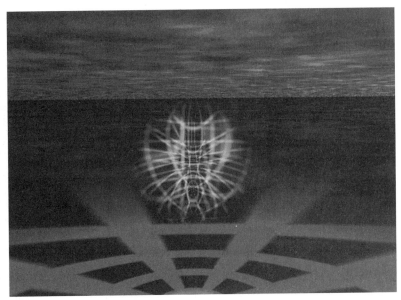

FIGURE *In this example, the Radial Light is both wrapped with the material and*
5.27 *projects the same material. It is also fuzzed out and soft in appearance.*

Cage material. Use the channel one marker in the Diffuse Color and Base
Density rows only. Input the following settings: Diffuse Value = 80, Am-
bient Value = 30, Specular Value = 22, Base Density = 55, Edge = 100,
Fuzzy Factor = 300, Quality/Speed = 30. Select the Flat Shaded type. Use
Spherical mapping and wrap the material to the light in Object Space.

RADIAL LIGHT STANDARD VOLUMETRIC WITH NO MATERIAL

To achieve the effect shown in Figure 5.28, do the following:

1. In the Edit dialog: Set Intensity and Fuzziness to 100. Make it a Volume
   Light and Infinite.
2. No need to do anything in the Materials Lab.

RADIAL LIGHT VOLUMETRIC WITH PICT GEL MAPPED TO IT

To achieve the effect shown in Figure 5.29, do the following:

1. In the Edit dialog: Set Intensity and Fuzziness to 100. Make it a Volume
   Light and Infinite. Click on Pict Gel and load the Watery Reflections
   item from the Gel folder in the Bryce 3D folder.

FIGURE   *In this example, the Radial Light is a standard Volumetric with no material*
5.28   *wrapped to it. Note that using a solid black sky emphasize the light's contrast.*

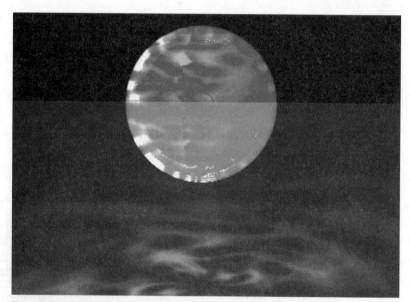

FIGURE   *In this example, the Radial Light is a Volumetric with a Pict Gel, Watery*
5.29   *Reflections, mapped to it. Some settings were altered in the material Lab.*

2. In the Materials Lab, do the following: Make it a Volume material with Full Shading. Place the texture marker in the Diffuse Color row and in the Diffusion Value row (setting = 100). Also set Ambience value to 50. Give it a Base Density of 16 and a Fuzzy factor of 100. Set Quality/Speed to the center (Air).

NOTE

Normally, you would not see the light itself, just the fractal Watery Reflections. The customization we did in the Materials Lab made the light visible. See Chapter 8 for water flx to appreciate this example in an animation.

RADIAL LIGHT VOLUMETRIC WITH TEXTURE GEL MAPPED TO IT

To achieve the effect shown in Figure 5.30, do the following:

1. In the Edit dialog: Set Intensity and Fuzziness to 100. Make it a Volume Light and Infinite. Click on Pict Gel and load the Luna file from the materials presets that pop up.

2. In the Materials Lab, do the following: Make it a Volume material with Flat Shading. Place the texture marker in the Diffuse Color row only. Set Diffusion value, Base Density, and Fuzzy Factor to 100. Set Quality/Speed to the center (Air).

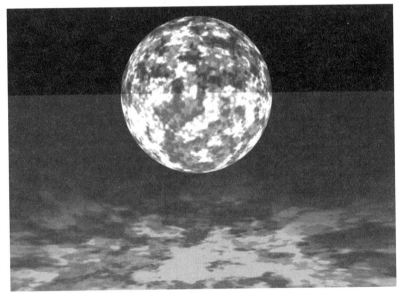

FIGURE *In this example, the Radial Light is a Volumetric with Texture Gel, Luna,*
5.30 *mapped to it. Some settings were altered in the Material Lab in order to make the light a visible object.*

NOTE

Important: Turning Atmosphere off in the Sky and Fog Toolbar enhances all projected light effects. If you need clouds, add them on an infinite cloud plane.

Sculpted Street Lamp Variation (Figure 5.31)

WHICH LIGHT TYPE IS BEST TO USE WITH A GEL?

There is no hard and fast answer to this question, because it depends upon what the project demands and how you configure the near infinite variables involved. There are a few guidelines to consider, however.

- Use Radial Lights when you want the Gel to influence objects that surround the light source, and the other types for targeted objects.
- Use Parallel Lights when you want to emulate slide and movie projectors in your scene.
- If you want to apply silhouetted light/dark images to objects, use PICT Gels. If you want to apply color washes, use Texture Gels.
- Consider the use of Alpha channel data when using PICT Gels when the image contains more than two colors (black and white).
- Use colorful materials when opting for Texture Gels, because that will enhance your targeted objects beyond the use of the light itself.

FIGURE 5.31 *All of the light in this scene is being provided by four sculpted street lamps. Each has the same "bulb" referenced in figure 5.30.*

Addendum Light Topics

A few more points concerning lights need to be made before we can move on to the next chapter. These concern a mention of which light type to best use with a gel, Material Preset Lights, Object Lights, and Grouping Lights to false light objects.

MATERIAL PRESET LIGHTS

There are two Material Presets that I find I am using constantly to target to spheres, for use as stars or false sun objects (the term "false" is used to distinguish these objects from the Bryce 3D Sun, a topic of the next chapter). These are the GreenLit and Marley's Ghost presets in the Complex f/x folder. I prefer GreenLit the most, because it can be easily customized and colored. Bring it up on your system and explore how it is put together in the Materials Lab.

OBJECT LIGHTS

Any object in Bryce 3D can be made into a light, or at least an element that has some of the attributes we expect from lights. This does not include illuminating other objects directly, but through a perceptual trick. What is the trick? Transparent objects that cause everything we see through them look brighter fool the eye into thinking they are lights. The three most common objects used for these pseudo-lights are spheres, cones, and very thin cylinders.

False Spherical Lights

These objects can be used effectively as suns and mapped with plain color or more evocative materials for use as background planets (see Figure 5.32). Used for this purpose, they are not usually transparent, but just fuzzy around the edges. If they are made transparent, they can be used as ghostly lights that can be placed anywhere in the scene. When you create a false spherical light, make sure you do the following:

- Make them Volumetric objects. This gives them more dimension.
- Use Flat Shading on them, which allows you to pay more attention to their color than their contents.
- Play with the Base Density slider to achieve the opacity or transparency you need.
- Set the Diffuse Color slider to whatever color you want and the Diffusion value to 100%. Set Ambience to zero.
- Resize and place the object as needed in your scene.

FIGURE *False spherical lights can act as effective stand-ins for suns and planets.*
5.32

False Conic Lights

Simply use a cone and select the Light Shading option in the Materials Lab (Surface material). Turn down ambience on all objects that the false conic light will seem to touch, or the image will lose contrast and the effect will be lost. Place the cones at an angle, so it seems they are emanating from the same source. In the Materials Lab, the Volume Color determines the color of the rays and Transparency Optics controls density. Move the Transparency slider to at least 65%, and even higher for more subtle effects. Make sure to pay attention to light directions and specular highlights in your scene, so the rays are coming from the same direction. Figure 5.33 illustrates this procedure.

This same effect can work for rays streaming from a globe, or even a Radial Light source. It can also be used for searchlights and spotlights, as long as true lights are grouped with the false ones.

False Laser Lights

Although the documentation advises you to use cylindrical primitives for lasers, I am going to suggest that there is a better way to go about it. True, if you are developing a scene in a laboratory showing a laser at work, you will definitely want to use the cylinder as suggested. But lasers, since their inception, have always had a close identification with particle beams and ray guns. For these project elements, the cylinder has no character.

FIGURE *Rays from a false sun illuminate a landscape.*
5.33

Bryce 3D contains the perfect object for more vociferous laser beam operations, and it isn't a cylinder. In the Imported Objects folder of the Objects library is a screw. Its threads act to give a light object just the right touch or variance and randomness. When stretched out, you can no longer tell what the object is, because the threads are stretched into flowing curves.

Look at Figure 5.34. There is a lot going on here with different lights. Let me describe some of the elements involved, although you should load the Fig5.34.br3 project and explore for yourself as well. Let's talk just about the light associated aspects of this graphic. First, because the Bryce 3D sun is illuminating this scene from the back, objects tend to be on the dark side. This being the case, the Specularity of texture channels was raised to 100%. This allows various parts of the material to literally glow in the dark. The Specularity of the simple color material used on the ship was raised as well, to pop it out of the dark. The internal glow emanating from the bottom of the ship is a Radial Light. It is toned down by the Torus that surrounds it, shielding the buildings from the light. A screw object is used as the beam. The beam is textured with the Volumetric Red Laser Beam on the Volume side of the Materials Lab. Flat, Additive Shading with a Volume Altitude Blend is used. The sliders are set to 100 for Diffusion and 17 for Ambient Value, a Base Density of 17, an Edge Softness of 50, a Fuzzy Factor of 142, and Quality/Speed at 5. Two volumetric

FIGURE *As described in the text, a variety of light types were used to create the lighting*
5.34   *effects in this scene.*

flames rise up from the target, while the ground is mapped with the fiery material. Load this project and investigate it further when you have a moment.

GROUPING LIGHTS TO OBJECTS

Just a few words need to be said about this topic. When you use false lighting of any kind, it usually helps to place a "real" light at the point the beam seems to be coming from. This allows you to use the false light at its maximum effectiveness, while using the real light to cast shadows and offer its contribution to the mix. The light coming from the bottom of the space ship in Figure 5.34 has a Radial Light grouped with the laser light. The creative use of lights carries us into the next chapter as well.

Moving On

You have courageously worked through all of the material presented in this chapter on the Camera and lights in Bryce 3D. In the next chapter, the focus continues with a detailed look at Bryce 3D's Atmospheric Sky Effects.

CHAPTER

6

Atmospheric Effects

Global Reality

What makes Bryce 3D users keep coming back time and time again to sculpt and shape their creations? Bryce 3D users are drawn into the wonder and mystery of world creating, of transforming the elements like a new age alchemist, and of watching as endless new worlds evolve out of the mist. Working in Bryce 3D has all of the lure of a challenging adventure. More than just spreading out new tools on the table in front of you, Bryce 3D invites you to pick them up and discover what you can do.

The way that Bryce 3D goes about this is to provide you with a number of one-stroke pathways to the virtual environment and letting the environment that results influence your options from that point onward. The dominant and most immediate pathway presented in Bryce 3D centers around atmospherics, so much so that a whole toolbar is provided for that singular purpose.

The Sky&Fog toolbar, shown in Figure 6.1, is usually your first stop in Bryce 3D. You could spend all of your time here, creating an infinite variety of awe-inspiring sky images that render very quickly and displaying the results to friends, clients, and colleagues. This is the place of atmospheric activity, where the sun, moon, clouds, and fog hold sway. The key numbers in Figure 6.1 outline the important features of this toolbar, so let's take a quick look at what's involved and why these features and tools are so important. Then we can take the next steps to using all that is provided here.

The Sky&Fog Toolbar

Looking at Figure 6.1, here are some things to pay attention to as you navigate the Sky&Fog toolbar. The numbers indicate callouts on the figure.

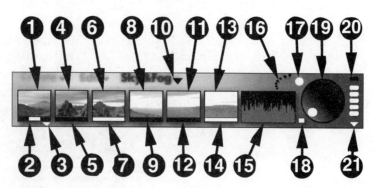

FIGURE *The Sky&Fog toolbar.*
6.1

CALLOUT 1

This is the Sky Mode controller. You can click and drag the mouse or access one of the four specific modes from the list (Callout 3): Softer, Darker, Custom, and Atmosphere Off. Clicking and dragging moves you through the four modes interactively.

CALLOUT 2

This is an eyedropper control that allows you to select a color from either a popup palette or from anywhere in a picture. It works only when you're in Custom Sky or Atmosphere Off.

CALLOUT 3

This arrow brings up the modes list: Softer Sky, Darker Sky, Custom Sky, and Atmosphere Off. Custom Sky and Atmosphere Off are the most important features for creating original sky elements, with Softer and Darker used as customizing options once you have a sky on the screen. Using the Custom Sky option, you can use the associated palettes and their Sky&Fog tools to create an original sky. Using Atmosphere Off (and manually moving any Haze and Fog settings to zero, as well as deleting any infinite planes), you can create one color backdrops.

TIP

Solid Color Backdrops are important for both compositing your Bryce 3D images for video (blue-screen/green-screen work) and also for developing text slides and overhead transparencies. Solid color backdrops also foster the ability to cut the image out in a paint application for 2D compositing.

Steps for Developing a Solid-color Backdrop

1. Delete all infinite planes and make sure Fog and Haze settings are at zero.
2. Select the Atmosphere Off option, or select the black or white backdrop from the Sky presets palette (which automatically gives you a solid black or white backdrop. Stop here if either black or white is your goal.)
3. Select the color of your choice from the eyedropper color palette (Callout 2).

CALLOUTS 4 AND 5

This is where you set the Ambient Shadow intensity and color of the atmosphere. This color sets a general emotional and atmospheric tone to the scene.

Important! Use a black color to have little or no effect on the scene and a white to wash out the atmosphere. Other colors tint the elements in the scene, as if the air was that specific color. As colors get darker, the effect is moderated and lessened.

TIP

CALLOUTS 6 AND 7

These options allow you to set the Fog intensity (click and drag the mouse right to increase from 0 to 100%) and height (click and drag the mouse vertically to increase from 0 to 100%). To see these modifications in the Nano Preview, you must be in either Camera or Director's mode.

In the Sky&Fog palette (accessed by clicking on Callout 21 in the figure, you can blend the fog intensity with the sun. Doing this allows the fog to "burn off" as the day progresses.

NOTE

A Fog Experiment

1. After having placed an object in your scene and deleted the ground plane, create a sphere and sink it half way in the Underground. Turn the Underground option off (right-hand toolbar).
2. Set the Fog intensity to 50% and the height to 3. Color it a medium green. Render the scene.
3. Increase the Fog height to 50 and render the scene. You should see the Fog creep up over part of your object. Doing animations with this basic technique allows you to cause the Fog to wash over objects.

See Chapter 8 and "Faking Water with Fog" to see how this same technique can be used in another way.

NOTE

CALLOUTS 8 AND 9

This is the Haze control. You should always have haze set to some amount (a good standard is 50) when you are developing a scene that shows the horizon line where the sky and ground meet. If you don't, that line will be far too evident and unreal. Haze also adjusts LOD (level of Detail), so that objects farther away from the camera are rendered more blurry than those close up. In selecting the color of the haze, opt for a color that matches the sky at its lowest point.

CALLOUT 10

This triangle triggers the appearance of the Sky&Fog presets library (see Figure 6.2). It's called Sky&Fog because the sky thumbnails you see come with Fog and Haze settings as well. Use the presets as they are pictured, or as basic ele-

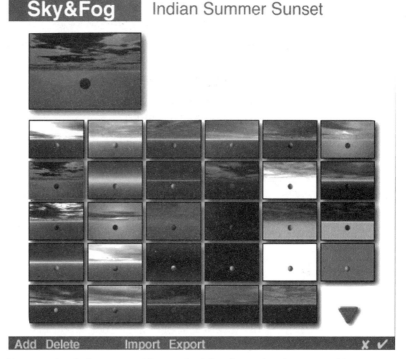

FIGURE   *The Sky&Fog presets library is loaded with new skies for instant addition to*
6.2   *your world.*

ments that can be customized. Remember to add (save) your own customized skies here for later use, or to export them to other directories for storage and sharing with other Bryce 3D Worlders.

CALLOUTS 11 AND 12

Cloud Height and Sky Dome Color can be modified from here. Alterations in Cloud Height cause radical changes in the look of your sky and also affect the light in a scene. If Cumulus Clouds are not switched on, the Stratus clouds will create different gradient washes when the Sky height is altered, but still based upon the color of the Cumulus Cloud setting. Sky Dome Color tints objects in the scene to simulate twilight and dawn lighting, but the effect is very subtle.

A Cloud height of 0 and a Cloud Coverage of 100 creates a solid color sky. Color is referenced to the Cumulus Color (Callout 14). Coupled with the middle palette bar in the Custom Sky option of the Sky Mode controller (Callout 1), a solid color is also added to the ground (as long as there is no terrain plane and no haze or fog). This gives you a solid two-color backdrop.

TIP

228   **THE BRYCE 3D HANDBOOK**

CALLOUTS 13 AND 14

Cloud Coverage and Cumulus Color are set here. A Coverage of 0, with Cumulus Clouds off, produces gradient wash skies. With Cumulus Clouds switched on, the higher the coverage the darker the sky, which is great for an impending storm. A gradual change in solid colors from light to dark takes place as you move upward in Cloud Coverage, as long as the frequency/amplitude settings are flatlined.

CALLOUT 15

Although you can watch the numbers at the bottom of the left-hand palette change as you drag the mouse horizontally and vertically in this interactive controller for cloud, it's far better to watch the waveforms so you can get an intuitive feel for how they influence cloud creation. Flatlining the waveform creates solid colors in the sky.

CALLOUT 16

Don't miss the chance to at least explore the use of the randomizing features in the toolbar. Clicking on these dots produces some very bizarre skies, which can be accepted or customized.

CALLOUT 17

This icon switches between sun and moon, telling you instantly if it's night or day. Instead of just working within this clock system, you are free to mix and match effects. For instance, you can create a daytime look with a night sky by simply adding a light source to illuminate the scene, even when this icon is showing the moon.

CALLOUT 18

Clicking and holding here gives you access to the color palette for the sun. Turning the sun black allows you to be in the Bryce 3D "day" with all of the effects of the night.

CALLOUT 19

This is the control you will use most in this toolbar, if not in Bryce 3D itself. This is the sun/moon positioning trackball. The moon is always on the opposite side as the sun. Make sure Link Sun to View is selected in the Sky&Fog options list, and make doubly sure that you have configured your camera as detailed in Chapter 5, Figure 5.2 to orient yourself properly.

CALLOUT 20

These are the sky memory dots, allowing you to save and instantly recall your skies. They are especially useful in animating skies, since you can target specific keyframes with a saved sky setting.

CALLOUT 21

It is vital that you understand all of the items and implications listed in this menu when you click (click and hold on the Mac) on this arrow. Listed here are Sky&Fog options, with the all important Sky&Fog Edit dialog at the bottom of the list.

Auto Update

Every time you alter the sky with this option checked, it will begin a rendering. Your work habits may differ from mine, but I would suggest leaving it off. You should use the Nano Preview instead of this annoying and time consuming alternative.

Link to View

Yes! Always leave this checked so you can orient yourself properly in your Bryce 3D world.

Stratus Clouds/Cumulus Clouds

As you create your customized skies, explore switching one and/or both of these options on and off. You can only appreciate the creative options Bryce 3D offers you when you explore them thoroughly and constantly.

Reset Sky

If you get totally lost and confused, use this option to return you to the beginning of the session.

Edit Sky&Fog   Edit Sky&Fog brings up a three tabbed Environmental Attributes dialog. The tabs are named Sun & Moon, Cloud Cover, and Atmosphere. Here are a few things to pay attention to in the options presented.

SUN & MOON

Figure 6.3 shows the Sun & Moon tab.

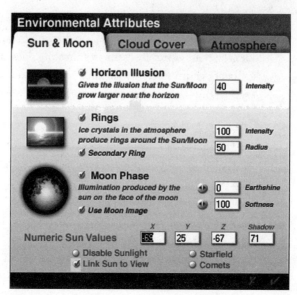

FIGURE *This is the Sun & Moon tab in the Environmental Attributes dialog.*
6.3

The following settings are recommended:

- Leave Horizon Illusion checked. The default value of 40 is OK, although you will want to enlarge this later to create larger suns when they are visible on the horizon.
- I prefer leaving this checked because rings of light look nice around the sun (they are too vague around the moon image). If you check this on, also check secondary rings. Explore what this looks like by placing a sun on the horizon in front of the camera.
- Moon Phase/Use Moon Image should also be checked on. Use an earthshine of 100% for sharper moons and lower settings for moons with blurry edges.
- Link Sun to View should always be on.
- Stars and Comets are not worth checking since they are far too washed out. There are better ways to create them, as we shall explore later in this chapter.

CLOUD COVER

Figure 6.4 shows the Cloud Cover tab.

Link Clouds to View is best always checked. The rest of the options presented here are best left to cloud animations, covered in Chapter 8.

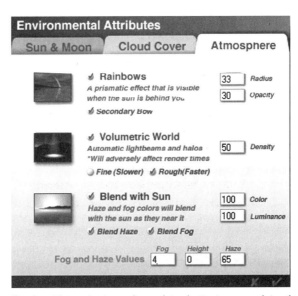

FIGURE *This is the Cloud Cover tab in the Environmental Attributes dialog.*
6.4

ATMOSPHERE

Rainbows will be covered later in this chapter. Volumetric World is definitely a Do Not Check. Bryce 3D renders volumetrics slowly enough. You don't have

FIGURE *This is the Atmosphere tab in the Environmental Attributes dialog.*
6.5

to punish yourself by making it render even more slowly. Blending Fog and Haze with the Sun is an option you should explore on a project-by-project basis, since there are too many possible variables to set any hard and fast rules for its use.

Creating Sky Types

There are so many variables to consider when creating a sky that laying out rules for all of the possibilities and variations is impossible. What we can do is to delineate a handful of examples that take some of the possible parameters into consideration. Table 6.1 shows some basic custom sky types and how they can be created by using the associated settings. All use the Custom Sky mode. Stratus and Cumulus is switched on for all examples unless otherwise noted. The Sun is positioned at the top center of the trackball, and a "Horizon Illusion" number of 70 is used throughout. You can use these examples as is, or as starting points for your own customizations. Figure 6.6 delineates the basic types.

You can load the basic scene from the project folder on the CD-ROM. It's called Fig6_06.br3.

Better Moons and Stars

The Moons and Stars that Bryce 3D allows you to add to your world are in many cases not suitable. Compared to the Sun, which can be positioned and colorized so that it becomes an integral part of the scene, the Moon often appears much too dim and the image of its surface is not at all well defined. The "stars" are far too dim, and just about disappear when printed out. These two natural elements do not tend to mix well with the startling content of a Bryce 3D scene, so we have to look for other alternatives for their creation.

MOONS

The best way to add a moon to a Bryce 3D world is to map a specific material to either a disk or a sphere and place it in the sky. Using a sphere is suggested if the moon is a place you want to visit, to actually fly around. The problem with spheres is that when placed at great distances from the camera (which may be a necessity with moon objects), they tend to distort. 2D disks do not distort, but may take the material in a way that doesn't look too convincing on first inspec-

TABLE 6.1 Basic Sky Types and How to Create Them

Sky Type	Fog & Haze	Height	Coverage & Cumulus Cover	Frequency & Amplitude	Comments
Mellow	Fog: 1/0 and Lt. Gray Haze: 12	Height: 24	Cover: 17 Orange	119 / 156	This is a peaceful sky, allowing you to breathe easy.
Murky	Fog: 22/30 Blue Gray Haze: 15	Height: 47	Cover: 50 Dark Green	9 / 322	You can almost feel the humidity.
Breakup	Fog: 0 / 0 Haze: 3	Height: 53	Cover: 42 Light Yellow	137 / 309	A sign of hope.
Doom	Fog: 3 / 9 Dark Red Haze: 10 Dark Red	Height: 0	Cover: 36 Dark Green	200 / 141 Black Sun	This sky uses a black sun. Don't go outside!
Yawn	Fog: 0 / 0 Haze: 4	Height: 70	Cover: 31 Pink	32 / 101 Light Blue Sun	I don't know why, but this one makes me want to go back to sleep.
Dream	Fog: 0 Haze: 100 Pink	Height: 0	Cover: 0	Flatlined White Sun	A walk in the dream world, with Stratus and Cumulus switched off.
Heat	Fog: 0 Haze: 50 Peach Color	Height: 0 Stratus and Cumulus switched off	Cover: 0 Yellow Sun with Horizon Illusion Off.	Flatlined	Loosen your shirt, it's going to be a scorcher! Shadows made yellow to emphasize the effect.
Blue Swoon	Fog: 0 Haze: 0	Cover: 0 Stratus On, Cumulus switched off	Height: 11 Dark Blue Shadows set to White	58 / 72	A blue sun and lavender sky assure us that we are not on Earth.
Aura	Fog: 0 Haze: 0	Height: 100 Red Purple	Cover: 12 Turquoise	4 / -125	A sky meant for prophetic visions.
Sol Etude	Fog: 0 Haze: 0	Height: 100 Dark Blue	Cover: 42 Turquoise	9 / -132	Dark, but not threatening. Violet Shadows

tion. If the moon object is to be seen from the surface of a planet, whether you use the 2D or 3D object, make sure to turn shadows off for both casting and receiving. Also make sure you don't have a local light in the scene with "No Falloff" selected, since that might illuminate the moon too. If the moon object is far enough away, Linear Falloff on a local light should be OK. Figures 6.7 and 6.8 give two examples.

FIGURE *These images refer to the Sky Types in Table 6.1 (from upper left): Mellow,*
6.6   *Murky, Breakup, Doom, Yawn, Dream, Heat, Blue Swoon, Aura, and Sol*
         Etude.

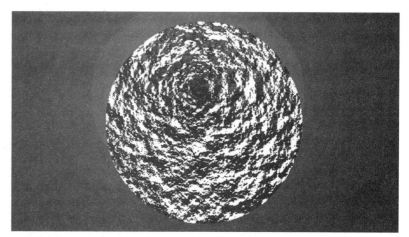

FIGURE   *Here is a 2D disk moon ready to place in your sky at a far distance. It has a*
6.7   *Volume Visible Radial Light behind it, sized at 3X the object, to give the moon*
          an aura.

FIGURE   *Using 3D Spheres for moons is a better idea and gives a 3D shadowing, but*
6.8   *watch out for distortion when the moon is placed too far in the distance.*

TIP

2D disks to be used as moons should be mapped with Object Top. Note that you could use a Boolean cylinder to cut the moon into the familiar quarter moon shape.

2D Moons from 3D Moons

How about the best of both worlds? Since a 2D moon can be placed in the far distance without distortion and a 3D moon has better shading, why not combine the two? Here's how:

1. Create a 3D moon. Use the Planet material to map it and use Parametric mapping. Render the moon on a solid white background, and save it out (export it) as a picture.

2. Create a Picture Plane disk. Go to the Materials Lab and map the 2D disk with the 3D moon graphic you just saved. Now you have the 3D moon's quality, with the 2D moon's usefulness.

STARS

Creating a field of stars is simple in Bryce 3D. Figure 6.9 shows an example. Just do the following.

1. Point the camera upward, so that the stars are created at the vault of the heavens. Set the Frequency/Amplitude of Clouds to zero for both, and uncheck Strata and Cumulus. Set the Sky mode to Atmosphere Off and color the sky dark blue.

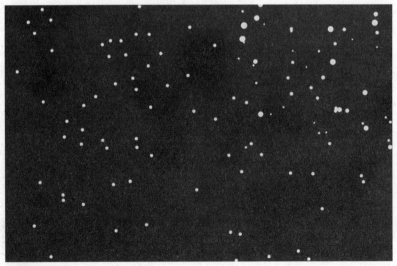

FIGURE   *A starry sky, created with 2D circular planes, multi-replication, and the*
6.9   *Randomize process.*

2. Place a horizontal disk primitive in the scene. Move it up to the sky and resize it so that it is very tiny. Assign a light blue material to it with a 100% Specularity.

3. With the disk selected, multi-replicate it 60 times in place.

4. Select the whole group of multi-replicated copies by extending a selection marquee around them. Go to the Randomize tool in the Edit toolbar, and with 2D Disperse Size selected, click and drag the mouse right to spatter the skies across the sky. Preview for a look.

You can repeat this procedure several times and then select some individual stars for color alterations. This makes a stunning and believable starry sky.

TIP

COMETS AND METEORS

When creating comets and meteors, we draw upon the same skills used thus far to create moons. There are only two differences. The first is that we have to find the proper material(s) for the tasks, and the second is that we may want to add some trail fire or debris. Comets are large balls of ice and rocks that trail vapor and ice chunks, while meteors are large chunks of stone that glow once they hit the friction of the atmosphere.

Comet (Figure 6.10)

1. Place a Bryce 3D Stone object on the screen from the Create toolbar. Use the Rocky Planet texture from the Rocks presets in the Material Lab. Use a light blue specular color. Set the Specular value to the texture and set the slider at 10. This makes the Comet ice glow.

2. Attach (Link) a stretched-out cone to the comet for the tail. In reality, the tail may be millions of miles long, but you don't have to try that in Bryce

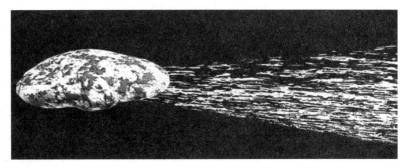

FIGURE *The Comet streaks along as its tail marks its path.*
6.10

3D for now. Make the tail about three times as long as the comet, with the small end of the cone stuck in the comet itself.

3. Now for the material of the tail. Open the Materials Lab with the tail section selected. Use a Marble texture from the Rocks list and make it a Volumetric texture. Place a channel marker for the marble texture next to Diffuse Color, Diffusion Value, and Base Density. Set the sliders as follows: Diffusion and Ambience Value to 100, Base Density to 13, Edge Softness and Fuzzy Factor to zero, and Quality/Speed to 30.5. Render and save the project to disk.

Meteor (Figure 6.11)

The meteor would just look like a rock if it were traveling in space, so we'll make this one appear as if it was interacting with the friction of an atmosphere.

1. Place a Bryce 3D Stone object on the screen from the Create toolbar. Use the Rocky Planet texture from the Rocks presets in the Material Lab. Use a yellow-orange specular color. Set the Specular value to the texture and set the slider at 10. This makes the meteor glow.

2. Duplicate the meteor, and without repositioning it, enlarge it by 10%. There is now a shell around the meteor that matches its form.

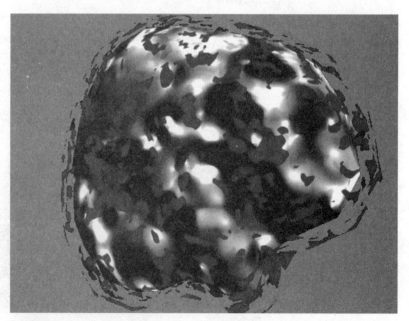

FIGURE   *The Meteor glows as flames flicker across its surface.*
6.11

3. In the Materials Lab, set a Volumetric material for the enlarged duplicate form. Use the rainbow texture from the Psychedelics folder. In the A channel, set the texture for Transparent Color, Ambient Value (100), and Base Density (40). Set Diffusion Value to 100, Edge Softness to 24, Fuzzy Factor to 30, and Quality/Speed to 40. Render and save to disk.

The duplicate form provides the meteor with flames that flicker across its surface.

DOUBLE SUNS AND DISTANT PLANETS

Using the same process we detailed above for creating moons, we can also create additional suns for the sky, or even large planets. Bryce 3D is set to an earthly environment, but most users at least explore the possibility of developing alien worlds. We know from astronomy that double suns and multitudes of moons are not uncommon features in the galaxy and most probably are familiar structures in other galaxies as well (see Figure 6.12). All it takes is the right texture and material, or bitmap, to evoke a multitude of other world features. We may not be able to travel to these places in our lifetime, but Bryce 3D and our own creative explorations can bring us as virtually close as possible.

If you want to explore Figure 6.12 further, load the Fig6_12.br3 project from the CD-ROM.

NOTE

FIGURE   *What place is this with double moons while in the sky a planet looms?*
6.12

Using Sky Planes

Remember that Bryce 3D offers two different ways to create skies. The first is the sky that can be created from modifying the parameters set in the Sky&Fog toolbar, already covered in this chapter. The other way to create a sky in Bryce 3D is through the use of an infinite Cloud Plane. Cloud Planes are useful for more than sky attributes, however. One of the best uses around is to use them to mist out terrain.

There are two ways to add a mist around mountains. One is to use a 3D object, like a squashed sphere, and map it with a Volumetric or Surface material. This is good for very localized effects, like a fiery cloud around a volcano, or a cloud around the mythic Mount Sinai while the Ten Commandments are being sculpted. The problem with Volumetrics is rendering time, and the problem with both is that you can always tell what the 3D form is, no matter how fuzzy. Using interleaved Cloud Planes for the same purpose leads to much more realistic results. The only drawback to using a Cloud plane to mist out terrain is that the plane is infinite, and panning the camera will reveal the Cloud Plane in all directions. So when you use this technique, don't pan the camera. You can also compound the effect by adding Haze and ground fog.

Misty Mountains

Here's one way to add a mist to a mountain or a whole range. Figure 6.13 shows an example.

FIGURE *The mountain range rises into the clouds, while a ground fog hovers near its*
6.13 *base.*

1. Create a mountain that fills your camera view and use a terrain material of your choosing to map it (Object Space).
2. Add four Surface Cloud Planes. Place three of them at different heights so that they intersect the summit of the mountain, and one so that it is raised a little above the mountain's base.
3. Use varying Cloud Presets on each plane to randomize the look and use different levels of transparency on each. Render and save to disk.

TIP

As an alternate method to using three Surface Cloud Planes to mask the summit, you could use one Volumetric Cloud Plane to do the same task. Rendering proceeds faster with Surface Planes, but if you wanted to fly through the mist, Volumetrics are the best choice.

Sky Rotation

You are already aware that the infinite planes can be rotated, but what about the sky itself? At first glance, this seems impossible. But is it? First, remember that you are looking at the Bryce 3D world through a camera, which represents your eye. The camera has controls, and one of those controls is banking. In any view, you can use the rotation tools to turn the camera on its side. When you couple this with your ability to rotate the camera so it's looking at the sky alone, you have the possibility for creating images that show the sky painted from the bottom to top of your screen, instead of from left to right.

OK, but what good does this do? What use could you possibly have for this capability? There are two uses that come to mind immediately. This is one way to generate "portrait" aspect work, as differentiated from Bryce 3D's standard "landscape" aspect graphics. Portrait aspect is often in demand for print output, and this is one way to generate it. That's the more conservative reason you might want to explore this technique, but there's a more creative answer as well. Since you can bank the camera at any angle, and since skies (like everything else in Bryce 3D) can be animated, you can create animations that show the sky moving at whatever angles you desire across the screen. The only challenge is that you will have to set your scene up at angles, too. Figure 6.14 shows an example. Here's how to do it:

1. Create a scene, complete with ground plane and objects.
2. Select the Camera and everything else (including the ground plane) and Group them.
3. Go to the Left or Right view, and point the Camera towards the sky. Everything else will also rotate.

FIGURE *Even this simple composition takes on a heightened interest level with the clouds*
6.14 *running vertically as opposed to their default horizontal orientation.*

4. Go to the Front view and bank the camera by rotating it on an angle left or right. Render a preview in the Nano Editor, and you will see an angled sky behind your scene. If you want a true portrait aspect image, the Camera must be banked 90 degrees left or right.

TIP

If you think Figure 6.14 looks interesting, wait until you check out the animation. It's on the CD-ROM as 6_14B.mov. The animated effect is not unlike smoke or fire rising from the ground. We'll look at it again in the Fire section of Chapter 8.

The Vortextron

Never allow the rules to dissuade you from exploring the impossible. Just as we have discovered that the impossible could be done by rotating the Sky, so impossible and unsuspected visuals can be created by resizing bitmap textures on a Cloud Plane. Since infinite planes go on forever, mapping a bitmap picture to an infinite plane at a 1:1 ratio results in an infinite tile of the image, as shown in Figure 6.15.

When you resize the bitmap however, strange things begin to occur. In addition to the image getting smaller to accommodate more samples, as the numbers increase you start to see patterns instead of just reduced copies of the original image. If you push the resizing to 500 or more, moiré type patterns emerge. These patterns become their own image, transparent sheets of energy

FIGURE   *Resizing a bitmap texture mapped to an infinite plane at 1000% or more*
6.15   *results in a series of interference patterns that look like energy fluctuations.*

that can suffice for simulating wave effects in a Bryce 3D project. Various percentages of resized bitmaps are shown in Figure 6.16.

The pattern is always dependent upon the Alpha transparency of the bitmap, so every bitmap will necessarily display its own interference pattern when more bitmaps are forced onto the infinite plane.

TIP

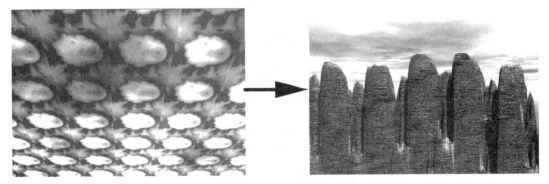

FIGURE   *At a 1:1 ratio, bitmapped graphics tile themselves forever on an infinite Cloud Plane (left) and can be used to*
6.16   *create mountains in the Terrain Editor (right).*

Rainbows

Everyone holds a special reverence for rainbows, whether from Dorothy's visit to Oz or from some archaic unconscious source. Rainbows have always been a sign of hope that tomorrow will be better than today. Bryce 3D has a wonderful rainbow generator, and it functions in accordance with the laws of optics. In our everyday world, the sun must be coming from the opposite direction from our perception of the rainbow. If we see a rainbow in the west, the sun must be in the east. This is exactly the way rainbows are configured in Bryce 3D. If you have positioned your camera as suggested in Chapter 5, and if you have checked the Link Sun to View option in the Sky&Fog toolbar menu, then we are ready to explore rainbow creation. Figure 6.17 shows the result. To create a rainbow, do the following:

1. Create a suitable scene for the rainbow to be placed in. Make sure the sun is at your back.
2. Open up the Sky&Fog Editing dialog and go to the Atmosphere tab. Check Rainbow, and if you want, Secondary Rainbow. Input the radius and intensity. A good default is a radius of 60 and an intensity of 70, but you may want to explore other settings.
3. Look at the Nano Preview and render when you have a good mix. Save to disk.

FIGURE *Creating rainbows in Bryce 3D is a snap, and the results can be quite alluring.*
6.17

To make rainbows more visible, try turning off Stratus and Cumulus clouds. Also, try raising the sun a little to move the rainbow lower to the horizon.

TIP

Foreground Planes

In a picture or an animation, the way target subjects are framed by other elements often becomes the major part of a composition. If you look at the Disney Studio's work over the years, you can appreciate this technique. Often, a black silhouetted foreground acts as a frame for color targets in a picture. Bryce 3D allows you to easily introduce these framing components into your work. Figure 6.18 shows an example. Here's how:

1. In a paint application, set your palette to work in two colors, black and white. Paint a silhouetted scene with black, allowing the dropout color to be white. One of the most common subjects of a foreground painting like this is a jungle scene, a silhouetted image of a group of trees, vines, and associated elements.
2. Save the image to disk in a format that Bryce 3D can read.
3. In the Picture Editor of the Materials Lab, import the image. You shouldn't have to do anything about the Alpha channel, since the white areas will be set for dropout automatically.

FIGURE *Using a 2D graphic to frame a 3D scene.*
6.18

4. Map this picture to a Picture Plane that covers your screen. Make sure there are no lights in back of the scene, including sunlight, so the foreground picture remains totally black except for the transparent cutouts. Place 3D elements in the scene in back of this picture plane. The final rendering should show your 3D world as framed by this 2D graphic. If the graphic is large enough, you'll be able to pan the camera to see different parts of the 3D scene showing through.

Another common foreground plane picture would be a window cutout, making it seem as if you were in a darkened room looking out on a colorful Bryce 3D world.

Moving On

In this chapter, we have explored a number of new ways to think about and use the Atmospheric effects in Bryce 3D. The next chapter begins the animation section, so get ready to make your worlds move!

Animating Your 3D Worlds

The Roots of Animation

Movement is the first seduction of the eye. The most primitive creatures who possess some form of visual perception see movement as the play of light and shadow, which tells them either to run from being eaten or that dinner is on the table. Our eyes are fine tuned to notice movement for the same initial reasons, though the "fight or flight" reaction has been enhanced to include new possibilities through the development of our consciousness. To the human eye, the detection of movement also includes the possibility that something interesting, or even awe inspiring, might be occurring. Movement to the human eye, and perhaps even to some animal's eyes, also means life. We intuit that anything that moves has a life of its own. This includes trees that sway in the breeze, as well as creatures that swim and fly. This is why cartoons and animated features of all kinds are so hypnotic and alluring, especially when created with the new computer graphics technology and tools. Everything is given the potential for life and a suspected consciousness. Just look at the magical visions communicated by the world of advertising, where frogs sing the praises of beer and all manner of inanimate objects dance and talk back. Anthropologists have given the name *animism* to the primal view that everything in the world, from rocks and trees to all of the animals, is conscious and alive, and *animism* is the root word and the motivating principle for *animation*.

As far as perception goes, we are able to trick the eye into believing that a series of projected images that change at the rate of ten times a second or more represent animated movement. Below that rate, movements look jerky, disbelief is fostered, and the magic is lost. This is the secret of creating animations. Animations, whether produced in Hollywood by a large bevy of professional animators or by anyone on a home computer, are nothing more than a stack of single frames played back at a frame rate that tricks the eye into seeing movement. This activity is enhanced by the fact that the single frames have some content that looks like it is not moving (or not moving much), and some elements that are displaced a good deal from frame to frame. We call the content that is not moving or moving very little the *background*, and the elements that are doing the most movement the *foreground* or even the *actors*.

In animation, the actors are alive (or some consciousness is suspected of being in the driver's seat), no matter what they appear to be. The planning that goes into bringing the actors in an animation to life is called *scripting* and *storyboarding*. Scripting refers to the verbal descriptions of what is going on from frame to frame, and storyboarding is the layout of the choreography, from one important nexus of movement (called a *keyframe*) to the next. With the computer, you choreograph the keyframes, the important points in the movement, and the computer figures out or interpolates the intervening frames, called *in-betweens*. This is different than creating an animation in the traditional manner with a series of drawings done by a collection or artists, where the in-betweens have to be manually drawn along with the keyframes. This is one reason for the explosion of computer animation, since being responsible for only the keyframes cuts the production time of an animation by 90%.

The Bryce 3D Animator

In Bryce versions 1 and 2, you could create wonderful and startling pictures. If you wanted to create an animation, you had to do it one frame at a time, a tedious and frustrating time-consuming process. There were no tools to automate the process, and all of the in-betweens had to be created manually. This has all changed with the release of Bryce 3D. Unlike other applications that start out as graphics oriented and gradually make the jump to animation over several releases, Bryce 3D has bridged the gap from images to moving pictures in one tremendous leap. Not satisfied to simply include a few nominal animation tools and options, the MetaCreations developers of Bryce 3D have included tools found in no other animation application on the market. The development was fostered by the release of Jan Nickman's stunning science fiction film, "Planetary Traveler," done with a customized version of Bryce. This fully animated feature film, rendered with commercially available desktop computers, has ignited worldwide interest in Bryce 3D as a software platform for animated storytelling. "Planetary Traveler" has also acted as a motivation for the thousands, and potentially millions, of computer animators who communicate personalized stories on their Web sites with smaller animations.

If you are new to Bryce, then Bryce 3D offers you a number of ways to create and texturize every element in a Bryce 3D world, with animation as a further add-on. If you are an experienced Bryce user, then the new animation potential of Bryce 3D is your main interest, why you bought the upgraded software, and the reason you purchased this book. In this section, the chapters will guide you through Bryce 3D's amazing new tools and options, so that you can become a knowledgeable Bryce 3D animator. Here we go . . .

CHAPTER

7

Bryce 3D Animation Basics

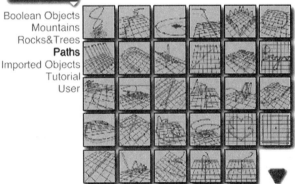

I n this chapter, the focus will center upon a collection of tools you must familiarize yourself with in order to feel comfortable in getting your animated story across in a timely manner. The whole section is bookended on one side by this chapter and on the other by Chapter 10, which deals with the intricacies of the Bryce 3D Motion Lab. In between, we look at what can be animated in Bryce 3D (which is everything), and some project-oriented examples. As always, it is assumed that you have already read the Bryce 3D documentation, and that you have either read or are familiar with the material referenced in all of the preceding chapters of this book as well.

The Animation Controls Palette

The new Animation Controls palette is where all of the decisions you make regarding the movement of the selected elements in your Bryce 3D world are put in place. Please refer to Figure 7.1 and the callouts as we detail some important features. It is expected that you have also worked through the Bryce 3D documentation concerning animation.

CALLOUT 1

Clicking and dragging this lozenge along the Timeline indicates the frame number you are interested in keyframing, or the place in the animation where some work needs to be done. Always pay attention to the data display at the left, which tells you the exact frame number and time where the sliding lozenge is.

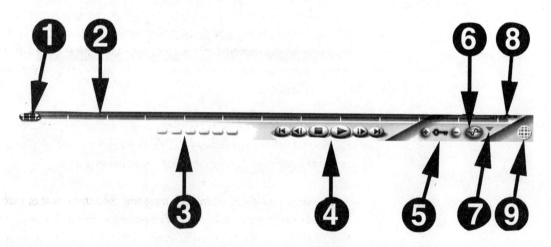

FIGURE *The Animation Controls palette, with callouts indicating its elements.*
7.1

CALLOUT 2

This is the Timeline. It is marked with tickers that indicate all of the separate frames in your animation, or the time involved. The lozenge relates to these ticks as places in the animation you want to add a keyframe or stop for additional editing of the selected object(s).

CALLOUT 3

This is the Memory Dot area, allowing you to store selected frame numbers from the Timeline, so you can instantly snap to that position. Though useful, it makes more sense to use the VCR keyframe buttons to get to keyframe positions quickly.

CALLOUT 4

This is the VCR controller, with buttons for start frame, previous keyframe, stop, play, next keyframe, and last frame as placed on the Timeline. When designing and choreographing an animation, this where you will spend the majority of your time. The animation can be played back as either wireframe objects or boxed areas. When the scene gets very complex, use boxes, unless you absolutely have to see the outline of specific objects.

CALLOUT 5

The plus and minus signs indicate Add and Delete Keyframes. The Key Symbol is there just so you can locate the plus and minus signs quickly. Holding on the plus or minus signs allows you access to specific parameters for the Camera, Sky, Sun, or selected object. These options allow you to control the specified parameters of the item, as opposed to the global controls that come into play when you simply hit the Plus keyframe button. Since these advanced controls are so important to your animation in Bryce 3D, it is important that they be more specifically detailed.

The Auto-Key Option should be checked when you use the advanced control options. You should also try to use as few Advanced Controls as possible in a single keyframe, as it's very easy to forget where you are and what actions you have taken.

TIP

It is suggested that you use global controls for animating these items, that is, with Auto Select checked on, move or manipulate the camera however you desire in its present keyframe. Then use the Advanced Controls to delete those specific actions in the selected keyframe that are not wanted. For instance, holding the minus sign down and accessing the Advanced Controls, you could selectively delete just the ro-

TIP

tation for the camera or any of the other items for the specific keyframe where you are, without bothering any repositioning that has been activated for that keyframe. Using the Advanced Controls in the Add keyframe mode (the plus sign) complicates matters more than needed.

Advanced Camera Controls

The options are: Position, Origin, Banking, Focal Length, Pan X or Y, and Zoom X or Y. Pans and Zooms will be covered later in this chapter under Camera animations. There is also an "ALL Timelines" selection, but that is rather redundant, since under global alterations, you already affect all of the timeline elements. You do not have to have the Camera selected to use the Advanced Controls to delete a specific camera function in the keyframe where you are. Here is an example of how to use the Advanced Controls to affect an animation:

1. Set the Camera at frame 1 as a keyframe.
2. Move the Lozenge to frame 30, and rotate and reposition the Camera.
3. Using the Advanced Control with the Delete Keyframe button, hold and select the Camera Rotation item.

The result will be that in frame 30, you will have removed the new rotation and have left the new position in place. If you did this globally by simply selecting the minus sign (remove keyframe), you would have removed both the new rotation and position from frame 30.

Advanced Sky Controls

The Sky Advanced Controls work exactly the same as the Camera Advanced Controls, with the difference being that you have 35 members of this list. Every sky parameter can be individually selected, though they can also be accessed through the Sky&Fog toolbar or the associated Sky&Fog Edit dialog already covered in the last chapter. Unless you enjoy applying effects from a list rather than individually and interactively from the Sky&Fog toolbar and dialog, it is suggested that you dispense with the use of this list.

Advanced Sun Controls

Here again, you have all of these controls offered in a more interactive manner in the Sky&Fog toolbar, so why complicate your life and access them in this manner?

Advanced Selected Object Controls

These Advanced Controls work on whatever object or group is selected in your scene, the options include Position, Rotation, Scale, Shear, and Origin. These controls are useful, especially when it comes to deleting one or more of these options from a keyframe. otherwise, deleting the entire keyframe with the global minus sign may not give you the more delicate result you are looking for. Use the Camera example above as an indication of how these controls can be put to use.

CALLOUT 6

This is the trigger for accessing the Advanced Motion Lab, a topic fully detailed in Chapter 10.

CALLOUT 7

This arrow triggers the Timeline Options menu. There are two options involved: Auto-Key on and off and what the ticker marks on the timeline indicate. Ticker marks can delineate either frames or various time markers in seconds. The time options include .25, .5, 1, 2, and 5 seconds. At the start of your animation, use the Frames option. Later, when the animation gets long and consumes more time, switch to whatever time marker allows you to see all of the tickers on screen at once.

CALLOUT 8

This is the almost invisible Scale Timeline controller. Clicking and dragging the mouse over it allows you to stretch out or squash how much of the Timeline can be seen at one time.

CALLOUT 9

This Globe Symbol toggles you between the Timeline and Selection palettes. In an editing session, it is often necessary to switch to the Selection palette in order to locate a specific object in your scene.

The Animation Setup Dialog

It's a good idea to access this dialog from the File menu before you start to design your animation (see Figure 7.2). That's because there are items here that will affect how your Timeline behaves.

The first and most important item to configure here is the FPS (frames per second) input. Never enter a number less than 10 or more than 30. The most common FPS rates are 15, 24, 29.97 (and other SMPTE rates), and 30. Bryce 3D does not offer interleaved 60 FPS Field rendering, commonly used in Broadcast Video productions. 30 FPS is the best video choice for NTSC (25 FPS for PAL), except for SMPTE work (called "drop frame"), which involves the capacity to add and edit synchronized audio with specific hardware.

Animation Setup

	Hour	Minute	Second	Frame		Frame #
Current ▼	0	:00	:00	.00		0
					FPS	
					15	
	Hour	Minute	Second	Frame		Frame #
Duration	0	:00	:00	.00		0

○ Scale   ◉ Extend or Clip

Play ◉ Once   Display ◉ SMPTE Time
      ○ Repeat   ○ Frame Count
      ○ Pendulum

FIGURE *The Animation Setup dialog gives you global control over specific parameters of*
7.2 *the animation.*

Under the Play list are three options that have an important effect on your animations: Once, Repeat, and Pendulum. These options affect how the animated objects in your scene will be displayed when previewed, and also how they will act in a rendered animation if the sequence is long enough. Play Once is the default, allowing your animation to move from start to finish as expected. Repeat plays the animation from start to finish over and over again until you hit the stop button. Pendulum (called "ping-pong" in the trade) plays the animation from start to finish and then finish to start, continuously, until you hit the stop button. These preview options are important because some multimedia and Web designers need their animations to play in a looping manner, and this allows a preview of those motions.

TO ASSIGN REPEATS AND PENDULUMS TO A RENDERED ANIMATION

If you want an object to either repeat its actions or to act as a pendulum in an animation, do the following:

1. Set up an object movement over ten frames that has keyframes at frame 1 and 10.
2. With the object selected, go to its Attributes dialog and the Animation tab, and click on Repeat or Pendulum as desired.
3. Go back to the timeline, deselect the object, and move the lozenge to frame 30. Preview the animation, and you will see the object either repeating its ten-frame action, or moving back and forth, in direct re-

sponse to your selection of either Repeat or Pendulum in the Animation Setup dialog.

CIRCLE

In an object's Animation tab in the Attributes dialog, you will see one more option that has an effect on the way the object moves along its path: Make Circular. This command creates a closed loop, so that the first frame of the animated object on its path will equal the last frame as far as position is concerned. Every time you move the object, it expands the circle (it's really a warped oval). Expanding the duration of the animation would show the object racing madly around, over and over again. This is one way you might create one object orbiting another.

TIP

Use the Make Circular option on standard paths, or rather with the object that is creating the path selected. If you turn this into a Ribbon Path, you will see two nodes close together if you zoom in (the first and last frame) instead of one smooth closed path. This is OK if you want to break the path, but it loses the unbreakable coherence of a closed path. If the first and last node are split on a Ribbon Path and you use the Make Circular option, the object will suddenly appear again at the first node when the action repeats. Of course, this may be an effect you want.

OK. Having covered all of the important preparatory material, we are ready to begin a detailed investigation of Bryce 3D's animation tools and techniques. We will center on four integrated topics for the balance of this chapter: Paths, Links, Targets, and animating the Camera.

Paths

Think for a moment about the word and meaning of a "path." A path is usually defined as a nonmovable accessway that is tied to the larger environment. A path is also associated with the elements that make it by their movements. The path that exists in the great north that marks the way of the migration of the elk was made by elk over hundreds of years of repeated movement. If the elks become influenced by constructs in their way as they traverse the path, they have two options. The first is to create another path around the disturbance, and the second is to bully their way through the potential barriers and try to stick to the path created over time. It is thinking about natural occurrences like these that gives the animator an insight into the tools he or she uses.

If a path is glued to specific geography, it is immovable. It is then defined not primarily by its shape, but by what surrounding elements it traverses over time. An east-west path across a bridge, for instance, is not defined so much by its orientation as it is by the fact that there may be only one bridge across a river. The fact that the river may bend so that the way across is north-south is of no consequence to those who must use a bridge to get across the river, unless there is another bridge at the north-south point. This is called an immovable path, because to get across the river, you must use specific items located in the geography, in this case, the bridge. Bryce 3D has immovable paths.

If, on the other hand, your primary aim is to get from south to north no matter what, then it doesn't matter if there is a bridge or not. Swimming or flying across the river is just as viable an option as traversing the bridge, as long as it doesn't lead to your demise. You could start anywhere in the south and simply select the shortest point to your northern destination. If you had to take a train, then you might build your track with south-north as your primary focus and decide later where the south-north tracks should be laid. In a sense, you have defined a movable path, because the options are open where it will interact with the geography, and there will be many options. Movable paths can have control nodes so that when a mountain or river is encountered, simply stretching the node will give you more path to go around or over the obstruction. Movable paths are more like objects than paths in that they can be modified and customized, and remain separate from the elements that travel on them. Bryce 3D has movable paths, called Ribbon Paths.

BASIC PATH CREATION

The standard paths that are simply the result of an object moving in space over time in Bryce 3D cannot be moved or otherwise modified, unless you reposition or rotate the object, camera, light, or other element that has created them. As standalone entities, they are immovable in every sense of the word. They are not objects at all, but rather the results of the actions of objects. Have you ever seen a cartoon character that is able to move a hole in the ground to a new place? The reason that this is impossible is that the hole, under Earth physics circumstances, anyway, is not a thing as such. It is rather the result of the result of an action of a thing or being who dug the hole. The hole can only be manipulated by actions of actors, who can cover it up, fill it in, or enlarge it. The hole, in a sense, is an immovable result of an action. In the same way, standard paths in Bryce 3D are the results of objects' actions.

If you set a keyframe for a sphere at frame 1 of an animation, and then set another at frame 30 after moving it, you will see a blue line that indicates its path, a timeline that stretches from frame 1 to its new position at frame 30. Previewing this animation with the VCR controls will show the object moving from its position at frame 1 to its new position at frame 30 over 30 frames of time. The time it takes will depend on how you set the FPS rate. If it was set at 15 FPS, then the object will travel from frame 1 to frame 30 in two seconds (30/15=2). If you set the frame rate at 30 FPS, then the journey will take only one second (30/30=1).

But what if you wanted the path to be a curve instead of a straight line? Clicking on the path to adjust its shape would do nothing. The path does not exist as a separate entity. Only the object exists at specific points on the timeline. To make the path a curve, you would have to do the following:

1. Go to the frame where the maximum point on the curve should exist, for example, frame 15.
2. Click on the object to select it and then move it to its new position for that frame.
3. Make that position a new keyframe for the object.

Having done this, and without ever touching the path directly, you would see that the path now has a new shape. This was caused by your actions on the object that made the path in the first place. The path cannot even be seen until the object that made it is selected. Figure 7.3 illustrates this point.

Note that the distance between keyframes on a path is an indication of the speed of an object. An object between two keyframes that are 10 frames apart has to travel that distance in the exact number of frames. Setting the same keyframes apart over a

TIP

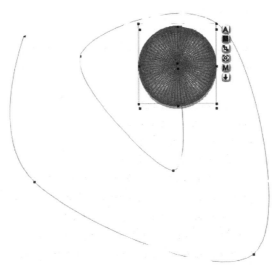

FIGURE   *With an object selected, you can see exactly how it will move over time in the*
7.3   *animation.*

longer distance will result in the object speeding up to make it to the next keyframe.
Setting a shorter distance between the same two keyframes will slow the object down.
If this is new information to you, explore the results by actually doing it.

RIBBON PATH CREATION

NOTE

Note that in the Bryce 3D documentation, the term Ribbon Path is used inter-
changeably with Motion Path.

Ribbon Paths are not only new to Bryce 3D, they are a new concept and way
of editing paths—period. Unlike standard paths, which are not things but only
the result of the action of things, Ribbon Paths are full-fledged objects. As an object, you can edit a Ribbon Path directly, without selecting any object(s) assigned
to it. Ribbon Paths can be created in two ways: by loading them from the Create Objects library or by transforming a standard path into a Ribbon Path.

To Create a Ribbon Path Separate from Any Object
(Figure 7.4)
1. Go to the Create toolbar and access the Objects library.
2. Activate the Paths folder, and select a Ribbon Path from one of the
   thumbnails. Click on the checkmark to place it on the screen.

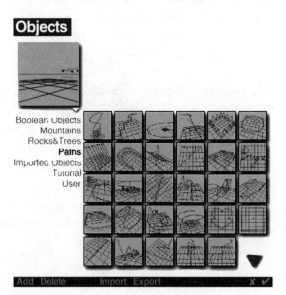

FIGURE *Ribbon Paths can be added directly from the Paths folder in the Create/Objects*
7.4 *library.*

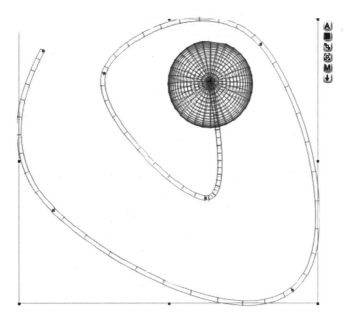

FIGURE   *The object's path has now become a Ribbon Path.*
7.5

To Create a Ribbon Path from a Selected Object Path (Figure 7.5)

1. Select the object whose path you want to become a Ribbon Path.
2. Go to the Objects menu and select Create Path. The object's path has now become a Ribbon Path.

DESIGNING, EDITING, AND ANIMATING RIBBON PATHS

Ribbon Paths have interesting properties. To begin with, they are full-fledged objects, and can be resized, rotated, or repositioned like any other object. Until and unless you take specific actions (defined later under Links), they are not related directly to the objects whose paths gave them birth. Moving the Ribbon Path, for example, will not move the object whose path created it. However, deleting the original object will also delete the new Ribbon Path. They are grouped in a strange relationship and cannot be ungrouped in the standard fashion.

To delete the original object from the new Ribbon Path, find and select it from the Selection toolbar. It will become highlighted. From there, it can be cleared without affecting the Ribbon Path.

TIP

Designing a Ribbon Path

To design an original Ribbon Path, do the following:

1. Place any object in your scene.
2. Keyframe it at frame 1. Move the Timeline lozenge to frame 30, move the object, and keyframe it again. You will see its path in blue, indicating the distance it moved from frame 1 to frame 30.
3. With the object selected, go to the Objects menu and select Create Path. Your new Ribbon path appears on screen.

You can select the Ribbon Path and add it to the Objects library in the Paths folder. Make sure, however, that you delete the original object first, as detailed previously.

Editing a Ribbon Path

You can edit your own Ribbon Paths, or any that you load from the Paths folder in the Objects library. Ribbon Paths have visible nodes that can be pushed and pulled just like a Bezier curve. In fact, Ribbon Paths are a form of Bezier curve, familiar to those who have worked in vector drawing applications like Illustrator, FreeHand, CorelDraw, or Canvas.

There are two kinds of nodes on a Ribbon Path. Resizing Nodes allow you to resize the Ribbon Path along an axis indicated by the node when your mouse cursor is over that node. If the node reads "Z", for example, dragging the mouse left or right will resize the path along the Z axis. If the node reads "X", then you can resize along the X axis. To resize it along all axes simultaneously, use the Resize tool in the Edit toolbar.

The other node is the Reshape type. These nodes are placed at keyframe intervals. Reshape allows you to alter the perimeter of the path, squashing it or stretching it at that point. A circle can become a heart, or you may decide to raise the point along the Y axis, creating a roller coaster path. To add or delete keyframe Reshape points from any path, standard or Ribbon, add or delete keyframes themselves. This adds and/or deletes associated points from the path. Some examples are shown in Figure 7.6.

NOTE

In the Attributes dialog of any selected object is the command Show as Ribbon Path. This allows you to see the standard path as if it were a Ribbon Path, but does not allow you to interact with the path as you could with a real Ribbon Path. The reason for this command, since it does nothing useful, is questionable.

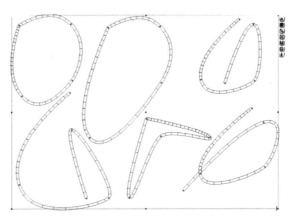

FIGURE **7.6**   *Ribbon Paths can be reshaped at any point in an infinite number of ways. These examples started out as circular paths.*

All paths have the Reshape nodes, placed at points where keyframes exist. The difference between standard and Ribbon Paths is that Ribbon Paths can be moved and resized independently of any object.

NOTE

Importing a Ribbon path from the Objects library always places the path so that it is parallel to the ground. Work in the Top view first to resize and reshape the path.

TIP

Animating Ribbon Paths

Aside from the objects that can be attached to a Ribbon Path (see the Links section later in this chapter), you can also animate the path itself. Here are some examples:

- Resize the path over time. Any objects traveling along the path would also be resized automatically.
- Rotate the path. Objects traveling along the path would also be rotated. This would result in an orbiting object whose path was spinning, like the old models of electrons around a nucleus.
- Reposition the path in an animation. This would foster things like a planet orbiting a sun, while the whole system moved through space.

Remember that Repeat, Pendulum, and Make Circular can also be applied in the Attributes dialog of a selected Ribbon Path, so that repetitive patterns can also occur over time.

NOTE

TIP

If you need a Ribbon Path to consume a determined amount of time, create it first with an object that you manipulate in the standard fashion. Then go to the Animation Setup dialog, and under Duration, enter that time in seconds and frames. The path is now active and will contain the time element you configured.

PLACING PATHS BEFORE OBJECTS

Here is a novel way to work with Ribbon Paths. Design the elements of a scene, but leave out the main actors. Instead, use an object to design a path that moves through the places in the scene you are interested in. Save the scene as you would any other scene. Now you have a scene with an active path, which can be used over and over again with many different actors assigned to that path.

ALIGNING OBJECTS TO A PATH

Selecting the Align function in an object's Attributes dialog is not always the wisest thing to do. For the most consistent results, it's better to deselect this option and align the object by hand in selected keyframes. DO NOT rotate the object in World Space, but in its own Object Space.

Links

Links are represented by the small chain-shaped icon in any selected object's Attributes list. By clicking on this icon and dragging the mouse to any other object, causing the target object to turn blue, a Link is established between the two objects. You can also Link objects by going to any object's Attributes dialog and to the Linking tab. Under Parent Object, find the name of the object you want to Link the selected object to. The object you link to does indeed become the parent object, so that it leads the child object by the hand. If the parent object is resized, rotated, or moved, the child object follows along. But all children have independence as well, and the same is true with Linked objects. Child objects can be resized, rotated, and repositioned on their own. There is always an invisible umbilical attached to the parent, however, no matter how far removed the child object may be.

A good example would be a moon linked to a planet which itself was linked to a sun. As the sun rotates, the planet, and its moon also rotate (think of the sun as the grandparent object). The planet, however, can also have its own rotation, which would cause its child, the moon, to rotate. The moon also has independence for its own actions and can be rotating as well. We could even complicate matters further by making a satellite the child of the parent moon. A guideline for complex animations like this is to set up the individual elements first, and then do the child/parent links.

Important! If you want to animate trains on a track, or any other object that has elongated dimensions along one axis, do not do this on a Ribbon Path. Instead, arrange and rotate the objects manually in a step-by-step fashion, and then transform the path into a Ribbon Path if you want to. Elongated objects on a Ribbon Path distort as they go around curves.

TIP

WHAT CAN BE LINKED?

Any object can be Linked to any other object in Bryce 3D. Objects can also be multi-linked, so that any parent object can have multiple children. A child object, however, can have only one parent. You could have a figure, for example, with two hands linked to one parent arm, but you could not have one hand linked to two Parent arms. You could, however, group the two arms, so that linking one hand to them would really be linking to one parent.

BODY PART MULTI-LINKS

Whether you are animating a robot, a spider, or a human model, you can (and should) link all of the parts together. This allows you to animate the objects one part at a time, so they can walk, sit, jump, and perform other feats.

DO NOT import DXF models for linking. DXFs often come in with groups mixed up, so that ungrouping the object to get to the parts can lead to unpredictable results. Import WaveFront OBJ objects instead. DXFs are OK to use, but not for ungrouping and linking parts. Besides, DXF models show unappealing facets when textured.

NOTE

WHAT IS THE DIFFERENCE BETWEEN LINKED OBJECTS AND GROUPED OBJECTS?

Attaching objects by grouping them is different than linking them. There are important considerations for both operations.

- Grouped objects have no parental hierarchies, so selecting one object for any transformation selects all in the group equally. There is one way around this. Using the Control key (Mac and PC) after selecting the group allows you to select an individual member for transformation, but that transformation is associated only with the selected object and not any others in a chain.

- Grouped objects can accept a material as one object, which usually results in a far different textured look than mapping each object individually. The only way to address this same situation in a linked hierarchy is by multi-selecting each object and then applying the material. The results, however, will not be the same, since the linked objects will retain their individuality.

- Boolean objects that are assigned Negative, Positive, or Intersect qualities must be grouped and not linked (see Chapter 9 on Boolean Animations).

If you use the Control key to select an individual object in a group, and then link it to one of the others in the group, it will no longer be part of the group.

THE PROPELLER PROBLEM SOLVED!

There are times when all of the logic and planning built into an application just isn't enough to tackle a persistent problem. If you take an elongated cylinder as a stand-in for a propeller and try to get it spinning, you will find that most of the ways you thought you could easily pull this off evaporate into a cloud of frustration. This is a problem that consumed myself and another Bryce 3D whiz for several hours each week for a period of months. We sent e-mail back and forth, evidencing the blind alleys we ran into. Using the Repeat function does no good at all, since it seems Repeat doesn't appreciate rotations much. Just rotating the propeller didn't help either, as more than a 180-degree rotation just wouldn't take. Then, while writing this chapter on Links, the solution came. Here's how to do it:

1. Create a Sphere and center it on your screen as seen from the Front view.
2. Create the propeller from an elongated cylinder, or import a propeller object if you have one.
3. Place the propeller against the mid-front of the sphere, as seen in the Front view. Link the propeller to the sphere. The sphere is now the parent object.
4. Keyframe this arrangement for frame 1, and go to the last frame in your animation duration (move the lozenge).
5. Select the sphere, and using the rotation tool in the Edit toolbar, rotate the sphere on the Z World Axis as many times as you like by dragging the mouse without letting up on the mouse button. A good number of rotations is 10 for a 5-second animation at 15 FPS.

When you play this back, you will have the almost impossible in Bryce 3D, a rotating propeller. A three- or four-bladed propeller looks nicer than a two-bladed one when animated.

Targets

What are the differences between Targets and Links? You cannot Link a targeted object back to the object that is tracking it. This would lead to an impossible loop, so that as the targeted object moved, it would move the targeting object, which would then move the original object. If you could do this, the computer would crash, since the computations would go on forever.

When a child object also targets the parent object in a link, much more useful orbits can be created. This is because as the child object orbits the linked parent, it also automatically rotates in position. This is an absolute must technique when the child object is to emulate our moon, which always turns the same face towards us as it orbits.

Animating the Camera

No matter what actors move in your Bryce 3D worlds, the way that you look at their actions is the difference between a boring ho-hum animation and one that will startle your audience. To create state-of-the-art animations, you have to know what the Camera is capable of and how to control it. The Camera has a close and creative relationship with everything we have discussed so far in this chapter, especially with Paths, Links, and Targets.

When creating Camera animations, there are a few things to keep in mind:

- If you want the animation to loop, to return to the place it started, set the last keyframe at the start to be the same as the first keyframe. It's easy to mistakenly alter keyframes without knowing it, so take care to do this at the start. This is also necessary to do with the Camera when you are looking at objects on a circular path.
- If something goes amiss, and the camera moves when you don't want it to, use the Undo command immediately. Do not attempt to reset the Camera manually. Chances are that 99.999% of the time you won't get it exact, and the render will show a jump. Sometimes using the Delete keyframe operation will fix it, too.
- Check to make sure you are at the first frame on the Timeline as a habit. Often, we forget to do this and throw a whole animation out of whack.
- Remember to make the Camera invisible when working on a complex scene as seen from the Front view. This can save a lot of time because you won't be selecting the camera by mistake and will be able to see more clearly. You could also Lock it in its Attributes dialog. When you need it unlocked, select it from the Selections palette by hitting the Globe symbol, and then going to the Selections list.

CAMERA ANIMATION EXAMPLES

There are infinite ways to create animations based upon camera movements alone. Here are some important examples:

Rotate Around a Selected Object (Figure 7.7)

To rotate the Camera around a selected object, do the following:

1. Select the camera.
2. Click and drag on the target icon in the Camera's Attributes list, until you are over the target object and the object's display box turns blue.
3. Set the frame 1 position of the Camera as a keyframe. Go to the camera's Attributes dialog, and under the Animation tab, select Make Circular.
4. Go to the Top view, and by moving the camera (which will always point to the Target automatically), describe a circular path of keyframes (which will also be drawn automatically in accordance with your Camera moves.)
5. You may want to alter the height of the camera at various keyframes, so your targeted object can be seen from other perspectives.

Repositioning the Camera

We could just as well call this example "investigation," because it allows you to view the intended subject from every possible angle and perspective. The inten-

FIGURE 7.7   *You may want to view or customize file Fig7_07.br3 on the CD in the projects folder to see how we crafted this example. You can also render it as an animation.*

tion is to give the viewer the best sense of the 3D nature of an object. It consists of creating keyframes that look at the object from any angle or distance that looks interesting. When doing an animation like this, make sure you extend the duration long enough so the view doesn't go by too quickly. One way to do this is to stay awhile at particular viewpoints, by moving the lozenge on the Timeline from one keyframe to another and setting another keyframe without moving the Camera. This allows the viewer to linger before moving on.

There are two rules for getting the most out of a Camera investigation:

1. Make the object different and interesting even as a silhouette.
2. Darken the lighting so that the object appears mysterious, so the audience has some heightened anticipation.

A Camera Light (Figure 7.8)

One way to make the investigative Camera even more useful is to link it to a spotlight. Don't make the spotlight too bright and make sure the edges of the beam are fuzzed out. Perhaps even give the light a mysterious color, like light blue or green. The light should not illuminate everything in the field of view, but just enough to whet the viewer's appetite for more clarity.

FIGURE
7.8
The investigative Camera is linked to a spotlight. A cloud plane was used as the ground, adding even more mystery to the scene. This image is from the project Fig7_08 on the CD-ROM. Load it, and create an animation that allows the Camera to "linger" before it moves on.

A guideline for Camera lingering is not to overstay your welcome. Several seconds is usually enough time in one place. Doing this three times in an animation is also a suggested limit.

A Moving Target

Whether it's a cannon tracking a flying behemoth, or the eyes in a figure tracking an insect, the ability of objects to track other objects is a well-used technique in computer animation. But the Camera can also track objects, and since the Camera is a stand-in for your eyes in Bryce 3D, the effect is like that experienced when you watch anything with care. There are two Camera tracking modes: Stand and Track, and Follow and Track.

- **Stand and Track:** In this mode, the Camera is placed in an optimum position, where it can see most of the actions of the targeted object. It may not see it when it goes into a tunnel, but keeps tracking anyway. The Camera never moves from its position. Unless there are times when the targeted object is hidden from the Camera, this technique can produce animations that instantly cure insomnia.
- **Follow and Track:** Follow and Track is best used when the Camera is at a fairly close range from the object. The object may be a ball traveling through a series of openings. The Camera becomes a ghost that follows the ball through the openings, giving the impression that the audience is to identify with the ball itself, like the personality of the ball. This is the mode used when the Camera is placed in a car or on a roller coaster. The Camera becomes a hitchhiker, and in some cases, the invisible personality behind the wheel.

Linking to an Object

Be very careful when linking the Camera to an object. Targeting an object is one thing, since the FOV (field of view) can take care of any erratic motions the object might display. When you link the Camera, however, every motion the object makes will be duplicated by the Camera. If you are going to link the Camera to the object, it is better linked close to the object than at a distance. It's also better if the object doesn't display too much bouncing or wiggling motion, because the Camera will imitate the motion and the viewer may get seasick.

Camera as Parent

This is a situation that has limited use because of the unexpected nature of the actions. If you make the Camera a parent link to an object (when the object is in center view of the Camera), then no matter where the Camera looks, the object will be center stage. The Camera actually becomes the puppet master of the object. The object itself will look like it is being tracked. You can actually emulate a sometimes used Hollywood effect by doing this. It is similar to the effect displayed when the camera is watching two people dance, and the room seems to be twirling around them. If you explore this option, create an animation that surveys the panorama of the scene, and takes in a section of the sky. At the very least, it's an option you should be aware of. The best thing about it is that the child object really defines no path at all, but just acts in accordance with Camera moves.

Linking to a Ribbon Path

This is a great way to get more use out of the paths stored in the Objects library. Besides controlling objects placed upon them, they can also act as tracks for the Camera. This capability is especially useful in Follow and Track animations, since both an object and the Camera can be linked on the same Ribbon Path.

A better way to accomplish more interesting results than just Camera and object linked to the same path is to duplicate the path first. Set the object to one path, and the Camera to the other. The Camera path can then follow the same general curve as the object path, but can do so from the side, top, bottom, or even from changing angles. Sometimes it will outrun the object and look at it from ahead, and sometimes it may lag behind. This is a method that is extremely useful when tracking vehicles in a race.

FOV Animations (Figure 7.9)

The larger the Camera's FOV (field of view) setting, the smaller all of the objects in the scene will become. If you alter the FOV over time, resizing it in the Camera's Attributes dialog, you will notice radical distortions near the edge of your visual plane. FOV animations look like zooms with distortion applied.

Load and render the project Fig7_09.br3 from the CD-ROM for an example of an FOV animation. This is an FOV animation with the camera's FOV changing from 20 at the start to 179 at the end.

If you are looking for some great sky renderings, use the maximum FOV settings with the camera pointed at the sky. The renderings will look like big sky country in the American West.

FIGURE 7.9 *The frame on the left features the FOV animation about 40% of the way through, with the objects appearing to be at a somewhat standard distance from the Camera. On the right is the last frame, with the FOV at 179. Because the sky is also centered, the zoom effect is enhanced.*

Camera Scale Factor Animations (Figure 7.10)

Playing with the FOV settings gives you distortions on both ends of the spectrum. On a scale of 1 to 180, 60 is the normal setting. Settings less and more than 60 result in distorted perspectives. The scale factor is different in that the highest setting, 100%, presents you with what you would expect the scene to look like, with no distortion applied to objects. A setting of 1%, however, is a radical zoom out. If all you want to do is to zoom in or out of a scene with a standard view as your starting or end point, alter the Scale setting of the Camera. If you want radical distortions on both ends of a zoom, use the FOV animation method.

Panning a Scene

You can do an animated Pan of a scene by altering the Camera Pan settings in the Attributes dialog. Pans can be horizontal or vertical. There are two types of panning operations: general and targeted. In general panning, all that you are interested in doing is to give the audience a feel for the panoramic environment on an incremental basis. With targeted panning, the object is to pan to an object of interest, like a special feature in the foreground on the left, or a vehicle traversing the sky. You should explore both types.

Repeat, Pendulum, Make Circular

In the Animation tab of the Camera's Attributes dialog, you will find the same options for applying these three animation types as with any other selected object. The same rules that we have discussed previously regarding the uses of

FIGURE   *The zoom effect when the scale of the Camera is altered is even more radical.*
7.10   *Here, the Scale is set to 10%, with 100% being the standard default setting.*
Compare the perspective look of the sky with this 10% Scale setting with the sky
as depicted in the right half of Figure 7.9

these options apply to the Camera. The difference is, since the Camera represents your eyes in the scene. you will feel that you are personally swinging your vision around and creating these effects.

Moving On   If you have worked diligently through this chapter and have also read and understood the Bryce 3D documentation on the potential of Paths, Links, Targets, the animations controls, and animating the Camera, you have all of the basic knowledge you need to start creating astounding animated sequences in Bryce 3D. The rest of the chapters in this section deal with creating a host of animation effects. The next chapter deals with animating the four elements, Earth, Air, Water, and Fire.

CHAPTER

8

Earth, Air, Water, and Fire

In the archaic alchemical and astrological traditions of the western world, Earth, Water, Air, and Fire were considered to be the four basic elements. Everything was said to be composed of a mixture of these four forces. In the East, especially in China, Wood was considered to be a separate fifth element. For our purposes in this chapter, we will stick with four, placing Wood with Earth, detailing 40 elemental effects.

Attention: This chapter is going to call upon all of the Bryce 3D skills you have accumulated thus far, both from the documentation as well as from this book and your own experience.

Earth f/x

There are four categories in Bryce 3D that relate to the element Earth: the Infinite Ground Plane, Terrain objects, Stones, and Materials associated with Earth-related textures. We will explore ten different Earth-associated f/x that look at all of these categories.

EMERGENCE (FIGURE 8.1)

In this animation, earthen objects emerge from the ground plane. Everything is mapped with the same material in Global Space, so the objects that emerge re-

FIGURE *In the Emergence example, the very ground looks like it is surging upward.*
8.1

ally look like parts of the terrain are bulging up. To use different materials would distinguish the objects from the plane, which is another possible effect altogether from the same saved Bryce 3D file. There are dozens of variations on this theme, of course. The idea of something appearing out of the ground could be applied to a graveyard mystery for instance, with semi-transparent Poser skeletons rising slowly. Not all animations that play upon this theme need to be that dire. In fact, generated in reverse, you could also show raindrops falling on the ground. You could also use this animation method to show the geological evolution of a specified terrain, the emergence of the Himalayas, for instance. Just so you know what to expect, using Global Space mapping on all of the elements will make it look as if the material is expanding and stretching to accommodate the rising objects. You can always use Object Space mapping on the objects if you don't want this.

The task of the animator is to do the unexpected, even with a fairly basic animation technique. When you develop an emergence animation, make sure that the elements that move are staggered in time, so they don't all move at once. It's also a good idea to vary their shapes, subtly or radically.

TIP

The Emergence example Fig8_01.br3 is included on the CD-ROM in the Project folder for your convenience. It is ready for you to animate and render.

NOTE

WALL EVOLVER (FIGURE 8.2)

This is a method for causing a wall to build itself from a collection of stones. Here's how:

1. Create a Stone from the Create toolbar, or import one from the Rocks and Trees folder in the Objects library.
2. Multi-replicate the stone 15 times. Move each stone into position as part of a vertical wall, varying the length of some of the stones. Select all of the stones by surrounding them with a dragged out marquee, and Group the wall into one object. Assign a Object Space mapped material to the wall (this makes the texturing of each stone a little different).
3. Create a 60-frame animation and make sure the last frame is a keyframe. This is very important, because we are going to work backwards.
4. Go to frame 1, Select half of the stones randomly, and each stone in succession (by holding down the Control key as you click on the separate stones). As each stone is selected, move it to some random position above or below the ground plane, and out of the view.

FIGURE   *The stones gradually fly up and create the wall.*
8.2

5. Now go to frame 20, and repeat the same movement on the remaining stones. If you set the keyframe for the last frame correctly, the last frame will show the wall built in place, and the first frame will show just the ground plane. If you render an animation from this project, it will show the rocks magically rising from the ground plane to assume their position in the wall.

6. To add more believable randomness to the animation, go to various random frames in the sequence and reposition and rotate selected stones.

This project, Wallbld.br3, is included on the CD-ROM ready for you to render.

NOTE

LIQUID ROCK (FIGURE 8.3)

In this example, we use variable material turbulence and other material f/x to move material across a rock surface. Placing a series of these animated rocks on a plane produces an eerie effect. When you use this method, attend to the following:

• Use a reflective ground surface, which will enhance the changes on the rock's surface.

FIGURE *The rock sits on a reflective plane to emphasize the changes taking place on its*
8.3   *surface.*

- Start with a fairly large-faceted texture, and then move to smaller components over time.
- Use the Rotation tool from the Materials Lab Transformation dialog in the texture animation.
- Explore reversing the bump map from positive to negative in the animated texture.

TIP

Try the rain Forest rock from the Materials Lab Objects library for this example.

See the Liqrk1.br3 project on the CD-ROM. Also see the Liqrk1 animation.

LIQUID WOOD (FIGURE 8.4)

Not only can you animate a single texture, as in the Liquid Rock example above, but you can also animate across material boundaries. This is a case in point. Do the following:

1. Build or import a table object, and place it within the boundaries o the camera view.
2. Create a 60-frame animation. There are four Wood materials in the Simple Materials presets folder that we will apply to the table. We will use Parametric mapping throughout.
3. Apply the four Wood presets so that they are separated by equal keyframes, at 1, 20, 40, and 60.

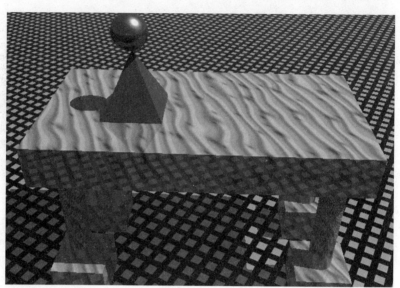

FIGURE **8.4** *The wood that the table is made of changes over time in this example.*

Rendering this animation, you will see that the material the table is seemingly made of changes over time. There is no reason you couldn't use any other material on the table as well.

NOTE

See the Tablex.br3 project on the CD-ROM. You can customize it by substituting whatever materials you prefer.

CRACK OF DOOM (FIGURE 8.5)

Open up the Earth on a fault line with this effect, creating a rift valley. This is your first opportunity in this book to work with animation in the Terrain Editor. Here's how:

1. Create a 60-frame animation. Place a Terrain object in your world, and with it selected, open up the Terrain Editor.
2. Lower the Terrain so it looks like gently rolling hills instead of a mountain. In the animation Timeline at the bottom of the Terrain Editor, make a keyframe of the terrain at the first frame.
3. Go to the last frame. With the Elevation Brush enabled, select a pure black color and a medium thin brush size. Paint a jagged line from the bottom of the topographical view to the top. As you look at the preview

FIGURE   *This rift valley is created while you watch. Just for effect, the Material is also*
8.5   *animated.*

model, you will see that a valley has been cut through the model. Return
to the workscreen.

4. Place a mountain behind the animated Terrain to add some interest and
   render the animation. You will see the rift valley created before your eyes.

*Check out the Doom1.br3 project on the CD-ROM. It's ready to animate a rift val-
ley being born.*

VOLUMETRIC EVAPORATION (FIGURE 8.6)

The Base Density control in the Volumetric Materials Lab is a magic wand that
can create some startling animation effects. Here's one example of its use:

1. Create a 60-frame animation. Place an egg-shaped object (an elongated
   sphere) on the ground plane so it can be seen clearly in the Camera view.

FIGURE   *As the egg shape evaporates, a symmetrical lattice object is revealed inside.*
8.6   *Volumetric Base Density controls it all.*

2. Create a Symmetrical lattice and map it with whatever material you like. Place it inside the egg-shaped object.

3. In the Materials Lab, assign a volumetric texture to the egg-shaped object. Set the Base Density to 100%, making it opaque.

4. Go to the last frame, and set the base Density to zero, so that the egg-shaped object disappears.

Always use Full Shading on volumetric textures that are set to evaporate, since that creates the most interesting patterns. Though there is a high rendering cost for volumetric materials, there is nothing quite like them for unusual effects. You might also think of this as the "beam-me-up-Scotty" effect.

NOTE

Volumetric textures do not map to a Terrain object in Bryce 3D, but can be used on any primitive. There is other great news, however. Imported objects DO take on volumetric materials. If you need to evaporate Terrain, design the Terrain object in another 3D application, and save it out in a 3D object format that Bryce 3D can read. Import it and evaporate away!

NOTE

Be sure and see the BD.br3 project on the CD-ROM. Create an animation from it with the knowledge that volumetric material take a much longer time to render. If you do decide to render it, make sure anti-aliasing is off.

TERRAMORPHS

Terramorphs are animations created in the Terrain Editor. The rift valley we created in the "Crack of Doom" example is a basic Terramorph. Complex Terramorphs, however, take advantage of the full range of features and tools in the Terrain Editor. You have already been exposed to these tools if you have read and worked through the exercises in Chapter 3 of this book, as well as any work you may have done on your own. Creating a Terramorph means using the Terrain Editor tools in reference to the timeline, so that your painted elevations and effects are set to various keyframes in an animation. You can accomplish absolute magic by morphing terrain over time. Here are some basic guidelines:

• Plan ahead by doing a rough storyboard of what you want to accomplish, especially as far as what your keyframes should look like.

• Make sure there is at least three seconds (at 30 FPS) between keyframes of a Terramorph. This allows the audience to appreciate a smooth transition.

• Try to design an intermediate keyframe, so that the audience is surprised by the final outcome. For example, if you want to transform a sharp peaked mountain into a volcano, show an intermediate keyframe that assigns maximum erosion to the mountain first. Then assign the crater to the last keyframe.

- Always preview the animation in the Terrain Editor, which shows you a full shaded rendering, and is much faster than rendering it first.
- It is suggested that you use only one Terramorph as the center of attention in your finished animation. More than one is, in most cases, overkill.

NOTE

Important! Make sure you view the five Terramorph animations included on the CD-ROM. They are short, but magical.

BOILING MUD (FIGURE 8.7)

Here is another Terramorph example, but one that uses a more subtle approach. The result is no less impressive. Do the following to create a sea or a puddle of boiling mud:

1. Create a 120-second animation (at 30 FPS). Place a Terrain object in your view, and go to the Terrain Editor.
2. Click on New and create a solid block by using the pure white elevation brush in the topographical area. Lower the block to about one-fifth of its size.

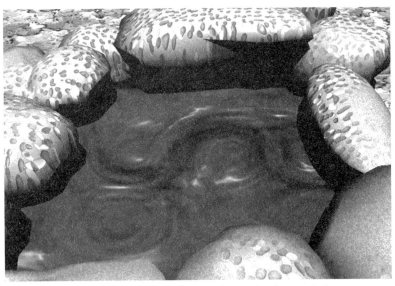

FIGURE   *Very realistic boiling mud can be created using the above method.*
8.7

3. Keyframe this solid block at the start and end frames.

4. Now the trick is to use an elevation brush matched just a tiny amount above the color of the block, because you want gentle bubbles, not spikes. At various points along the timeline, place random-sized elevation brush circles on the block. Erase them for succeeding keyframes, and place others in different areas. Preview the animated results, and adjust any parts of the animation that need it.

5. After returning to your screen, place a ring of rocks around the Mud Block. Place the Oily Bronze material on the Mud Block and get a good view of the composition in the Camera view. Render and save the animation.

You can just as easily make this boiling water or lava by placing the right material on the Mud Block.

NOTE

See the Mud1.br3 project on the CD-ROM, and view the associated animation.

A/B IMPACTS

A number of things can happen when object A is hurtling through space and meets object B, all depending upon the mass of either object.

- Object A can bounce away from object B, with B remaining in place, or objects A and B can both bounce away from each other after the impact.
- Object A can break up, object B can break up, or they both can break up.
- In computer graphics worlds, object A can pass without notice right through object B.

In the following two animated scenarios, we take a look at two A/B interactions.

Slam Hammer

In this scenario, object A meets object B while object B is on the ground. The resulting impact causes object A to bounce off object B, but not without acting as a hammer that drives object B further into the ground. Do the following:

1. Create a 60-frame animation at 15 FPS. Create two rocks. The moving one will be called Rock A and the stable one Rock B.

2. Plant Rock B in the ground about one-third of the way. Move Rock A out of the scene and above Rock B.

3. Set a keyframe at the beginning of the animation for Rock A. Move Rock A so that it touches Rock B at frame 20 of the animation. Set a keyframe

for both Rock A and B at this point. From frame 21 to 60, Rock A should bounce off Rock B and bounce out of the scene. Rock B should be driven vertically into the ground about two-third of the way from frames 21 to frame 45.

Ker-pow! (Figure 8.8)

This time, object B proves to be no match for the inertia of object A, and it breaks up. This leaves object A on the ground in its place. Do the following:

1. Create a 120-frame animation at 30 FPS. Create Rock A and move it out of the scene vertically, keyframing it.
2. The creation of Rock B will be a little different. Create it by combining twelve smaller rocks to form one large one. After Rock B is complete, Group all of the components of Rock B and assign a suitable rock material to it using Object Space mapping. Global Space mapping would slide the material around the rock when it shatters. Ungroup all of the components of Rock B so it can shatter.
3. Move Rock A so that it touches Rock B at frame 40 of the animation. Set a keyframe for both Rock A and B at this point. From frame 41 to 120, Rock A should be planted firmly in the ground without moving. But what about Rock B?
4. Rock B should remain stable right up to the moment it is struck, and a keyframe should be set for Rock B at that moment. Then you should

FIGURE *A view of Rock B before and during being struck by Rock A.*
8.8

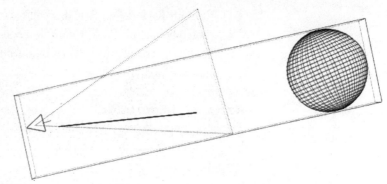

FIGURE   *This figure shows the placement of the elements in the scene.*
8.9

move to the last frame. With Rock B selected, use the 3D dispersion tool to scatter the components randomly with the 3D and Rotation option. After you do this, you will need to manually move all of the components off screen, and move those that seem to penetrate Rock A as well. The resulting animation will show Rock B being smashed by Rock A. Use a variation of this method to show one object being obliterated by another, especially when hit by a projectile.

SOLVING THE HORIZON/DISTANCE PROBLEM

Commonly, your ground planes have horizons that are in the infinite distance. You cannot place anything at or beyond the observed horizon line in Bryce 3D, using an infinite ground plane. Unless you move objects a huge distance from the Camera from the top view, you can't even come close to object placement near the horizon. But like every other problem you may face in Bryce 3D, there is a solution. To place an object near the horizon without moving it very far from the Camera, do the following:

1. Place a Ground Plane and a primitive Sphere in your scene.
2. Multi-select the Camera, Ground Plane, and the Sphere, and Group them.
3. Move the group upward, about three screen inches away from the Underground boundary, and tilt the group 15 degrees on the X axis. See Figure 8.9.
4. Use a 75% Haze setting, and turn Cast Shadows Off on the object in the Materials Lab.

You can achieve close to the same result just by rotating the Camera so its FOV skims the ground, but the horizon line is usually too apparent.

FIGURE *On the left is the tilted infinite ground plane method, and on the right is the*
8.10 *Terrain object substitution, with an intervening vertical Cloud Plane (50%*
transparent). The right-hand object is also a Fuzzy object, emphasizing the
distance.

If you must show an object rising from below the horizon line to above it, a
false sun or a more esoteric object, replace the Infinite Ground Plane with a
flattened Terrain object (give it a Y size of 2). Elevating and tilting the components as in the previous example should still be followed, though some exploration of the variables is important for each project. This time, however, you
can place objects so they are totally or partially hidden by the false horizon line
and animate them to interact with it. Figure 8.10 shows the results.

TIP

If you elongate terrain Plane substitutes far enough on their Z axis, they can also
show Haze and Fog effects. You can also use an intervening Infinite Cloud Plane
placed vertically between the end of the Terrain plane and the object to show clouds
passing in front of the object, which adds to the believability of the depth and dis-
tance involved. If you do this, explore the use of the Tea Kettle Steam material.

TREES

If you have to add a good number of trees to your world, *do not* use the trees included in the Objects library. Most are Boolean constructs, and rendering
them can tie up your system for days. Instead, consider mapping bitmap trees
to a series of 2D Picture planes. The only time this doesn't work is when you
have to fly over them. In that case, map a Picture plane with a bitmap that
shows a forest from above. The best tree designing application around, for both
DXF 3D models as well as 2D bitmaps, is Tree Professional from Onyx Software. See Appendix C at the end of this book.

Air f/x

Air f/x center upon everything we can do to customize or effect the look of the
sky in Bryce 3D. This includes Haze and Fog effects, since the sky is not just
something "up there," but takes in general atmospherics.

FIGURE *A collection of skies created by Deep Texture Editing explorations displays*
8.11 *unusual and unfamiliar precincts of the air.*

DEEP SKY EDITING (FIGURE 8.11)

When you simply have to have a sky that you can not create from the present components, and the random generator isn't providing you with what you need, there is another more personal alternative. The same Deep Texture Editing process that allows you to get to the very roots of texture generation when it comes to customizing materials is also available for creating sky textures. There are no limits to the unique looks available, as long as you are conversant with the Deep Texture Editing process (see Chapter 4).

If your Deep Sky textures are not rendering, try the following:

- Turn Cumulus off. Stratus clouds often take better advantage of this procedure.
- Try setting Cloud Height to 10 and Cover to 5. This seems to clarify the new patterns.
- Try altering the Custom Colors. More contrasted colors seem to show the patterns better.
- Make sure the material you assign to the sky has an Alpha channel in the Deep Texture Editor. If it doesn't, create one. This allows "holes" in the sky plane.

In general, these effects are more limited in terms of clarity and meeting your expectations than it would be to apply procedural textures to an intervening Cloud Plane. Cloud Planes offer much more procedural texture control, because you can work with four interleaved channels as well as the Deep Texture Editor for each.

DE-FOGGER

Using fog settings, we can generate animations that reveal things that were previously hidden in a progressive manner. A very effective, yet simple to create Fog effect is to watch the Fog burn off in front of our eyes, going from 100% to 0%. If you plan on using this effect, make sure there is something interesting that gets revealed.

HAZE LIGHTER

Using a 75% haze, alter the Haze color over time. Haze adds a strange glow to objects in the distance and altering the Haze color accentuates this effect. You can also explore different haze percentages for more subtle or enhanced variations.

STONE SKY

This effect is best applied to an intervening Cloud Plane, leaving the background sky set to No Atmosphere and a solid color or a gradient (by switching Cumulus off, and using Custom Sky).

SKY STACK TRIP

This animation is similar to the effect at the end of Stanley Kubrik's *2001: A Space Odyssey*, when the spacecraft moves through a series of infinite planes. The difference is, this effect moves you vertically through the planes. Here's what to do:

1. Create a stack of six Infinite Cloud Planes, separated by the height of the camera on your screen.
2. Map each of the planes with a different Cloud material, making sure that about 35% to 50% of the materials show transparent areas.
3. In the first frame of a 120-frame 15 FPS animation, place the Camera at the bottom of the lowest Cloud Plane, facing straight ahead, and keyframe it. In the last frame of the animation, move the Camera vertically, so it is above the top Cloud Plane. Render and save.

AURORA BOREALIS WITH SHIMMER (FIGURE 8.12)

This one's a real beauty. It should be composited against a dark sky. Here in the North, we consider the aurora a sign of hope, though it often indicates very cold weather for the coming winter. Here's how to do it:

FIGURE   *The beauty of the Aurora Borealis is captured by Bryce 3D.*
8.12

1. Create a scene with a few mountains and a dark blue sky.
2. Place a 2D vertical plane in the scene in back of the mountains. Make it large enough so you can't see any edges when viewed from the Camera.
3. With the 2D Plane selected, open the Materials Lab. Load the Waves2 texture from the list into channel A. Activate Diffuse, Specular, Specular Halo, and Transparent Colors; Diffusion (100), Ambience (82), and Specularity (53) Values; Transparency Optics (22). Notice that we leave the Specular button in the color palette mode, because this allows us to alter the color of the Aurora over time and to see that color against a dark sky.
4. Create a 120-frame animation at 30 FPS. At random places on the time line, alter the Specular color and the size of the Aurora. Render and save to disk.

Be sure to Open the Aurora.br3 project on the CD-ROM to investigate all of the parameters of this spectacular effect further. Also see the Aurora1 animation. If you are going to use this project file to animate the scene, try rotating the material on the 2D plane as part of the animation and also explore stretching and/or contracting the 2D Plane in a left-right direction.

TORNADO

Tornadoes are tremendously destructive forces, born of sky and wind. Their power and terror is exactly what attracts us to them as a symbol. The flight of

Dorothy to Oz still thrills us, because the tornado is also a vehicle of transformation. In Bryce 3D, tornado-shaped objects are not the easiest thing to create, though they can be generated with a little effort.

The most basic tornado shape is based on a jagged cone. In Bryce 3D, to create the tornado with the primitive objects available, a cone must be included. Since there are no options for creating jagged shapes, we must think in terms of Boolean constructs as part of the solution.

If you use a negative Boolean cube to cut away the narrow ends of a rotated cone, the resulting object can be fitted inside of another cone at its base. Do this a couple of times, and the 3D object starts to look like a jagged tornado. When you have the convincing components put in place, you can Group everything. Then it's just a matter of finding the right material. This is where a Volumetric comes in really handy, since it can be broken up with the Base Density slider and made partially transparent as well. A tornado is swirling dirt, so use materials like Volumetric Pollution to map it. Set it in motion, and use 3D Dispersion to make objects fly when it hits. Figure 8.13 shows the results.

The Torn1.br3 project on the CD-ROM contains a tornado object ready for placement and animation. Investigate its construction and use it in your own animations.

NOTE

CLEARING

This effect is easy to understand and apply, but the results can be spectacular. Switch Cumulus on and create an animation that moves from 100% cloud

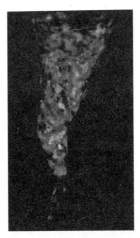

FIGURE   *On the left is the tornado, constructed from primitive cones and negative*
8.13   *Boolean cubes. On the right, the Volumetrically mapped object is placed against a black backdrop for effect.*

cover at the first frame to 0% at the last frame. Turn Stratus off. The best version of this effect is the one that displays an enlarged sun shining behind the clouds, with halos turned on. If your scene has some interesting terrain and objects, you will be amazed by the results. Work with a 30 FPS 240-frame animation as a minimum, to allow the effect to take place slowly.

24 HOURS

This is another easy to understand and apply effect. It emulates day passing into night and again into day. All that it takes is an interesting scene, so shadows get cast as the sun moves. Water is nice to add to the scene, because there are different reflections that occur as the sun moves.

PULSAR

A Pulsar is a star that revolves in a steady repetitive cycle, so that it produces radiation "noise" that can be picked up by radio telescopes here on earth. In our Bryce 3D Pulsar example, we will change the size and color of the Sun object to emulate this effect. Figure 8.14 shows the results. Do the following:

1. Create a 120-frame animation at 30 FPS.
2. Create an alien landscape and make the sky color red with either no clouds, or a few bizarre clouds created by using the Deep Sky Edit dialog (activated by clicking on the Edit button in the Sky&Fog palette).

FIGURE *A Pulsar reigns over an alien landscape.*
8.14

3. Move the Sun so that it is on the horizon in front of the camera. Go to the Sky&Fog Edit dialog and switch the Horizon Enlargement option on, with a percentage of 100 for the first frame. Select a yellow color for the sun.

4. At frames 20, 40, 60, 80, 100, and the last frame, alter the size and color of the sun, so that it gets larger and smaller and exhibits different colors. Render the animation and save it to disk.

The Pulsar1.br3 project is on the CD-ROM, ready for you to configure and animate.

ALIEN STORM

Bryce 3D not only offers you the capacity to animate sky planes by manipulating the light and patterns, but in addition, you can create animations that use completely different skies on separate keyframes. The result is that one sky type gradually washes over another. The Randomize buttons at the upper right of the Sky&Fog toolbar allow you to march through a series of unexpected sky parameters and patterns. Adding these two capacities together, the ability to keyframe different skies and the ability to generate random skies results in strange animations that show one unique sky morphing into another. All you need to do is to hit the Randomize button and watch the Nano Preview. When you find interesting skies, Add them to the Sky&Fog presets library. When you have half a dozen favorites, select each one in turn, and keyframe it as part of an animated sequence.

See the project and animation Skywash1 on the CD-ROM for a look at this procedure in action.

Water f/x

Water is the elixir of life. As far as we know, life cannot exist in any form comparable to ours without it, though off-planet explorations await. Water effects in Bryce 3D offer some of the most stunning renderings and animations. There's something about reflections and transparencies at the same time that makes us dream. Here are ten suggestions for utilizing Water f/x in your Bryce 3D projects.

AGUA TERRA

When you think of Water in Bryce 3D, do not confine your thoughts to Infinite Water Planes alone. As we have seen in the Mud project detailed earlier,

FIGURE *This is a close-up of the Terrain Ripple effect.*
8.15

Terrain objects are great objects for a host of needs. Water is no exception. Referring to the previous Terramorph examples, it's just as easy to sculpt Terrain to look like water f/x. Figure 8.15 shows the result. Here's how:

1. Create a 120-frame animation at 30 FPS. Place a Terrain object on the screen and go to the Terrain Editor.
2. In the Terrain Editor, first create a solid block by clicking New and then Invert. Lower the block to about one-tenth of its size by dragging right over the Raise/Lower control.
3. This time, we'll create animated ripples. Use the Elevation Brush to paint concentric rings at frame 60 on the Terrain. Alternate between black (low elevation) and medium gray (higher elevation) until you have a series of concentric rings.
4. Allow the last keyframe to return to the flat surface you started with. Preview the animation in the Terrain Editor. After you quit the Terrain Editor, map the Swimming Pool material to the terrain slab and set the camera view. Render the animation, and save it to disk.

Take a look at the Rippler.br3 project on the disk, and render the animation if you like.

NOTE

FOG WATER

You don't need water to achieve a water effect. Under the right circumstances, that is, with the right environmental look in your scene, you can generate water by using low altitude Fog. Off the Maine coast in the early morning, there are times when to ocean is subject to large patches of low level fog, and the water as such is completely obliterated. Fantasizing oceans in far away worlds, there may be seas of ammonia or other non-water elements that rise and fall with the tides created by more than one moon. In both of these situations, our appreciation of a liquid surface may be enhanced not so much by the constituent components of the sea, as by its actions. Seas that we are familiar with have specific motions, waves and rising-falling actions. You can use Fog in Bryce 3D to emulate a sea, one that is either covered over with Fog, or a non-water liquid. Figure 8.16 shows the result.

See the Fogwat.br3 project on the CD-ROM to explore and customize this effect. Substituting Fog for Water saves a lot of rendering time, since Fog takes little to no time to render.

NOTE

One reason to use Symmetrical Lattice objects in a water scene is that they are symmetrical on their vertical axis, so placing them in a transparent or partially transparent material makes it seem as if they always have a reflection. It takes less time to render a Symmetrical Lattice than it does to compute and render a reflective surface, so you get the same effect without the cost.

TIP

FIGURE *In some compositions, Fog can substitute for Water, and renders faster.*
8.16

FIGURE
8.17
As if radiating energy, the pool seems to reflect patterns on everything in the vicinity. It's really the hidden Radial Light causing this fractal water effect, projecting the wavy procedural texture.

RADIAL REFLECTIONS

As we discovered in Chapter 5, Radial Lights can be mapped with procedural textures. As long as the texture has an Alpha channel, the Radial Light will project eerie fractal patterns on the surrounding area. Figure 8.17 shows an example. When using this method, attend to the following:

- Place the Radial Light over a water surface, causing the water to glow as if under its own power.
- Create a scene that has thoughtfully placed and interesting objects in the vicinity, so the reflections will play on all of the surfaces.
- Always use Linear Falloff.
- Do not apply this texture as a Gel in the Radial Light's Edit dialog, but instead apply it as a procedural texture in the Materials Lab. Make sure the Alpha channel for the texture is activated in the Deep Texture Editor.
- The best way to animate these reflections is to rotate the Radial Light over time.
- Always use moonlight to enhance the power of textures projected through a Radial Light, as the Sun will tend to dilute and wash out the effect.

FIGURE *By tilting the Infinite Water Plane from side to side, you can simulate a rolling*
8.18 *sea.*

NOTE

See the Watref1.br3 project on the CD-ROM. Rendering Radial Light procedural texture projections is expensive, but no other method can produce this effect.

SEASICK

The rocking motion of the sea is solace to some, and nauseating to others. Bryce 3D allows you to simulate this motion by tilting the Infinite Water Plane from side to side, as seen through the Camera view. To emphasize this effect, build a small boat and place it in the water (see Figure 8.18). Bon voyage!

NOTE

When your Water Plane tilts one way, rotate any craft on the surface the opposite way to enhance the rocking motion. See the Seasick1.br3 project on the CD-ROM if you want the elements necessary to create an animation displaying this effect, including a small boat. Warning: Don't watch the animation too long after you render it, unless you've brought along some seasick remedies.

RIPPLE PROJECTION

Here's another water procedural texture projection effect for use with a Radial Light. You can also use this on non-water surface to create energy waves. Figure 8.19 shows an example.

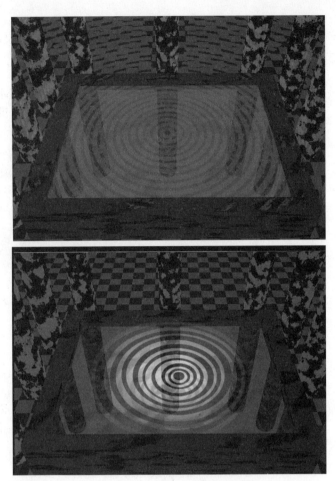

FIGURE **8.19** *On the top is a Procedural ripple applied to a Radial Light. Just to see the difference, the bottom graphic displays a PICT Gel applied to a Square Light. With a Square Light, the effect does not bleed over onto the surrounding objects, but is contained within the water pool.*

TIP

Radial Lights accept procedural textures like any other object, while other Lights do not project them as effectively. Use PICT Gels to project patterns with other lights.

1. Create a scene that has water in it, either in a closed container or as an Infinite Water Plane.
2. Place a Radial Light above the water so its cone can be seen in the Camera view pointing downward. Use a Yellow Bands Material to map the Spotlight, adjusting the size of the texture as needed.

Important! Do not use a standard Spotlight to project a ripple effect PICT Gel on a water object, since the pattern will distort. Use a Square Light instead.

NOTE

THROWN ROCKS AND RAIN

Use an Infinite Water Plane as the target for the following effects, which are based upon the previously described Square Light PICT Gel projections. To mimic a pebble being thrown in the water, move the Square Light with the concentric rings projection Gel as close as possible in frame 1 of an animation, and then move it far enough away vertically, at the last frame, that the Linear Falloff causes the projection to disappear. As the light moves to the last frame, decrease its intensity and increase the fuzziness. The result will be an expanding ripple that fades at the end. Do this with ten or more randomly placed Square Lights on a water plane, and you have Rain.

You can control the density of square Light projections by altering the intensity of the light, while adding fuzzy edges to the light will make the projected images fade at their extremities.

TIP

WATERFALL

Waterfall simulations are some of the most sought-after effects in computer graphics. This water effect is usually added in a post-production phase of the animation by another application, like Adobe After Effects. You can, however, create an interesting, though basic, waterfall effect in Bryce 3D (see Figure 8.20). Do the following:

1. Create a 240-frame animation at 30 FPS. Create a scene that has a rocky cliff, which will be the home of your waterfall. Create a pool at the bottom of the cliff, a reservoir for the tons of falling water.

2. Create a cylinder object, set on its side as facing the Camera view, and place it in the area of the cliff that is to evidence falling water.

3. Map it with a Volumetric water material. The Polluted Waterfall material is a good choice. You can go into its Deep Texture Editor and recolor the yellow-brown texture a light blue, instantly correcting the pollution.

4. At the base, where the water meets the pond, place a sphere. Map the sphere with a Volumetric cloud texture, which will be the spray evaporating as the water hits.

5. There are two components of this scene that you will want to animate, the waterfall and the spray cloud. Animate the waterfall itself by simply revolving the cylinder, and altering the Base Density of the texture over time. Animate the spray cloud by altering its Base Density over time.

FIGURE *A Bryce 3D waterfall pours its water into a waiting pond.*
8.20

If the waterfall is very high, consider using a series of cylinders, so it looks like the water is cascading from one to the next. See the Watfall1.br3 file in the Projects folder on the CD-ROM for an example of how the waterfall can be created.

TIP

THE WHIRLPOOL EFFECT

Like tornadoes, whirlpools are forces of nature with a lot of power. Also like tornadoes, whirlpools can be constructed from basic cone primitive objects, only this time, in the water. Figure 8.21 shows an example. Do the following:

1. Create a Terrain block in the Terrain Editor. Make it about twice as deep as the Camera is high.
2. Use the Elevation brush to dig a series of concentric holes in it, making each ring a little deeper as you reach the center.
3. Map it with the Caribbean water material, but turn the reflection down to 30%.

Render for a preview. If everything looks OK, it's time to render the animation. For this animation, rotate the material mapped to the water in the Transformation palette of the Materials Lab. The effect is subtle because the Caribbean material is not as patterned as other materials.

See the Wrlpl1.br3 project on the CD-ROM, ready for you to customize, adjust the parameters, and render as an animation.

NOTE

FIGURE   *The whirlpool opens and waits for the forgetful fisherman.*
8.21

TAP WATER

Here's a water effect that's small by comparison to oceans and waterfalls. It's simple to set up, with perhaps the most challenging part being the modeling of the faucet. If you load the project, Tapwtr1.br3, from the CD-ROM, you can take the faucet object apart to see how basic Bryce 3D primitive objects were used in its construction. figure 8.22 shows the result.

What about the water? A screw object, included in the Bryce 3D Imported Objects library folder, was used. It was mapped with a 96% transparent Swimming Pool Water material in the Materials Lab.

Animation Suggestions

If you want to animate this scene, what should you target for movement, and how?

- Animate the faucet handle turning. It is a separate Group from the rest of the faucet, and can be rotated by using the rotation tool on the Y World axis.
- Animate the "water" coming out. This can be accomplished by simply reducing the vertical height of the "water" until it disappears into the

FIGURE *A close-up shot of the faucet reveals its structure and the usefulness of the*
8.22 *inverted screw as a stream of water.*

faucet, and then elongating that length over time. You should also rotate
the water on the World Y axis as it leaves the faucet.

*Load the Tapwtr1.br3 project on the CD-ROM to see this scene in detail and to
customize and animate it.*

NOTE

SEE TO BOTTOM

This project (see Figures 8.23 and 8.24) uses a Volumetric transparent water
block with a sandy bottom and moving "fish." Here's how this project was created.

1. The Valley Terrain Map, from the Bryce 3D Terrain Maps folder, was
   imported in the Terrain Editor. It was resized to about one-quarter of its
   height and placed in the scene. It was mapped with the Rainforest Rock
   material, which was sized to 1000% to make the textures smaller and
   more numerous.
2. A rectangular block was added for the water and mapped with a **XX%**
   transparent Aqua Glass material, with a bump map channel added
   (Waves Bump texture).
3. A sandy bottom with pebbles was added at the lowest level of the water,
   using another rectangular object embedded in the Terrain "river." It was

FIGURE
8.23
A DXF public domain model of a shark was reconfigured as this somewhat unique fish.

FIGURE
8.24
A school of fish swims near the sandy bottom of a stream.

mapped with the Riverbed textured material from the Sand materials folder. It was resized to 625% and turned 35 degrees on the Y World axis, so that mechanical symmetry could be broken. The texture was darkened in the Deep Texture Editor to give it a wetter look, although it is only visible at the bottom of the rendering.

4. Stones were added to the composition to give it more viewer interest.

5. A public domain DXF "Fish" object was added and duplicated for a school. Camera and lighting were adjusted for filming.

The "water" you place in your scene need not be derived from a standard water material. As in this case, you can use a transparent glass, and perhaps add a bump channel. You can, in fact, use a mirror.

See the Bfish1.br3 project on the CD-ROM to study and animate this scenario.

Very Important! When you want multiple copies of a DXF model you have reconfigured, do not use either Duplicate or Replicate, or the copy will suffer serious re-alignment. Instead, use Copy and Paste. Then move the clone into position.

SPLASH

You can use the same process that was presented in the Earth section of this chapter on dispersal explosions to explode water as well. The difference is that this is not called an explosion, but a splash. All you have to do is to embed small spheres mapped with a transparent water material under your watery surface. Multi-replicate the spherical particles 30 times or so. When you throw a virtual pebble in the water, and at the very moment it hits the surface, begin the dispersion of the spheres. You can move any by hand later that don't meet your visual requirements. All you have to remember is to map the spheres with a very high transparency level, and perhaps to elongate them into more teardrop shapes as well. Use the 3D Move, Rotate, Resize dispersion method.

EXTRA! TV RAIN AND SNOW

Before the dawn of computer graphics and animation, TV productions would simulate rain and snow mechanically. They would place a cylindrical roll with white or black markings and a drop-out blue background in front of a second camera, and superimpose the markings over a scene shot by camera 1 as the cylinder was turned. In computer animation, this is called Alpha Channel Compositing, so it's something learned from the historical tradition of animation. We can certainly accomplish this same process in Bryce 3D. Here's how:

1. Create a 320 x 480 grayscale graphic in a paint application. On a white backdrop, add black anti-aliased streaks that are randomly placed and randomly sized, and that are on an approximate 15 degree angle. This will be our rain map.
2. Create a cylinder that is lying on its side as seen in the Camera view. Resize it so that it covers the whole scene and move it so that the Camera is inside of it (as seen in the top view).
3. In the 2D Picture Editor in the Materials Lab, import the rain graphic and wrap it on the Cylinder (cylindrical mapping). If anything looks dis-

oriented, use the Rotation tool to correct it. The image should come in with white acting as an Alpha dropout. If not, simply copy the graphic to the Alpha channel in the 2D Picture Editor.

4. You can map it a multiple number of times, which will create repetitive sheets of rain (a monsoon?). When you create the animation simply keyframe the starting position at the start and end of the animation, and make sure the cylinder rotates 360 degrees (on the X World axis) to make the streaks look like falling rain.

TIP

To create a gentle snowstorm, use snowflake designs instead of streaks in the bitmap, making sure they are randomly placed and sized. To create a blizzard, use white dots instead of designed flakes. To create a meteorite storm, use red-orange streaks with a somewhat bulbous end. To create a cats-and-dogs rain, use cat and dog graphics as the image map.

Fire f/x

Fire, like water, has a dual personality. It can be life-giving when it resides in a stove or a candle and life-threatening when it is the heat and power of an explosion. Fire f/x are a mainstay of computer animations, since they allow the sudden removal of objects from the scene, and can also display lighting factors not possible with artificial lighting components. There are many more ways to use fire f/x than the examples presented here, but these should give you a good overall view of what is possible with fire designs in Bryce 3D, and how to create them.

SPARKY

Glance one flinty stone off another and the friction causes sparks. Campfires also release sparks into the air, as do electrical mishaps. You already have the technique for creating sparks down pat if you have worked through the Doom and Splash examples earlier in this chapter. All that's new is to create the initial spark object itself.

The Spark object, unlike stars placed in the sky, should be a 3D object. If you are going to create it in Bryce 3D, use three crossed elongated squares grouped together and very tiny. Map them with a very high Specular Red-Orange color, so they appear no matter how dark it is. Also use a high Red-Orange Diffuse color. The rest of the operation is the same as those already mentioned. Just select the object and multi-replicate it in place and use the dispersion 3D/Move/Rotate operation on them. There may be some occasions, like an exploding rocket, that demand a Resized Dispersion as well. Use your judgment to fit the project you're working on. Figure 8.25 shows an example.

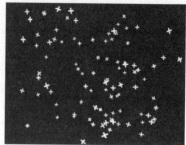

FIGURE *Evolution of a Spark.*
8.25

FIREHEAD

In this example, we'll replace a MetaCreations Poser head with a fireball (see Figure 8.26). You can use any imported humanoid figure you have access to, but obviously, if you want to use a Poser figure you'll have to own Poser. Do the following:

1. Import the Poser or other figure. Ungroup it and delete the head.
2. Place a sphere where the head was. If you desire to animate the whole figure, link the parts properly before Grouping it again.

FIGURE *Firehead glows in the dark.*
8.26

3. Select the figure and Control-select the sphere, which selects it from the Groups.

4. With the sphere selected, go to the Materials Lab, and select the Fire material from the Complex f/x folder. Apply it using a Object Space mapping, leaving the defaults set as they are. Render an animation that shows the fire with different turbulence settings over time and save the animation to disk.

See the Firehd1.br3 project file on the CD-ROM.

NOTE

CANDLE

Candles have been used for millennia, both to light the darkness and as symbols of hope and faith. Candles in Bryce 3D can be constructed so that their flame casts light on receptive objects in the surrounding scene (see Figure 8.27). Here's how to do it:

1. A candle starts with a cylinder. Attach six or so elongated spheres to the sides of the cylinder to represent melted wax, and Group everything. Place a black cylindrical wick in the candle.

2. Assign a Psychoactive Christmas Ball material to the candle body with the following settings: Object Front mapping; Ambient color alone is activated for the channel; Diffusion (100), Ambience (28), Specularity (75); Transparency Optics (35).

FIGURE *The candle glows in a composition because of the embedded Radial Light.*
8.27

3. Design a Candle Holder from two flattened cylinders to make a plate and use a Polished Bronze material on it (Metals folder).

4. For the flame's gases, place an elongated sphere on the wick. Map it with a clear glass material with the following settings: Fuzzy, Object Space mapping,

5. Use a small Radial Light on top of the wick for the flame itself. Color it light blue, and make it volume visible. Set intensity to 50, and fuzziness to 35 in the Light's Edit dialog.

Group everything as one candle object when it's done. Place it in a scene on a table with some objects around it. To animate the flame, elongate and shorten the gases at various keyframe points along the Timeline, and allow the flame itself to pulse with less and more intensity.

See the Candle1.br3 project on the CD-ROM.

NOTE

GLOWING COALS

Glowing coals, whether experienced as the remnants of a campfire or as the main actors in a barbecue pit, can be easily created in Bryce 3D. All that you need is a suitable rock material with a high deep-red Specularity. To make the glowing coal a more esoteric object, like a recently landed cosmic object, just make sure that the Specular Color channel relates to only one texture in a mix of two or more. This gives you patches of light, as opposed to having a whole object that glows.

FIREPLACE

Computer greetings cards, whether printed out and sent through the mail or used as part of a Web page, are very popular ways of displaying your expertise as a 3D artist and animator. If a fireplace is to be used as an animation element, the flame has to be moving. Let's look at how a fireplace with burning logs can be created in Bryce 3D. The result is shown in Figure 8.28.

1. Use a Boolean negative cube to cut away a Boolean positive cube to construct a basic fireplace. You can place a mantle on top, made from another cubic primitive. Set a wall behind it.

2. Use cylinders mapped with a wood material and a very high bump map channel for stacked logs.

3. Place a sphere over the logs for the fire. Map a Wood material to the sphere.

4. Place a yellow Radial Light in the flames so the light will be cast into the

FIGURE   *The warmth and light of a fireplace casts a spell on everything in the vicinity.*
8.28

surrounding room and onto whatever artifacts you decide to place near the fireplace.

NOTE

See the Fireplac.br3 project on the CD-ROM.

LIGHTNING

Lightning is the ultimate spark. Usually we associate it with a sky occurrence, but varieties of lightning can also be useful to science and fantasy scenes, like the power surges that brought the Frankenstein monster to life in an underground laboratory. You can create some pretty realistic lightning in Bryce 3D (see Figure 8.29). Here's how:

1. Open your favorite paint application and draw a lightning bolt. Use whatever copy you need if you are unaccustomed to drawing. Draw it as a bright blue graphic on a white backdrop. Save it to disk.

2. Now use your paint application's Magic Wand Tool to select the background and invert it. The bolt should now be outlined. Paint it solid black. Save it as the graphic's Alpha channel.

3. Configure a scene in Bryce 3D appropriate for lightning, with a darkened sky. Place a 2D Picture Plane in the background where you want the lightning to occur. Select it, and in the Materials Lab, map the bolt to the 2D Picture Plane.

FIGURE *Lightning has always been a symbol of power.*
8.29

If you want to animate this effect, make sure the 2D Picture Plane is in view for two or three frames when the lightning is to be seen. The rest of the time, make sure it is out of the view. You don't want it to slide into view, but to suddenly appear. This means that you should keyframe it as not in the frame on either side of the keyframes that show it as present. It will suddenly appear and seem to flash. Do this two or three times in an animation.

Important! If you see a picture plane border around your image and you can't get rid of it, then you are not using the 2D Picture Plane, but another 2D Plane. Make sure you are using the 2D Picture Plane, the vertical circular icon.

TIP

See the Liteng1.br3 project on the CD-ROM.

NOTE

FIREBALL DISINTEGRATOR

How about creating a fireball that reacts to altitude, so that as it gets lower to the Earth, it burns more intensely? You can do it in Bryce 3D (Figure 8.30), and here's how:

1. Create your fire object. Commonly this is a Rock, but it can be anything you desire (a rocket, a cube, a Poser head, etc.). Map it with a material that has a specular channel, because we want it to glow against a dark backdrop.

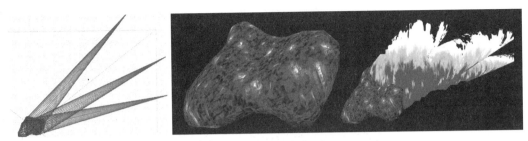

FIGURE   *A cosmic fireball streaks across the night sky, burning more reddish as it gets closer to impact.*
8.30

2. Place a Cone primitive on the screen. Resize its larger end to be as large as the back end of the fireball object and rotate it into place over the fireball object.

3. Use the following Volumetric material map on the Cone: Channel A—the Fading texture, with markers for Ambient Color, Diffusion (80) and Ambient (60) Value; Channel B—the Fire texture, Diffuse Color and Base Density Volume (75). Other settings not tied to channel markers are Specularity value of 80, Edge Softness and Fuzzy factor at 40, and Quality/Speed at 5.

NOTE

If you would like to explore this effect further, or customize it for your own use, see the Fireball.br3 project on the CD-ROM. To add even more realism, set the Base Density of the cone textures to zero before the object impacts (if it does), which turns the trailing fire off.

ROCKET EXHAUST

All that might be mentioned regarding simulating exhaust from a rocket that we haven't already covered is that making a Spotlight a visible light with a Linear Dropoff can add realism to rocket exhaust. It also adds light to the inside of the engines. Whenever possible, try to achieve this effect without using Volumetric smoke or fire if possible, because of the render times needed. Figure 8.31 shows an example.

VOLCANIC FIRE

Following the previous Fireplace and Firehead examples, you can use either standard Fire materials or the Volumetric Fire material to map a spherical object for fire from a volcano. Another alternative is presented in the VolcoFire

FIGURE **8.31** *The close-up of the engine exhaust on the left was generated using a Spotlight inside, shining through the Fuzzy texture of the flame. On the right is the finished ship with all engines fired up.*

project in Section III, Chapter 11. Fire and explosions can also be added to a Bryce 3D production from commercial CD-ROM content, as included in the Pyromania CD-ROM mentioned later in this book.

NOTE

For information on the Pyromania CD-ROM, see Chapter 11 and Appendix C.

LAVA FLOW

Our final Fire f/x might also be listed under Earth f/x, since lava is a mixture of the temperaments of both Earth and Fire. The concern here is twofold: first, to use a suitable material to wrap a surface that simulates lava, and second, to move a series of these surfaces to emulate the flow. Figure 8.32 shows an example. By the way, using the same procedure that was detailed for the Waterfall project, we could also create a river of lava. For simulating moving lava surfaces, here's what to do:

1. Create seven 2D disks and elongate them on their X axes so they are all a little different.
2. Use the Lava Rock texture in channel A to map the ovals and set channel markers in Diffuse and Ambient Color. Set the Diffusion and Ambience values to 100, and do the same for Bump map value. The XYZ texture size should be set at 10%.
3. Create a volcano in the Terrain Editor and use the Elevation brush to slice away part of the slope, so it can "leak" lava. Place the volcano in your scene and stack the lava mapped ovals under it. You may need to resize them smaller to do this.

FIGURE *Lava spreads across the landscape from an active volcano.*
8.32

Make sure all of the lava ovals have a name, so you can locate them easily (such as lava1, lava2, etc.).

TIP

4. Place a cylinder of "lava" inside the volcano and create a radial Light at the top, over the cylinder, to light it up (Linear Falloff and no Surface or Volumetric options).
5. Create the rest of the elements in your scene. You should use a reddish sky to emphasize the fiery nature of the environment.
6. Make sure your ground plane is beneath the sliding lava flows. Set an animation length and get ready to set keyframes for an animation.

The Lava Flow Animation

When you animate this scene, attend to the following procedures:

- As the animation progresses, the lava cylinder inside of the volcano should move up and down about 10% each way. This gives the illusion that the lava is active.
- The intensity of the Radial Light inside the volcano should vary in intensity. It can flash or throb, depending upon what you want to show.

- A 2D Disk mapped with surface reddish clouds should be set above the calendra of the volcano, to catch the variations in the Radial Light.
- If you like, you can add exploding sparks and lightning flashes, as detailed in previous examples.
- The Lava Planes beneath the volcano should gradually move across the ground plane, from the direction that shows the split in the volcano. One by one they should creep out, with some overlapping others as they move. Given enough frames to take advantage of the slow movement of the lava (no less than a 10-second animation will do), this will create a startling scene.

See the Lavaflo.br3 project on the CD-ROM to explore your own customized creations with this example.

Moving On

If you have worked through this chapter, you are well on your way to understanding many of the intricacies of Bryce 3D and how to apply its creative power to elemental f/x generation. In the next chapter, we take a look at Animating Objects: Singular, Composite, and Boolean.

CHAPTER

Object
Animation

A nimation brings your Bryce 3D objects to life. Though it's interesting to animate the camera and fly around a scenic Bryce 3D world, appreciating the textured landscape as it comes into view, depending upon this for sustained audience excitement is not enough. We are storytellers and story-listeners, and we demand empathy with the actors in the stories we tell, not with their environments alone. The actors may be human or animal, robotic, or even basic geometric forms. What they must do however, is to somehow navigate within the confines of the world they live in. They must be seen to move on their own, because we intuit that their movement indicates life. There are different classes of object types that can be animated in Bryce 3D. In this chapter, we investigate three general animated object categories: Singular, Composite, and Boolean.

Singular Object Animations

A singular object is defined as one that cannot be ungrouped to form more than one object element. No matter if primitive-based or imported, singular objects are the most basic forms that can be animated in Bryce 3D. If possible, however, it's always a good idea to keep your use of primitive objects for structures, and to use imported objects in your animations. Primitive objects tend to warp and skew more than imported ones, though this is more true for composite objects than for non-composited ones. You can use basic primitive objects for simple animation tasks, however, and they offer the best way to explore the Bryce 3D animation functions when you are at the start of the learning curve.

THE BRYCE 3D PRIMITIVES

All of the Bryce 3D primitives are singular objects. Aside from all of the primitives we have already identified as such in Bryce 3D, we should also add the Symmetrical Lattice to this list, because it too is a singular object. Even Terrain objects themselves are singular objects and can be used as such (set on an animation path) when they are reconfigured in the Terrain Editor. As standard terrain (hills, valleys, and mountains), however, there is no known need to race them along paths, though your own reasons may force them to do exactly this. As singular objects in an animation, Terrain and Symmetrical Lattice objects are usually given a new shape personality in the Terrain Editor first. See Figure 9.1

The best Terrain to use for designing a customized object in Bryce 3D is the Symmetrical Lattice, because it appears in the Terrain Editor without a base. This makes it perfect for sculpting into customized shapes.

FIGURE *A Terrain object and a Symmetrical Lattice object transformed into suitable*
9.1   *forms for animating.*

LINKING AND GROUPING SINGULAR OBJECTS

Linking and Grouping can be used interchangeably if all you are interested in
is moving objects around to get a better single shot. But when used as animation methods, they produce very different results. For more on Grouped and
Linked objects, see the section on Composite Objects that follows in this chapter. In general, here are the rules:

- If you want the object to act as one unit, Group all of its separate parts.
  To select any single element in a Grouped object, hold down the Control
  key when selecting with the mouse.
- When Linking objects together, pay strict attention to hierarchies, and
  what object is a Child of a specific Parent in the chain. Moving, resizing,
  or rotating a Parent is always applied to all of the Children and other off-
  spring (grandchildren, great grandchildren, etc.) in a chain. Moving, resizing, or Rotating a Child that does not have Children of its own just
  acts on that Child.
- You can always Link any singular or composite object to a stable element
  in the scene, even if that element is hidden. This element then acts as a
  global control over the object. For instance, Linking an orbiting sphere
  to a central sphere and rotating the central sphere can produce perfect
  circular orbits. Perfect circular orbits are not possible just by using
  keyframes to move an object.
- Link a Light to an object if you want the object lit in the same manner
  no matter where it is or what the global lighting is doing. See Figure 9.2.

FIGURE   *This globe is illuminated by six separate spotlights and each is Linked to the*
9.2   *globe. No matter where it moves in the scene or how dark the scene gets, the*
          spotlights will illuminate the same orientation of the globe.

SINGULAR OBJECTS AND STANDARD PATHS

Standard animations paths are created by selecting a new time on the Timeline
and rotating, moving, or resizing an object. This creates a new keyframe at that
point. This is done automatically with Auto-Key switched on. With Auto-Key
off, you must hit the keyframe plus button to create the new keyframe. Standard paths are not objects, so they cannot be moved by themselves, nor can
they be resized or rotated. They are merely indicators of how the objects that
created them move over time.

You can, however, alter the shape of a standard animation path. Simply
move its control point, the point that creating a keyframe generates. This is
useful when you need to alter the path to get around or through other elements
in a scene.

Making Sharp Corners on a Standard Animation Path

Normally, the shape of a path from one keyframe to the next is either a straight
line or a smooth curve. What about creating a sharp corner in an animated
movement? This can be done very simply. Just set two keyframes for the object
while it is in the same place. You may have to straighten out a little loop that
forms on the path, but you will see that it produces a square corner.

SINGULAR OBJECTS AND RIBBON PATHS

There are more reasons for creating an object path than just to set the objects movement in an animation. Your purpose may be quite different, because the object itself may be dispensable. You may want only the path itself. If this is the case, then create the path by moving the object and select Create Path from the Object menu while the object is still selected. A new Ribbon Path will be created over the standard path. Then all you have to do is to select the object separately and select Clear from the Edit menu. Now you have only the path, and as a Ribbon Path it can be manipulated like any other object.

Animating Singular Objects on Ribbon Paths

To assign a Singular object to a Ribbon Path, simply Link it to the path. You will see it snap to a position on the path. If you move it, it will only move to another position on the path, unless unlinked. It will not, however, use the path as an animation path unless you first set it for specific keyframes on the path. The easiest thing to do is to set its beginning keyframe at the start of the path and a second keyframe at the path's end. This makes it follow the path from beginning to end in an animation.

In animation, farther equals faster. The farther you move something between two keyframes, the faster the object must go in order to make its targeted destination at that moment. The guideline in non-computer animations is to move an object only a small amount at a time if you want it to move smoothly, while movements that cover larger distances produce more erratic and jerky movements. This same rule is true when creating computer-based animations. Also remember that on a Ribbon Path, an object can reverse or bounce back and forth between any two keyframes, without affecting the path one bit.

THE IMPORTANCE OF ORIGIN POINTS IN ANIMATIONS

There is no more important placement to understand when animating objects (Singular or Boolean) than that of their Origin Points. By now, you are aware that an object's Origin Point can be viewed by toggling it on in the object's Attributes dialog. Doing so turns it green so you can move it. Any Child object Linked to a Parent object is linked to the parent's Origin Point, so if you move the Origin Point, the Child object points to the new Origin Point's position. It is actually an object's Origin Point that is used to place points on a path when you move the object in a keyframe sequence.

Animating with a Singular Object's Origin Point

There are two ways to use Origin Point movements on an object to create animations. The first is to animate the object and the second is to animate any Linked Children.

Origin Point Animation on the Object

An object's Origin Point is its center of rotation, so moving its Origin Point allows it to revolve and be resized from the new placement. You can place the Origin Point inside any other object, and the initial object will then orbit the second object like a planet around a sun. Moving the Origin Point again will give the object a new center of rotation. For instance, setting a planet's Origin Point at the center of one "sun" and then moving it to the center of another "sun" would make it orbit first one than the other in an animation.

Origin Point Animation on an Object's Children

A Linked Child points to a Parent object's Origin Point, so it is that Origin Point that controls the placement of the Child object. Although the Parent object may manifest no movement of its own (like a mountainous terrain), it can be control the Child objects by the mere displacement of the Parent's Origin Point over time.

If the object is a Terrain object, you can only move its Origin Point once, producing a linear movement in an animation.

NOTE

SINGULAR OBJECT ANIMATION TIPS

When animating Singular Objects in Bryce 3D, attend to the following:

- Create your initial animation path by first keyframing just the start and end. Then go back and create keyframes at points where the path has to move around objects or other things and move the resulting points of the path into place. This usually saves a lot of time and makes the process clearer to customize.
- Use as few keyframes as possible to prevent jerky jumps in the animation.
- If you want the object to make a sudden or angular move, place two keyframes at the same point on the Timeline and adjust them afterwards to remove unwanted loops in the path.
- When adding keyframes to adjust and fine tuning the animation, work with Auto-Key off. The only time not to do this is when animating the camera, since Auto-Key usually needs to be on to track all of the Camera moves and turns.

- Remember that, as objects, Ribbon Paths can also be linked to other Ribbon Paths or objects and that extremely complex movements can be generated in this manner.

- You must select **Constrain to Path** in the Objects Attributes dialog if you want the Linked object to be on the Parent path. Otherwise, it will relate to the path from whatever distance it is at.

- In the object's Attributes dialog, next to the **Constrain to Path** check item, is a percentage input area. This tells the object what part of the path it is to be attached to at that keyframe: 0% is the start of the path and 100% is the end. At the start of an animation, when the object is Constrain-Linked to a path, it is common to use a 0% keyframe at the beginning and a 100% keyframe at the end of the animation. This allows the object to make one complete revolution on the path.

- When you Link multiple singular objects, their Child/Parent hierarchy is all important. For instance, you can Link a satellite to a moon, so that rotating the moon rotates the satellite. Link the moon to a planet, so that rotating the planet rotates moon and satellite. Link the planet to a sun, so that rotating the sun rotates the rest of the hierarchy. Then Link the sun to a prescribed Ribbon Path so that everything moves through space while maintaining its own motion.

See the Linky1 animation on the CD-ROM for an example of multiple singular objects linked to a Ribbon Path and each other, and explore their hierarchies by opening and investigating the Linky1.br3 project.

NOTE

SOLVING THE MULTIPLE ORBIT SPEED PROBLEM

Linking multiple children to a central object and rotating that Parent object will cause all of the Children to orbit the parent at the same keyframe rate. Objects further out from the parent will orbit faster, because they have a longer distance to cover between the start and end of the animation, and objects closer to the parent will orbit slower for the same reason. But what about planets around a sun? Most times, the rate of their orbits should vary radically, so that some planets orbit a few times while others orbit just once. How can we solve this problem?

Actually, there is more than one way to do it.

- You could just Link everything to appropriate Parent objects and rotate the Parent as necessary. That, however, would not give you any variance in the orbital speeds of Child objects (planets) positioned around a common parent.

- You might select to place invisible spheres inside of the Parent (sun) object, and name them as controllers for each Child (planet). That would work to give you specific control over each Child (planet), but it would be a bit cumbersome.

- You could also select to import a circular Ribbon Path for each Child (planet). That would work OK, but again, it would be a bit cumbersome. You would also have to make sure that you set the repeats as needed for each Child (planet).

- The best way is to use a combination of Origin Point moves and Links. Move the Origin Point in every Parent/Child relationship so that the Child's Origin Point is placed in the center of the Parent object. Then Link the Child to the Parent. Nothing has to be Linked to the central sun, since moving a Child's Origin Point will do the trick by itself. See Figure 9.3.

NOTE

See the SolSys.br3 project and the SolSys animation on the CD-ROM to explore this approach to multiple orbit speeds and solar system objects.

NOTE

If an object needs to revolve around its own center as well as around another object, moving the Origin Point may not be the best method. In that case, use another control sphere at the Child object's center, and simply Link it to the Parent.

THE SPIRAL PROJECT

One of the most challenging object animations is that of creating an object that spirals towards a target, perhaps a gravity well. By using the now-familiar Ori-

FIGURE
9.3 *This is a frame from the SolSys animation on the CD-ROM, which demonstrates the Origin Point/Link collaboration method.*

FIGURE   *The Spiro1.br3 project on the CD-ROM is there for you to explore, challenging*
9.4   *you to make the ball spiral into the hole.*

gin Point relocation method, you can create interesting spiral animations. See
Figure 9.4.

*Be sure to load the Spiro1.br3 project from the CD-ROM and customize it to make
the ball spiral into the hole.*

NOTE

Composite Object Animations

A Composite object is one made up of grouped elements that can be ungrouped and relinked in Bryce 3D. The best thing about composite objects is
that they can have their own movements, aside from path-associated animation. A composite spider object, for example, can show all of its legs and an-
tennae moving, while it is also moving on an assigned path. Composite objects
are those that we identify most with living forms. You must be knowledgeable
about Linking methods in Bryce 3D to make full use of composite objects.

Stay away from composited primitives if possible, because they tend to do
strange things when used as animated objects, like flipping object parts around
on their own. The best composite objects you can work with in an animation
are those that have been imported as either 3D Studio or WaveFront (OBJ) formats. DXFs work well as animated objects, too, aside from their uncorrectable
faceted look (which you may like), but there are sometimes problems in the way
that DXF objects are grouped when they are imported. This leads to problems
with ungrouping and animated links. If you have a composite DXF object you

really like and need in a scene, the best thing to do is to import it into an application that can save it out again in a 3DS or OBJ object file format.

COMPOSITE SYMMETRICAL LATTICE OBJECTS

These objects represent the most complex objects that can be created inside Bryce 3D. Unlike Terrain objects, Symmetrical Lattice objects have no base plane to worry about or erase. Their top and bottom sections are perfectly matched. Using Elevation and Effects Brushes in the Terrain Editor, you can create extremely convoluted shapes for compositing into larger objects. The results are rather mechanical, so they work best when used to glue together parts for robotic figures and vehicles. The best thing about using the Terrain Editor and Symmetrical Lattice objects as elements for 3D animated actors is that there is no need to use Boolean operations to shape holes (unless you want to do that in addition to what the Elevation Brush offers). It is more common to Group parts of a Symmetrical Lattice composite together than to Link them, as long as no animation is needed within the object itself. If you do require animated parts (flapping wings or moving appendages), then select to Link the parts.

To create Symmetrical Lattice objects with organic folded skin, use the Erode operation on them.

Load the SymLat1.br3 and SymLat2.br3 projects from the CD-ROM, and animate both of the objects in Figure 9.5. If you find render times too long, try replacing the materials with simple colors. Pay special attention to the Linking on the movable figure.

LINKING AND GROUPING COMPOSITES

The rule, as previously stated, is simple. If the composite object is to have moving parts, then use Linking to attach the moving elements. All non-moving parts can be Grouped. In general, Grouped objects have more stable behavior than Linked objects, but each composite object has to be judged on its own. The placement of the Origin Point is absolutely vital for Linking, since that determines the fulcrum point that the moving element relates to.

Extremely Important! When you need to clone a Linked chain of objects, select just the main Parent, and use Copy/Paste. Then you can rename the cloned parts to keep everything clear. Using other methods to clone Linked hierarchies will result in skewed and distorted elements.

FIGURE   *On the top is a Symmetrical Lattice grouped object, and on the bottom is a*
9.5   *Linked object in several views, composed of Symmetrical Lattice parts.*

NOTE

Very Important! Note that grouped elements have no accessible Origin Points. To move a grouped element in a composite object, first Link it to a sphere as Parent to act as a ball joint and then rotate the sphere.

COMPOSITE OBJECTS AND STANDARD PATHS

There are few special rules that apply to composite objects that don't apply as well to singular objects. The only caution is that composite objects may have their own moving parts that have nothing to do with the path of the composited whole. One of the best ways to handle this is to create the animated composite object first and save it out as a complete object, including the necessary Timeline information that tells the object what to move and when. When you load it in and alter its rotation, size, or position in the standard path creation manner, you can increase the size of the animation and use the Repeat or Pendulum functions to make the animated object repeat its internal movement while also moving on a path (a common procedure for walking and other motions).

COMPOSITE OBJECTS AND RIBBON PATHS

There are no special rules for Linking a composite object to a Ribbon Path that are not covered in the standard path concerns above.

COMPOSITE OBJECT ANIMATION TIPS

- Group the parts together when you are designing a Composite object that has no moving parts, like a spaceship. If the object does have moving parts (like the tires of a pickup truck), Link those parts to the whole.
- Pay attention to where you place the Origin Point when Linking one element of a Composite object to the whole.
- Choose one main Parent as the central element when designing a Composite object with moving parts. This is normally the torso on humanoid and most animal forms. This is the element that must be keyframed when the object is to be rotated, scaled, or repositioned on a path. It controls the global rotation, global resizing, and global re-positioning of the object and all Linked Child objects.
- When Linking elements of a Composite object together, it is essential that you use spheres or cylinders as ball joint parents between the moving elements. To link these elements directly is guaranteed to cause unwanted shearing and warping of the elements.

Boolean Object Animations

Boolean animations are f/x-oriented animations and stand out as a completely separate animation category. In a Boolean animation, an invisible force seems to be present in the animation, causing objects to magically disappear and reappear. There are two types of Boolean animations in Bryce 3D: Negative/Positive and Intersecting. Each creates a unique effect.

There is one major rule for configuring all Boolean objects and animation elements: Create all of the separate elements first, and tag them as Booleans in the object's Attributes dialog; following that, group all of the items together that will participate as either object or animation elements.

NEGATIVE/POSITIVE BOOLEAN ANIMATIONS

A typical Negative/Positive Boolean animation shows a Negative Boolean drilling a hole in a Positive Boolean object. This is interesting, but like any f/x, it grows tiring and anticipated after one or two showings. In order to spice up your Negative/Positive Boolean animations, here are some suggestions for creating variations on the theme:

- Use a variety of forms as negative components. Cubes, Cones, Spheres, Rods, and other forms add interest because the holes they drill change size and shape as the animation progresses.
- Stagger a group of Negative Booleans so that as one hole is part way through, another is just beginning.

- Use multiple Negative and Positive Booleans in more complex choreographies, so that unexpected interactions take place.
- Rotate the Positive element(s) so that the viewer sees a hole being started on one end of an object and also sees the exiting negative on the other end afterwards.

INTERSECTING BOOLEAN ANIMATIONS

Intersecting Boolean animations do the opposite of Negative/Positive types. They too require a Positive Boolean partner or partners, but the Positive object(s) remain hidden until the Intersecting object displays all or part of them. The animated result is stranger, because it reveals something in the 3D world not visible before.

LINKING AND GROUPING BOOLEANS

All of the components that are to take part in a Boolean animation have to be grouped, just as they are in a Boolean object. In fact, you can take any Boolean object and instantly make it into an animation. Simply move the parts closer or farther from each other over time, or rotate or resize them, keyframing as you go.

Do not Link elements in a Boolean Group to each other, as this will ungroup elements in the group, and destroy the Boolean construct. If you do this by mistake, you may have to clear the screen and start over, since the elements may not be reconfigurable.

CAUTION

You can Link the entire group to an object not in the group however.

BOOLEAN OBJECTS AND STANDARD PATHS

There are no special rules for creating animation paths with Boolean objects. Any member of a Boolean group can be repositioned, resized, or rotated over time and keyframed to form an animated sequence. It is only the interactions of the members within the Boolean group that will cause Boolean interactions to be displayed as the animation progresses.

BOOLEAN OBJECTS AND RIBBON PATHS

As above, no special considerations need be cautioned when using Boolean Groups on a Ribbon Path.

WHEN TO USE BOOLEAN ANIMATION TECHNIQUES

Here are some project ideas that give you some sense of where Boolean animations might serve useful.

- **Beam-me-up/Beam-me-down.** Using a light source with a visible beam pointed at an object that sits on the ground, you can use a Negative/Positive Boolean animation to make the object seem to be vaporized in the beam. Using an Intersect Boolean method would work to make an object suddenly materialize out of thin air.
- **Laser-cutter.** Shine a column light on an area of an object and use a Negative/Positive Boolean to cut a hole where the beam makes contact.
- **Set the table.** Design a dishes and utensils setting that sits on a table. Group each place setting as Positive Booleans, along with a Negative Boolean object large enough to cover each. In an animation, slowly move the Negative Booleans to reveal the settings slowly materializing.
- **Flicker-flames.** Wherever you use flames that need to be animated, whether from a candle wick or the nozzle of a rocket engine, think about using Boolean interactions. If you make the flame object Positive and group it with a Negative Boolean, you can control the size and seeming flicker of the flame over time.
- The strangest animated results can be generated when you use all three Boolean types in one group: Positive, Negative, and Intersecting. Imagine that the computer is calculating that the Positive object can only be seen when it is covered by the Intersecting object, but the Negative object wants to hide it at the same time. You will find that size wins out. If the Intersecting or Negative shell is larger than the other, it will affect the Positive object in a dominant manner at those junctures. Experiment with this technique. At the very least, your animation will be unique.

Be sure to view the Citbool1 and Citbool2 animations on the CD-ROM. They display some of what can be expected from Negative/Positive and Intersecting Boolean animations.

NOTE

THE CAMERA DRILL

Here is a perfect use for Negative/Positive Boolean techniques. Do the following.

1. Create a series of five Cubes that are lined up in front of the Camera, so that the closest one hides the rest. Color each of the cubes with a different hue. Reshape the Cubes so that each one is wider and longer than it is deep, and separate them by a space equal to their depth. Make each of them Positive Booleans.

2. Place a Cone primitive in the scene so that its apex faces in the same di-

rection as the Camera. Make it a Negative Boolean and Group it with all of the resized rectangles. This Cone is our drill.

3. As seen from the top view, place the camera just inside of the base of the Cone. Do not Link or otherwise Group it. Place a Spotlight in front of the Camera (100% intensity and fade, with Linear drop-off, and colored as you like). Link the Spotlight to the Camera. This is like the lamp on a miner's hat, lighting the hole that the Cone drills.

4. Now this is very important. If you were to Link the Camera to the Cone drill, it would warp, due to the rotation and resizing of the Cone. From the top view (or the Right or Left view) select just the Cone from the Group (Control/Click after selecting the Group). With the Cone selected, shift-select the Camera. Now the Camera, Cone drill, and Spotlight will move as one, as long as you use the position controls and not the mouse to move this group of objects.

5. Place some sort of treasure scene beyond the walls, so that when the hole breaks through, the camera has something to look at. Start the animation with the camera behind all of the walls and end it at a point where the Camera drill breaks through, and you can only see the treasure. This same technique can be used to drill through a mountain or any other "solid" object. If you want to see textures as the drill goes along, it is best used with Volumetric objects, as long as you are aware that this takes up a lot of rendering time. See Figures 9.6 and 9.7.

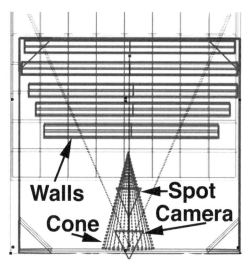

Walls **←Spot**

Cone **Camera**

FIGURE *This is a top view of the Camera drill project.*
9.6

FIGURE *The Camera drill moves through a series of walls to reveal the treasure on the*
9.7   *other side*

See the Camdrl.br3 project on the CD-ROM, and the Camdrl animation.

THE MOVING PEN

The "moving pen" animation is a standard in the industry. Basically, it shows a moving pen, pencil, or brush that seems to be magically writing as it moves with no hand attached. This animation is a perfect place to use Boolean Intersections in Bryce 3D, since what is displayed is at first hidden. Simply create the "message" first and make it a Positive Boolean object. Next create your writing implement. As it passes over selected parts of the message, use an Intersection Boolean, grouped with the message, to display the text.

Moving On

In this chapter, we have investigated a number of ways that Singular, Composite, and Boolean objects can be animated using paths, both standard and Ribbon. The next chapter is the last in the animation section of the book, and it involves your mastery of the Bryce 3D Motion lab.

CHAPTER

10 Mastering the Advanced Motion Lab

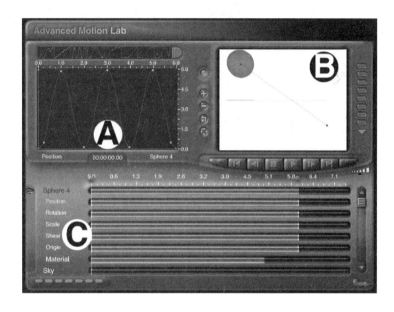

The Advanced Motion Lab is the third special editing screen in Bryce 3D. It customizes animations like the Materials Lab and the Terrain Editor address materials and terrain objects. The Advanced Motion Lab has animation controls for every aspect of your Bryce 3D world. Because the Advanced Motion Lab represents the final step in customizing your Bryce 3D animations, it is fitting that this is the final chapter in the animation section of the book.

Although you can input some parameters for controlling your animations in the Animation tab in an object's Attributes dialog and also by selective keyframing (accessed by holding down the plus or minus buttons), it is far better to do all of your animation fine-tuning in the Advanced Motion Lab. This is because everything is at your fingertips, and you are presented with an instant preview of any alterations made. There are also animation tools here that can be found nowhere else.

Mastering the Interface

The Advanced Motion Lab is activated when you click on its icon in the Animation Palette (Figure 10.1).

It is important for both experienced and new Bryce users to spend some time getting acclimated to the new options presented in the Advanced Motion Lab interface, as shown in Figure 10.2.

MOTION WAVE ASSIGNMENTS

This is the central control feature, the heart of the Advanced Motion Lab. By clicking on any of the wave thumbnails, that particular wave shape is placed on the screen below. From there, you can move the shape's control points to re-shape it, or use the pencil tool that appears when the mouse is over a non-shape area to draw your own wave. All customized wave shapes can be saved to an empty slot in the thumbnail section simply by clicking on that empty slot.

FIGURE *The Advanced Motion Lab icon.*
10.1

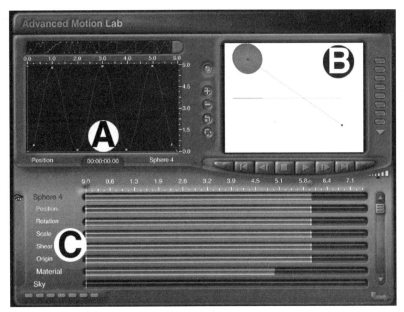

FIGURE   *The Advanced Motion Lab interface has three basic sections: (A) Motion Wave*
10.2   *Assignments, (B) Preview/Playback Screen, and (C) Object/Item Selection*

Each wave shape determines the movement of the selected object or item feature over time. The bottom border of the shape shows the selected item's attribute at the start of the animation, while the top border is the last frame of the animation. The left-right parameter shows the time from the first to last frame. A non-customized wave shape would be a straight diagonal line that travels from bottom left to upper right. This would cause the selected object or item attribute to move from whatever setting you dictated at the start of the animation smoothly to its targeted attribute at the end of the animation. If, for instance, an object's color was set as red at the start of the animation and blue at the end, setting this default wave shape would show a steady movement from red to blue as the animation progressed.

Understanding at a glance what different wave shapes force an attribute to do is necessary for the mastery of Motion Wave Assignments. Let's take our previous example. What if you wanted an object's color to move evenly from red to blue back to red in an animation, although you only assigned it red at the start and blue at the end? Do you have to re-assign the colors all over again? No. You simply have to apply the appropriate motion wave in the object's color attribute channel. In this case, the proper motion wave would be a smooth curve that started at the lower left (the object's color channel assigned to red), moved at the middle of the animation to the top (the object's color channel equated with the assigned blue color), and finished at the lower right (back to red again). Any attribute listed in the object's attributes channels could be played with in the same manner.

Understanding Motion Wave Shapes

Remember that Motion Waves can only customize attributes that have at least two set keyframes in an animation, assigned normally while you are creating the animation. The Advanced Motion Lab may therefore be thought of as a secondary or post-creation process.

With a little exploration and time spent in the Advanced Motion Lab, you will begin to see exactly how the shape you import or create will affect the selected object or item attribute. Starting with the default assignment, the straight diagonal line that moves from lower left to upper right, you can learn to "see" time. Here are some pointers to observe:

- If lowest points assign starting attribute conditions to the selected object or item, and the topmost point assigns a targeted state, then points in the middle of any line or curve indicate a blend of the two conditions. In our example of color animation used above, a midpoint would force the object to be a blend of red and blue.
- Vertical lines force the object to move very quickly between the assigned attributes. In the case of colors for instance, straight vertical lines in your wave shape will cause them to flash. Many vertical lines in the wave shape will cause the attributes to change quickly and repeatedly.
- Straight horizontal lines in your wave shape will cause the selected attribute to remain stable at that state. In our color example, for instance, a horizontal line at the middle of the wave would cause the object to remain at a set red-blue color for the amount of time indicated by the length of the horizontal line.
- Small fluctuations in a motion wave will cause the selected object attribute to fluctuate between the lower and upper points of the smaller curve. Assigned to a color attribute, an object or light would flash just a bit. Assigned to a brightness attribute, a light would dim and brighten. Assigned to a position attribute, an object or item would take steps back and forth, though moving gradually towards a targeted position. All other attributes would be treated in a similar manner.

- If you go past the vertical when moving control points, the curve will be reshaped as a smooth curve containing the points of the vertical line. This prevents a non-allowed time reversal.

PREVIEW/PLAYBACK SCREEN

The Preview/Playback screen allows you to preview whatever adjustments you are making to the animation. The VCR controls below are the same as those you have grown accustomed to in the Animation palette, the Terrain Editor, and the Materials Lab.

OBJECT/ITEM SELECTION OPTIONS

Three categories are listed here: selected objects, Sky, and Sun. Each of the three can be expanded by simply clicking on its name in the list. Object options are included for every animated object in your scene, including the camera and any lights. The parameters of a selected item must be animated, so that the way the animation unfolds can be tweaked in the Advanced Motion Lab. If an object's position, for instance, is not animated over time but its rotation is, then you can only customize its animated rotation in the Advanced Motion Lab. All animated attributes can be reconfigured in the Advanced Motion Lab.

Object Attribute Options

Using the Advanced Motion Lab Motion Curves "in the Motion Graph", you can alter the selected Object's Position, Rotation, Scale, Shear, Origin, or Material by selecting that attribute in the Object/Item list (letter C in Figure 10.2).

Material Attribute Options

When you need to alter an Object's Material, a separate Attribute list becomes available. You can alter every item in the material's Color, Value, and Optics channel attributes. As you might expect, all of the attributes in a volumetric material's attributes can be customized as well.

Camera Attribute Options

The camera attributes that can be Motion Graph influenced in the Advanced Motion Lab include Position, Origin, Rotation, Banking, Focal Length, Pan XY, and Zoom XY.

Light Attribute Options

If your selected object is a light, the following attributes can be animation-tweaked in the Advanced Motion Lab: Position, Rotation, Scale, Shear, Origin, Color, and Intensity.

SKY OPTIONS

Remember that Sky options are keyframed when nothing else is selected in your scene. There are thirty-four sky attributes that can be animation-customized in the Advanced Motion Lab by applying or creating a Motion Graph. You could also do this by assigning multiple keyframes from the Sky&Fog palette, but it would take a lot longer. All you need to access these parameters in the Advanced Motion Lab is to have assigned a beginning and ending keyframe in the animation. These include: Sky Level, Cumulous Color, Stratus Color, Cover, Amplitude, Frequency, Base Color, Horizontal Color, Dome Color, Def Color, Shadow Intensity, Ambient Color, Ambient Intensity, Haze Color, Haze Amount, Fog Color, Fog Density, Fog Amount, Moon Angle, Earthshine, Moon Tilt, Moon Hardness, Illusion Max, Link Color Blend, Link Value Blend, Ring Intensity, Ring 1 Width, Ring 2 Width, Rainbow Visibility, Rainbow 1 Width, Rainbow 2 Width, Visible Air, Wind Direction, Wind Speed, Wind Turbulence.

SUN OPTIONS

Using the Advanced Motion Lab and a Motion Wave, you can alter the Sun's Color, Intensity, Disc and Halo colors, and Direction.

COMPLICATED MOTION SANDWICHES

This is one of the most important methods that you can use Bryce 3D to co-operatively alter the movements of your animated objects, camera, and/or lights. This method involves the Animation Setup dialog, the Animation tab settings from the Attributes dialog, and the Advanced Motion Lab. All three of these setup areas can work together to influence how selected objects move in your Bryce 3D world. The order in which you do things however, is vital. Your priority should be:

1. Length of animation setting in the Animation Setup dialog.
2. Animation tab of the object's Attributes dialog.
3. Return to length of animation setting in the Animation Setup dialog.
4. Advanced Motion Lab settings.

Here's why this order of operation is important. Let's say you have a sphere on the screen that is to be animated. The movement it goes through is determined to be 1 second long at 15 FPS. You would first set that animation length in the Animation Setup dialog. Next, the sphere would be moved on whatever path you create from its initial frame to the last frame.

Following that, with the object selected, you would open its Attributes dialog and go to the Animation tab. There, you might click on Make Pendulum. If it takes one second for the sphere to traverse from its initial position to its end position, Make Pendulum means that it will take two seconds for it to travel from the target position back to the source. But with only 1 second as the length of the animation so far, the sphere has just enough time to travel only once from source to target, so we have to lengthen the animation.

We open the Animation Setup dialog again, and this time make the animation 8 seconds long. How will this affect the sphere? Well, since we have Make Pendulum checked, and since it will take the sphere 2 seconds to make one pendulum swing from source to target and back again, it will repeat this process four times (8 ÷ 2) for the length of the animation.

And now to complicate the issue even more. With all of the above done, we bring the lozenge on the Timeline back to the start of the animation and open the Advanced Motion Lab. The sphere is listed there as whatever name you have given it. Clicking on that name opens up all of the sphere's attributes for animation. Since all we have done is to change the sphere's position, we click on the sphere's Position tab. In the Motion Graph display, a straight diagonal line is shown. This means that the sphere is set to move from its initial position to its end position over the length of the animation, even though the Make Pendulum option is not indicated on the graph.

Selecting the triple sine wave graph will force the chosen attribute of the sphere, its position, to move from initial to target position back and forth six times in the animation. Since Pendulum is already indicated in the object's own Attributes dialog, this means the pendulum effect will also be multiplied. This makes the object move faster between the initial and target points eighteen times during the animation (3 × 6). Why eighteen? The first number 3 is the number of times it would have moved anyway, due to the Pendulum setting. The 6 used as a multiplier comes from the Motion Graph applied to whatever is happening on the sphere's path during the animation, in this case three sine waves. Each sine wave, however, will move the sphere twice, once on the upward curve and once on the downward curve.

If you read this and remain confused, the only (and best) way to get a clear idea of what is going on is to explore the possibilities by doing the project in Bryce 3D. There are infinite variations, depending on the length of the animation, an object's Animation attributes, and the quality of the Motion Graph applied in the Advanced Motion Lab.

Important! If you have multiple objects in your animated scene that need to be targeted for more complex movements as in the above example, their initial movements should be set before the final animation length is set so they repeat according to the final Advanced Motion Lab settings.

Suggested Projects to Explore

The following project ideas are not contained on the CD-ROM as examples, but are left up to you to explore. All make use of the options possible in the Advanced Motion Lab. The solution will be given, but you will have to explore the uses of the Advanced Motion Lab processes to create the steps to get to the solution.

PULSAR

A pulsar is a star that pulses in brightness and sometimes in color as well. The solution is based upon altering the Sun's color and brightness attributes.

PISTON

A piston is an object that moves up and down on an attached rod. The solution in creating a piston motion cycle is in the application of the piston's position attribute.

PENDULUM

A pendulum swings back and forth on an attached line. Over time, the pendulum's swing deteriorates because of friction and other forces. The pendulum can be made to deteriorate by adjusting the shape of the curve used to address the lines rotation in the Advanced Motion Lab.

CANNON BALL

A projectile shot from a muzzle has a trajectory that is defined by the force of ejection and the way that gravity pulls on the mass of the projectile. This changes the projectile's path in space. The force works to fire the projectile in a straight line at its maximum height, but gravity seeks to bring it to the ground. By adjusting the projectile's position over time in the Advanced Motion Lab, you can alter its animated motion curve.

Hint: Start the motion curve as a horizontal straight line to represent the minimal lack of gravity.

PUTT-PUTT

A vehicle may exhibit a start-and-stop motion when it's running out of gas or in other trouble, though it may eventually reach its destination. By programming stop points in an animation in the Advanced Motion Lab, you can achieve this effect.

Hint: Using short horizontal straight lines in the motion curve stops motion intermittently.

TIP

DUAL STATE

Some objects look good as a blend of two diverse materials, remaining that way over time. Create an object that is a blend of wood and glass, without blending the materials in the Materials Lab.

SCHIZO-CLOUDS

For a strange effect, clouds can reverse their movement across the sky a number of times in an animation. Use the Sky item in the Advanced Motion Lab to create this effect.

WALK CYCLES

One of the most challenging animations to set up is an animated walk cycle. Using the Advanced Motion Lab, you need only set up the start and end points of the cycle to generate the entire animated result.

This project is actually included on the CD-ROM for your study and evaluation, though you may wish to create it on your own first. Then your work can be compared to the way it is done on the referenced project. The project is called Sym-Lat3.br3 on the CD-ROM. The animation is also on the CD-ROM as Runz1.

NOTE

Moving On

In this chapter, the last of the animation section of the book, we have explored the Advanced Motion Lab. You should continue to explore this new Bryce 3D feature until you feel comfortable concerning its use. The next section of the book is devoted to solving advanced problems in Bryce 3D animations.

SECTION III

Advanced Topics

This section of the book assumes that you have worked through and have accumulated an understanding of the topics covered in Sections I and II, as well as the Bryce 3D documentation. The chapters in this section push your project options a little further, and also allow you to create more complex Bryce 3D worlds.

CHAPTER

11

Wrong Materials for the Right Reasons

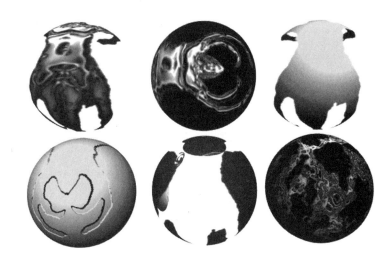

On the Way to Personalization

An artist needs to know all of the rules when working with any media. As a computer artist and animator, you need to know how to use your computer, from how to turn it on to how to load software. As a Bryce 3D user, you need to read the documentation thoroughly, so you are aware of what to do when the creative idea hits you. But there is another reason for learning the rules when it comes to working within media constraints: You need to know the rules so you can creatively break them when the time comes.

This is especially true when it comes to customizing and applying materials. If you use only the materials you are "supposed to"—those most logical for the task—then how will your work differ from everyone else's? It won't, and your work will have no discernible signature of originality. This is actually the central criticism leveled at computer art, because it is seen as the programmer's signature, not the artist's. Bryce 3D is no exception to this, especially since it's so easy to accomplish basic tasks. Click on a sky parameter, and the sky is painted in. Place primitive objects in the scene, and they magically appear. Without a little stretching of the rules, it won't matter who is responsible for the resulting artwork, you, another person, or the computer itself.

But every time you spend part of your creative juices on customizing the components of a scene, you start to develop work that bears the mark of your own mind and hand. That is why Bryce 3D is such a massive creative tool. You are given every opportunity to stray from the expected path and to mark the resulting work with your personal signature. The objects that you create, the way you compose them in space and time, and the global parameters of your scenes—all of these play a part in your personal artistic watermark. One area especially stands out in Bryce 3D as having the potential for customization: materials.

Creating Customized Materials

At the start of your Bryce 3D experience, you will probably be in a hurry to see your rendered worlds. Some of the more subtleties aspects and options may be passed over in a rush to render. But as you become more familiar with how fast you can do the basics, the subtitles may start to attract you, and you will spend more time tweaking the smaller points. In our visit to the Materials Lab (Chapter 4), we have already explored the ways that materials can be composed through the use of multiple channels and even customized further by using a channel's Deep Texture Editing and Picture Editor processes. Perhaps you have already attempted some materials creation on your own, and you may even have a personal library that contains hundreds of your own material creations.

Let's delve further into some generalities, before pushing the topic to a more specific and unique creative edge.

SURFACE MATERIALS CREATION TIPS

When you are creating Surface materials on your own, here are some points to take note of:

- Think of Ambient as "glow." Ambient color will act as a glow color, especially when the object is placed against a dark backdrop. Any part of the object that is in a shadow, even a self-shadow, will show the Ambient color, while the part of the object that remains in the light will show the Diffuse color. If the Ambient Value is taken from an assigned channel texture, then that texture will glow whenever the object is in the dark or shadow. If you are using a pattern from a channel texture, keep the Ambience value related to the value and the Ambient Color related to the color palette. This gives you a patterned texture that will be visible in both light and dark environments.

- As a general rule, keep a texture size set from 0 to 10 if you want to see the details of the texture. Larger sizes are good for effects, but look very speckled when used on small objects or when animated (especially without antialiasing).

- Multi-color patterns (like RGB Fabric) can behave better in the light and dark by attaching both the Diffuse and Ambient color to the channel texture, while leaving the Value set to the color palette.

- Keep Ambience value to 50% or less when applying a deep Bumpmap (50–100%), or the Ambience will wash out the Bumpmap shadowing. See Figure 11.1.

- Any smooth metallic texture looks like worn metal when you assign a Bumpmap from an appropriate texture channel.

NOTE

If you add the Bumpmap referenced in Figure 11.2 in an animation, with 0% at the start and 100% at the end, the object will look like it is being blistered by heat. A great use for this would be a ring of rocks too close to a departing rocket.

- Set the Ambient color to a darker hue (dark blue or even black) to preserve the underlying texture pattern, even when the Ambience value is set at 100%.

- With transparency set to 100% and all other sliders set to 0%, the color of the transparent object will be a blend of its Transparent Color and the Volume Color. Moving the Diffusion value slider up at this point adds

FIGURE
11.1
On the left, the Ambience is set to 30%, while on the right it is set to 100%. In both cases, the Bumpmap is set to 100%. Keep the Ambience setting low to emphasize the Bumpmap.

the Diffuse Color to the blended mix. Setting the Transparent Color to black effectively makes an object opaque, no matter what the other colors are set to.

- There may be a time when you want to turn on an object in the dark as if it were a light. This can be done with or without textures in the Ambient Color channel, since the Ambient Color will represent the light as a color or a texture. All you have to do is to set the Ambience Value to 100% and use the Transparency Optics slider as the "light switch." The higher the transparency setting, the dimmer the object light, so at a transparency of 100% the light will be invisible. Material Options should be set to blend Transparency.

FIGURE
11.2
On the left is the default gold metallic material, while on the right it has been modified by adding a texture channel Bump Height map (the texture used was BlackWhite from the Basic folder in the Materials Lab).

VOLUMETRIC MATERIALS CREATION TIPS

NOTE

Be very careful about applying volumetric materials to large objects, as this will send rendering time through the roof. As a caution, make objects mapped with volumetric materials no more than 15% of your total screen size, especially for animations.

When you are creating Volumetric materials on your own, here are some points to take note of:

- Multiple layered volumetric materials can be used as layers with holes in them by controlling the material's Base Density. These are best used unanimated since the rendering times are very high. Make sure shadowing is on to increase the depth perception of the layers.
- Do not push the Quality/Speed slider all the way to the left or you will be in danger of hanging up your system because the preview render will take too much time.
- Setting the Fuzzy factor to zero produces the most brilliant texture colors.
- By simply switching from Surface to Volume in the Materials Lab, all of your procedural surface materials can become volumetric.
- Use Flat Shaded Volumetrics for layered objects with holes in them and Full Shaded Volumetrics if you are going to move the camera through them. See Figure 11.3.

BITMAP MATERIALS CREATION TIPS

The first step in creating interesting materials that utilize bitmap pictures is to create or customize interesting bitmap pictures in your paint application. In

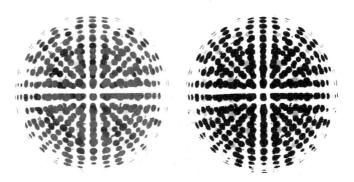

FIGURE
11.3
The same volumetric material appears flat shaded on the left and full shaded on the right. Full Shading creates 3D material pieces, but rendering times are much longer.

general, they should be defaulted to 72 DPI for use in Bryce 3D, with a size of 640 × 480 or 430 × 240. Use the larger size when the camera is going to zoom in on the material, and use the smaller size when the material will remain a backdrop element. You can use any DPI ratio, but 72 DPI will suffice in most cases. When you are creating bitmap-based materials on your own, here are some points to take note of:

- Except for cases in which the entire image, background included, is necessary for use in Bryce 3D, make sure to create an Alpha mask for the selected image area. The Alpha mask tells Bryce 3D which parts of the image are to be opaque and which parts are to be read as transparent. The way to create the Alpha mask is to select those parts of the image you want to use in Bryce 3D and remove the rest, substituting a solid white area, then saving the image to disk. Next, using the same image, make the selected area a solid black (RGB = 0, 0, 0). Save the image again with an Alpha name, perhaps as myimage1A. In Bryce 3D's Picture Editor, import the image and its Alpha equivalent for mapping to a selected object.

- If you are importing an image series into Bryce 3D for an animated sequence, each image should have its own Alpha image as well.

- Bitmap images will tile when you use any mapping but the Random option if they are resized to address the object more than once. The higher or lower you alter their size in the Materials Lab, the larger or smaller the tiles will be.

- Using Random Mapping with a bitmap creates color patterns from the bitmap that can substitute for similar procedural texture looks. This works best if the image is constrained to no more than four hues, since more colors result in a random dot pattern (unless you are looking for a random dot pattern, of course).

Alpha Stand-alones

An Alpha image is a mask, and it does not have to have an accompanying cloned color image to be a valuable tool in the creation of a material. It can also serve to mask out an underlying procedural texture, or a totally different bitmap image. In this way, you can create bitmapped areas on an object (like labels and other effects), mapped over another bitmap or a procedural textured material. See Figure 11.4 and 11.5.

NOTE

See the Alpha1.br3 project on the CD-ROM.

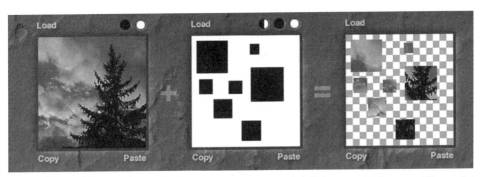

FIGURE **11.4** *The color image was loaded on the left and the rectangular Alpha image in the center. The result is an image that displays parts of the color image inserted in rectangular areas, as shown in Figure 11.5.*

Placing the Bitmap in a Channel

Normally, the Bitmap picture activates the Diffuse Color channel, so that all of the color data in the image comes through. There are more options than this, however. The following figure shows the bitmap image attached to different channels on the Material Editor. See Figure 11.6.

Bitmap Logos

There is no reason that your bitmapped picture material can't be your personal or corporate logo. Tile mapped logos are a rage on the Web, used most often for

FIGURE **11.5** *The Alpha masked image shown in Figure 11.4 inserted in a Bryce 3D scene, wrapped on a sphere with a color sphere inside.*

FIGURE **11.6** *The same bitmap image as addressed to the following channel attributes: Diffuse (Transparency = 100%), Ambient, Transparent, Bump, Reflection, and Diffuse Random.*

FIGURE **11.7** *A plane tiled with bitmapped logos casts shadows on another plane below, mapped with a procedural texture material.*

a page backdrop. Using the bitmap techniques already described, you can create infinite logo backdrops in Bryce 3D.

BITMAP-PROCEDURAL COMBINATION MATERIALS CREATION TIPS

This material effect uses a bitmap picture in one or more Color, Value, or Optics channels (Surface) in the Materials Lab. When you are creating bitmap-procedural mixed materials on your own, here are some points to take note of:

- The most common way to fold in the bitmap is in the diffuse color channel, since this allows you to get all of the color from the image. Another suggested alternative is to apply the bitmap as a bumpmap, especially if it is composed of an image that can be recognized in silhouette. This creates an embossed effect and is especially attractive when tiled.
- The cloned object method allows you to paste the bitmap to a clone of the original object that is just a few percent larger than the original object. This makes the bumpmapped image look like a solid cutout above the object. See Figure 11.8.
- The multiple channel method allows you to mix procedural and bitmapped textures in one material, so the effect is a blend rather than a segmented layering. This is what was done in Figure 11.9, using the following parameters: Channel A and B are activated for Diffuse Color and Diffusion value. Channel B is also activated for Ambient Color and Ambience Value. Channel A holds the bitmap image (the LEO picture), which is mapped Object Front. Channel B holds the galaxy texture from the Basics library. Diffusion and Ambience sliders are set at 100%.

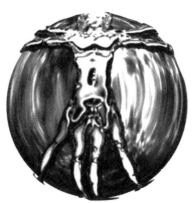

FIGURE **11.8** *This bitmapped object is mapped to a clone of the original object, sized a few percentage points larger. Notice its 3D appearance, especially at the edges.*

FIGURE *An example of multiple channel mapping.*
11.9

To explore Figure 11.9 further, load the Bmapx2.br3 project from the CD-ROM.

NOTE

LAMINATES

Exotic Laminates

True laminated materials present a different problem. A laminate is a combination of two materials, both of which must be present on the object. You cannot create two different materials in Bryce 3D using just the Materials Lab, so another way has to be found to do this. The elegant solution incorporates the use of the Advanced Motion Lab. Here's how:

1. Select one material, or create one, for frame 1 of an animation (animation length is your choice), and map it to an object. Select or create a second material for the last frame.
2. Open the Advanced Motion Lab with the object selected. Find the object in the list, and click on Material. For all of the parameters listed under material, draw a straight horizontal line midway in the Motion Curve area. This effectively blends the two materials into one for the entire animation.

Use this technique to create the following exotic laminates: Double Wood, Wood-Stone, Double Stone, Cloud-Stone, Water-Cloud, Water-Stone, Rock-Psychedelic, Mirror-Wood, Cloud-Metal, and more. See Figure 11.10.

NOTE

Animated Laminates

The difference between animated laminates and the stable laminates covered above is that the line you draw in the Motion Curve area of the Advanced Mo-

FIGURE   *From upper left to bottom right, these exotic laminates blend Rock and Wood,*
11.10   *Red Fractal and Vortex, Carnival Tent and Clown Collar, and Gilded Cage*
　　　　and Disco Kelp.

tion Lab should have a slight slope to it, between 10% and 15%. This will keep
the flavor of the laminated material throughout the animation, while causing it
to fluctuate a small amount.

MULTIPLES OF ONE

I have called this effect "Multiples of One" because you need only one material
mapped to a selected object to achieve this effect. This effect allows you to max-
imize the variability of one assigned material by using it up to four times in different ways in each of the four (ABCD) channels in the Materials Lab. Do the
following:

1. Place a sphere in your scene and select it. Open the Materials Lab.
2. Activate the A, B, and C channels for Diffuse and Ambient Color, and
   Diffusion and Ambience value (click on channel C for these attributes
   with Shift/Control held down). Activate the D channel for Bump
   height.
3. Use only one texture of your choice in all four channels. Vary the size, rotation, and mapping type in each channel. You now have a four-layered
   material that is based upon different elements of the same texture. See
   Figure 11.11.

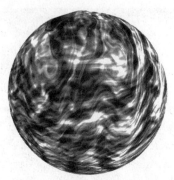

FIGURE **11.11** *Startling material maps can result when you use the same material configured in different ways in each of the four ABCD channels in the Materials Lab, like this quadruple mapping of the Abalone texture from the Psychedelic folder. Each channel can also be independently animated, producing complex layered movements.*

Investigate Figure 11.11 further by loading the Mthr_prl.br3 project from the CD-ROM, and viewing the Mthr_prl animation.

Employing the Creative Mistake

Why would you want to use the "wrong" materials on an object in the first place? There are two reasons. The first is that the "wrong" material might have a more "right" look than the "right" material. Let's take a simple case in point. Bryce 3D features both a Terrain/Plane materials library and a Rocks/Stones library. Placing material on a mountain, however, especially on the foreground, may work better if you use a Rocks/Stones material than one meant specifically for terrain. The Rocks/Stones material may display a more realistic and discernible texture at some distances than the "right" material from the Terrain materials choices.

The second reason that might make you at least explore assigning the "wrong" material, however, is more personal. It may be that a certain material expresses your compositional and aesthetic needs more than a standard material. You may want to assign a cloud material to a solid in order to make the composition appear more ethereal or alien, or the opposite, assigning a metallic or rock material to a cloud plane. We will therefore incorporate both of these categories of use in our deliberations about the use of "wrong" materials.

USING THE WRONG MATERIALS FOR MORE REALITY

"Reality" is a nebulous affair at best. Reality can be a monster that lurks in your bedroom, until the light reveals a bundle of clothes draped over a chair. Reality is broken all of the time by what we perceive at the moment. If you have been taught that red is evil, then the most striking red sunset will have overtones of evil intent. Some aspects of perception are ingrained in us because of what we have been taught, so reality can depend upon mental and emotional attitudes as well. "Reality" also depends upon experience. You might discover that the swastika has a deep history as a symbol of transformation in Indian culture, but if your parents escaped the terror of the Nazis, the "real" nature of the swastika will be forever colored by the stories you were told and the horrors that the swastika of experience evokes. Reality is not a neutral ground, but is colored by suspicion, education, cultural bias, personal experience, and more.

How might all of this affect your work in Bryce 3D, when you are deciding what material looks to apply to an object? The answer might depend upon who you are doing your work for. If you are creating art or animation for a client, then you have to listen carefully to that client's critiques. If that person says that your "brick doesn't look like real brick," you have to find out what their definition of "real" brick means and reshape the composition accordingly. If the Bryce 3D work you are involved in is to bring your own vision to pass and the brick material you just rendered doesn't look or feel "real" enough for you, then your own exploration will continue until it does.

Knowing all of this means that some of the following suggested alterations for achieving greater reality or optional reality may not work for all of your perceptive needs. If these suggestions leave you feeling unsatisfied, then simply use this as a procedure for exploration and seek further for examples that satisfy you.

Simulating Materials Realism

"Materials realism" is a term invented by a sculptor friend of mine (Dave Huber) to indicate that the materials used in a sculpted piece are to be used as is and not painted. I am using it in a slightly different context to indicate that what a material's name is does not always determine its uses in a Bryce 3D composition. There is an alchemist's way of perception that also is used as the basis for this exploration, which is "like begets like." Keeping in mind all of the perceptual inconsistencies already discussed, there is one cardinal rule when you want to use the "wrong" materials in order to simulate an enhanced realism in your Bryce 3D work.

NOTE

The Cardinal Rule: When you need to assign a material to an object in your Bryce 3D world, do not read the names of the materials. Instead, look at their thumbnails and see which ones look like the real-world material you have in mind. Select them accordingly.

A General Cloud Formula

If you load a Cloud material from the Materials library, you will see that only its Bump Height and Transparency is allocated to a texture channel. The rest of the texture draws its look from color palette assignments, with both Diffusion and Ambience sliders set around 30%. This emphasizes the wispy nature of a cloud or smoke. The type is always set to fuzzy. If you follow these standard settings, you can apply more than the standard Cloud textures to the Bump and Transparency channels.

You can, for instance, apply a Rock texture, as long as you make sure it has Alpha and Bump attributes. Color doesn't matter, because clouds normally draw their color references from diffuse and ambient palette settings. If your alternate texture doesn't have bump and alpha attributes, just add them in the texture's Deep Texture Editor. See Figure 11.12.

Note that stand-alone "realistic" clouds in the Bryce 3D sky are normally addressed to spheres, distorted spheres, or grouped spheres. Stand-alone clouds also work great in an animation when you set them in motion so they cast shadows across a landscape.

"Realistic" Planets

Basically, just about any material wrapped to a sphere can be a planet, except perhaps a logo or other recognizable textures. However, some materials work better than others for this purpose, and many are not in the standard planetary categories (rocks and other terrains). What features does a material need to possess to be believable as a planetary texture, according to what we have been trained to expect of "reality"?

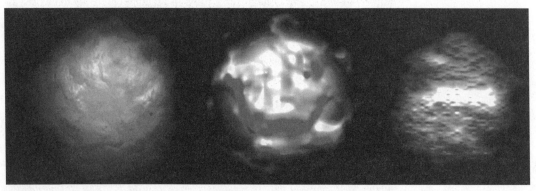

FIGURE *At the left is the Cloud texture LowSmog5 and in the middle is the Rock texture, StuccoBump. On the right is a*
11.12 *texture from the Bump folder, Polychrome Bump. All make interesting clouds.*

- It should fall into one of the three basic planetary classes: cratered, gas, or potentially "habitable" (by human-like creatures). Habitable planets look more believable if they have cloud-like atmospheres and also show some water areas.
- The features should not be too small, or the lack of detailed areas will detract from their believability.
- "Strange" anomalous features should be confined to smaller areas of the display (like the Red Spot on Jupiter). If stranger features dominate, they can detract from the believability factor. See Figure 11.13.

For Gas Planets, make the sphere a Fuzzy type.

If you want a planet to show the lights of civilization when it rotates into darkness, use an Ambient texture with small gridded artifacts to map its dark side. The Ambience elements will not show when the planet is in the light.

To create snowy poles on planets, embed spheres at the northern and southern hemispheres, and use a snowy material map.

FIGURE **11.13** *Here is a selection of planetary objects (left top to right bottom), created with the following "wrong" materials: Red Fractal, Mushrooms, Barnacles (Sand), Cliffy Sand, Foamy Water, and Bleached Wood (recolorized in the Deep Texture Editor).*

USING THE WRONG MATERIALS FOR A PERSONALIZED REALITY

Whose reality is it anyway? If you purchased Bryce 3D in order to simulate only what your camera sees on a summer afternoon on earth, you are missing a major part of the creative fun. As seen in the groundbreaking animated movie, "Planetary Traveler" from Third Planet Productions, Bryce is capable of more horizons than the one we see when we look out on our familiar world. Bryce 3D is also a tool for the surrealistic artist and animator. The goal of surrealism is to use seemingly identifiable elements to construct dream-like visions, and Bryce 3D (with a modicum of creative effort on your part) fits this role perfectly. Yes, you can use Bryce 3D to generate lovely animations that take you for a ride on the Colorado river, with the Grand Canyon rising up majestically on each side. But pushed just a bit further, you can also be riding on a lake of liquid mercury, past empty shards of lost civilizations. It is when you select the latter experience that your creation, customization, selection, and use of stranger more variable materials can come into play.

Simulating Materials Surrealism

There are no rules that will guide you in the application of surrealistic materials, only the persistence of your own visions and dreams. Some Bryce 3D users will move toward a radical materials approach, while others will prefer to subtly alter the materials in their scenes. In my experience, I find myself pushing materials towards radical variations, and then adjusting them until I feel satisfied that the scene looks and feels right. Exactly what "right" is eludes any verbal description, because each Bryce 3D world is so different.

Figure 11.14 Mapping Details

The three variations shown in Figure 11.14 are mapped as follows (from the top):

    A. Terrain = Office Building; Ground = Leopard; Figure = Mirror (Reflection turned down).

    B. Terrain = Green Bump Glass; Ground = GridRock; Figure = Water Puddles.

    C. Terrain = Dreams of Xanades Lake; Ground = Tyrell Building; Figure = Dali Bee Stripes.

The full color painting is on the CD-ROM as Bigscn1.TIF.

NOTE

FIGURE   *These scenes are based upon the same composition, with only the materials*
11.14   *differentiating the three. The materials give each variation a totally different*
          look and feel.

FIGURE **11.15** *This graphic shows two spheres, each mapped with the checkered texture. The top sphere is a little larger than the center sphere, and is partially transparent. The pattern is created by the moiré interaction of both textures, creating a moiré material look*

Moirés by Choice

In the traditional and desktop publishing world, everyone wants to avoid moirés. Moirés are the patterns that result when one halftone screen, made up of tiny dots, is placed at an angle above another halftone screen. The resulting pattern shows a tiled array of dots that detracts from the image being halftoned. You can use moirés in your Bryce 3D work to create some very interesting and hypnotic animated effects. While moirés in a printed graphic are distracting, moirés in an animation can prove quite interesting, resulting in shimmering surface features on the selected object. Here's an animated moiré experiment:

1. Create two spheres on the same center. Make one about 10% larger than the other.
2. Map both spheres with a 35% transparent checkered texture resized to 400%, and turn the outer sphere so that it does not have the same orientation as the inner one.
3. Animate just the outer sphere so it turns on its Y world axis, and watch as the moiré patterns interact. See Figure 11.15.

One way to enhance this material effect is to place a light or lights behind the object, and to darken the rest of the light in the scene.

Moving On

Hopefully, by reading and working through this chapter, your knowledge of and appreciation for customizing Bryce 3D materials has been extended. In the next chapter, we'll deal with the customized linking of Poser figure appendages.

A rendering from the Zland project from chapter 14.

Strange fish swimming up-stream.

A rendering from the Space-warp project from chapter 14.

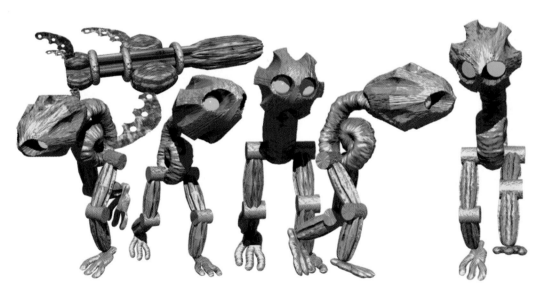

Animated figures modeled in Bryce 3D.

A Bryce 3D planetscape.

The approaching storm.

A Bryce 3D still life.

A rainbow lights the vault of the sky.

A selection of Bryce 3D rendered images.

More Bryce 3D rendered images.

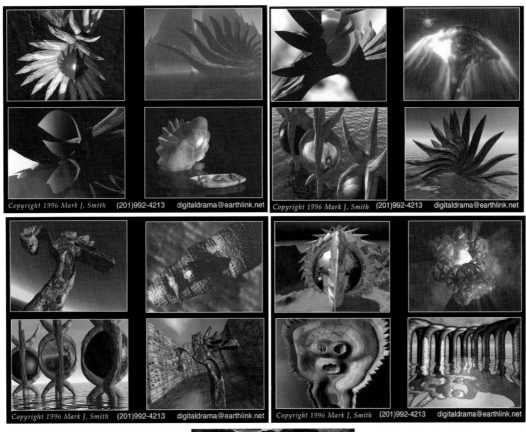

Copyright 1996 Mark J, Smith   (201)992-4213   digitaldrama@earthlink.net

The Bryce master work of Mark Smith.

The Bryce master work of Cecilia Ziemer.

CHAPTER

12 Advanced Animation Techniques

361

Animating Appendages

Whether you build creatures in Bryce 3D using available object primitives, import them from CD-ROM collections, or bring in Poser figures, you are going to be faced with Linking the parts so you can develop animated characters. Unless you Link the parts of an animated figure together in the correct fashion, all sorts of unpleasant warping and skewing of the parts will occur.

NOTE

Important! This material is absolutely vital for creating animations that include moving figures in Bryce 3D, and it is not referenced anywhere in the Bryce 3D documentation.

Mastering Animated Links

There is a new term that you should become familiar with, in order to optimize your animation work in Bryce 3D. The term is "Appendage Control." An Appendage Control is an object, most commonly a sphere, inserted between the moving Child object in a Linked hierarchy and its Parent (see Figures 12.1 and 12.2).

NOTE

It is advisable to remove the "neck" from a Poser figure, and substitute a visible spherical Appendage Control in its place.

If the Appendage Controls are visible, they should be resized so that they are not obvious on the finished model.

HOW TO LINK APPENDAGE CONTROLS

This information is absolutely vital and even not hinted at in the Bryce 3D documentation. When you Link the parts of a model together that has Ap-

FIGURE **12.1** *Here is a Poser figure with all of its parts ungrouped and ready for Linking.*

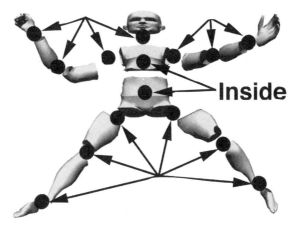

FIGURE *Spherical Appendage Controls are inserted in the Poser figure, as indicated,*
12.2 *between the Linked parts. In many cases the spherical Appendage Controls are textured with the same material as the parts linked together, or they can be made invisible.*

pendage Controls inserted, **DO NOT** Link the Appendage Controls to objects in the hierarchy. Let's take a hand–lower arm–upper arm example. Link the hand to the Appendage Control between the hand and the lower arm. Link the Appendage Control between the hand and Lower arm to the Appendage Control between the lower and upper arm. Link the lower arm to the Appendage Control between the lower and upper arm. Link the Appendage Control between the lower and upper arm to the Appendage Control that is between the upper arm and the body. Finally, Link the upper arm to the Appendage Control that is between the upper arm and the body. When you are set to create keyframes based on the rotation of the parts, select the Appendage Controls for rotation, and not their associated body parts. This gives you smooth animated movement with no warping or skewing of the parts.

Name all of the Appendage Controls to fit their task. For example, "LHandC", "LowerLArmC", etc.

NOTE

ALWAYS USE APPENDAGE CONTROLS

There are times when you can go without using Appendage Controls inserted between the hierarchical parts of your animated object, but they are rare. Because Bryce 3D does not have a "Bones" utility (a way of allowing you to move object parts without separating them first), and because in most cases rotated elements can warp and deform, it is necessary to insert intervening control elements.

Visible or Invisible

Appendage Controls are invisible most of the time (see the section on Null Objects later in this chapter). There may be times, however, when you want them to be visible. If they are objects that are part of a larger collection of objects, for instance, they can act as the master choreographer, so their movements visibly influence the movements of others in the collection or tribe. The advantage of making them invisible is that their shape need not have anything to do with the animated objects you want the audience to see. Usually, invisible Appendage Controls are spheres or cylinders, but any object at all will do.

Why would you make appendage controls visible? There are two reasons. First, you may notice that when a specific appendage, an arm or leg part, is rotated past about 20 degrees, an obvious split becomes apparent. It may look as if the part has separated from its parent element. In this case, the Appendage Control (usually a sphere) can serve as a material fill-in object, so no split in the object takes place. The other instance for making the Appendage Control visible is when the rotating appendage is a grouped element, so no movement of the Origin Point is possible. In that case, the grouped element rotates around its center, which is usually not the place you want it to. An Appendage Control element is always desirable in this situation, and since without it an obvious split in the parts takes place, the Appendage Control element is made visible and textured with the same material as one or both of the connecting parts.

PROPAGATION: WHAT IT IS AND WHEN TO USE IT

The Propagation toggles are the four options under the Linking member name in the Animation tab of the object's Attributes dialog. They appear when you set the linked Parent's name. They are Distance, Offset, Rotation, and Size. They take any or all of these attributes from what you do to the parent. If you activate Rotation, for instance, you will rotate the Linked Child when the Parent of that Child is rotated. If size is activated, then resizing the Parent will also resize the Child object accordingly. Propagation components are hereditary traits that tell the object what it will inherit from its Parent object.

Although each object can offer its own complications where animated parts are concerned, switching Size off on animated Child elements prevents warping of appendages in most instances.

It's always best to select the propagation features you want before moving an object into place in a hierarchical chain. If you do all sorts of moving and rotation first, the object will have to be resized and repositioned after it is Linked, because of propagation components.

Primitive Constructs

There is a way to animate primitive objects that are not grouped to minimize potential problems later. This consists of turning Rotation and Size propagation off in all Child objects. Child objects can be rotated singly by moving their Origin Points to a fulcrum position, usually at the top center of the Child object. This means that it takes more effort to set the keyframes (since the Child objects of the rotated element do not automatically rotate), but results in a distortion-free animation.

This same method can be used on some imported objects that have been ungrouped, though each case may react differently.

Save the resizing of object primitives until after the Linking and positioning has been accomplished. Resizing a Parent will move the Child objects in the chain, however, as long as Distance and Offset propagations are switched on.

Remember: Origin Points can be animated to smooth over unwanted anomalies that result when object parts are rotated at different angles.

Imported Models

Try not to work with imported DXF models that are to be animated. There are dozens of DXF formats, and some cause strange relationships among their elements when they are ungrouped. Work with 3DS (3D Studio) and OBJ (Alias WaveFront) models whenever possible in Bryce 3D.

Some models that you import will not be open to ungrouping. Ungroupable models are not suitable for animation, because there is no way to move their elements separately. One solution is to take them apart in a separate 3D modeling application and export them again to Bryce 3D.

Conglomerate Objects

What is a conglomerate object or model? It is any object or model made up of a mix of parts, either from separate models, or between Bryce 3D object primitives and imported components. Because there are an infinite number of ways that conglomerate objects can be stitched together, there are many problems that can crop up when the object is animated. In general, here are some rules to keep in mind when creating a conglomerate object whose parts are to be animated:

- Always use Appendage Controls between elements if either one of the elements is a Grouped object.

- Don't forget to move the Origin Point of selected elements so that rotation takes place around the correct axis fulcrum.
- Use the Advanced Motion Lab whenever possible to apply suitable and/or repetitive Motion Curves to the selected elements. This saves a lot of time and handwork.

Load the Ballfly1 animation from the CD-ROM and look at the Ballfly1.br3 project file. This object is composed of a Bryce 3D primitive sphere and grouped wings from an imported model, utilizing Appendage Controls for the wing movement.

NOTE

The Conglomerate Linking and modeling methods described here are also valuable when working with the new animal models in Poser 3.

NOTE

COLLECTING BODY PARTS

This sounds like a rather macabre practice at first hearing, but it is a rather benign activity. What it means is that in order to create interesting composite animated models, you have to have interesting parts. The most common parts to collect and store in the Bryce 3D object library are wings and heads, followed in order by anything else that interests you.

3D Acuworlds

Acuris, Inc. created a CD-ROM of a variety of animals for Bryce 2 in the Bryce format. Unfortunately, though it would be interesting to animate the models in this collection, few can be ungrouped so you can get to their parts, and then to top it all off, the division of Acuris responsible for this collection (3D Acuworlds) went out of business. You can still find the collection offered by various mail order houses, however, and there are a few models very valuable in Bryce 3D for animated component parts. The Hawk and Dove models can be ungrouped and offer some superlative wings that you can add to any model that needs them. The same collection also features a large library of DXF models useful for adding nonanimated components to a scene. See Figure 12.3.

Linked Material Shells

Just as clouds can be mapped to an outer sphere that revolves around a planet object, so any object can also have its own outer shell. Shells can be used for clothing on a human figure or more esoteric looks. You can, for instance, wrap a shell on a human, animal, or robotic figure and map it with a fuzzy light, giving the figure a perceptible aura as it moves in the scene. See Figures 12.4 and 12.5.

FIGURE   *The Acuworlds' Dove's wings were ungrouped, added to this sphere, and*
12.3   *animated.*

FIGURE   *A Linked cloud shell revolves around a planet.*
12.4

FIGURE   *Steel Cage, Dali Bee Stripes, and Random Basic material shells are Linked over*
12.5   *a Poser figure.*

When building a shell for a Poser figure, it's best to select the parts in the grouped model one by one to enlarge them before applying a material. Otherwise, the parts will not fit correctly over the whole figure.

Null Objects

Null object may be a brand new concept to you, and besides being a word you've never heard before, you are sure you haven't used them in Bryce 3D. But if you've worked through the previous section in this chapter concerning Appendage Controls, you have already begun using one type of Null object. Appendage Controls are one type of Null objects. A Null object is any object in a scene that has power over other objects or facets of an animation without itself having to be rendered. Null objects are usually invisible and vital for certain animation actions and effects.

TYPES OF NULL OBJECTS

There can be an infinite array of Null objects, but for our purposes in Bryce 3D, let's classify five important ones: Appendage Controls, Gravity Wells, Negative and Intersecting Booleans, Camera Targets, and Propagation Engines.

Appendage Controls

We have already investigated Appendage Controls in the first part of this chapter. Appendage Controls, especially when they are made invisible in their Attributes dialog, are perfect examples of a Null object. They control every aspect of an animated figure without being noticed in the rendering.

Gravity Wells

A Gravity Well Null is an object, usually not rendered, that controls a number of moving object in a scene. A Gravity Well Null can simulate the power of a black hole or a super-magnet, attracting and influencing objects that are Linked to it. As a core parent object, its effects can be seen, while the Null object itself remains hidden.

A Gravity Well Experiment

Here is a basic Null Gravity Well animation that you can create to study this effect:

1. Create a Positive Boolean Cube, drilled from the top by a Negative Boolean Cylinder to create the well. Use a stone material on the cube and a basic red on the cylinder.

2. Place a radial light at the bottom of the well, tinted yellow at a 50% intensity, to give the well some depth character.

3. Make the project a 150 frame animation, 30FPS at 5 seconds.

4. In frame 1, create a sphere that sits in the air above the well. Create a cube, which will be our Null object, at the midpoint of the well. Link the sphere to the cube. Note that this Null cube can be visible because it is hidden in the well.

5. Move the Null cube from the midpoint of the well at frame 1 to the bottom of the well at the last frame. This will pull the sphere along with it.

6. On the last frame, make sure the sphere is in the well so it cannot be seen by the camera. Stretch the sphere in the last frame to four times its vertical height. This makes the sphere look like it is being distorted by the pull of the well as it is being drawn into it.

7. Render the animation, and save it to disk.

Note that when a Gravity Well tugs on objects, they usually distort in the direction of the attractor. This can be seen in the Gwell animation and in the Gwell.br3 project on the CD-ROM.

Negative and Intersecting Booleans

By their very nature and actions, Boolean Negative and Intersecting objects are Null objects. They are invisible, but their influence on the Positive objects grouped with them is readily apparent in a rendering.

Invisible Targets

Objects, lights, or the camera can be Linked to a Null object to control their movement, rotation, and other animation factors. In addition, a Null object can be used as a target for the camera, so that instead of moving the camera itself to create an animation path, you can move the target. This forces the camera to follow along, which, many times, is easier to do than moving the actual camera. This is especially useful if you have a scene, perhaps a room, full of objects that you want to focus on one at a time. By using an invisible Null object as a target for the Camera, you can pause on different objects as long as necessary before moving on to the next one. This would be extremely complicated to do by moving the Camera itself.

Dispersion Engines

We have already investigated the Dispersion tool in the Edit toolbar. You know that by using the Dispersion routines, you can act on any number of selected objects. Why use a Null object to control dispersed objects?

If you select a number of objects and disperse them, they remain single objects if they are not grouped. As single objects, using the Rotation tool on them rotates them in place, around their own Origin Points. Grouping them and using the Rotation tool rotates them around a common Origin Point (see the Disnull animation on the CD-ROM). Using a Null object that every member of the group is Linked to gives you both options. With the Null object selected, using the Rotation tool rotates all of the objects around the Null's Origin Point. Because the objects remain ungrouped, however, marquee-selecting all of the objects also allows you to rotate the objects individually around their own Origin Points. This gives you the best of both options. See Figure 12.6.

Null Material Palettes

Here's a novel use for Null objects. You may have the occasion to need to copy a selection of materials already used in your scene to more than one additional object. You can find the object that has the required material, select it, Copy its material, select the target object, and Paste the material. All of that is doable, but it takes time. Using a Null Palette method, you can accomplish this task much more quickly. Just use a portion of your workspace that is not included in the rendering to set up as many Null objects as you need, naming them according to their materials. Select them by name when you need to Copy/Paste materials and proceed with the Copy/Paste operations. You can save them out with the scene for future reference.

FIGURE *This collection of dispersed floating cubes is rotation controlled by a hidden*
12.6 *Null object*

Partially and Totally Visible Nulls

Null objects can be rendered along with your other objects in a scene if you want them to be. Just turn off the "Hidden" item in each Null object's Attributes dialog, and treat it the way you would treat any other object (making them display a material and other light sensitive attributes). This is especially effective when the Null object is of a different type than the objects linked to it. A Null cloud, for instance, can be used to control the rotation and path movements of a flock of birds. The viewer is less likely to suspect the cloud as having this power than they would a bird leading the pack. When you do make a Null object visible in the render, try to shape it into an object that the viewer does not suspect as the controlling influence.

Moving On

In this chapter, we have explored some advanced techniques for Linking animations and using Null objects. In the next chapter, we will list a number of additional hints and tips, as well as to display the Bryce 3D work and thinking of two professional Bryce 3D masters.

CHAPTER 13

Hints, Tips, and Master Users

I n this chapter, we've included a number of hints and tips to push your Bryce 3D work even farther. In the second half of the chapter, you'll be able to read about the work of two Bryce 3D masters and see some examples of their astounding work.

Hints and Tips for Optimizing Your Bryce 3D Work

The following collection of hints and tips cover many of the Bryce 3D tools, options, and techniques. A few are important reminders that need to be underlined and followed. It is assumed that you have worked through both the documentation and this book thoroughly, so that you can use these hints and tips to push your Bryce 3D work to the edge.

LIGHTS

- Using squared Falloff on a light makes its cone of illumination drop off very fast. Use this option when you need to illuminate just a small section of an object, without effecting nearby objects.
- Use the following procedure for creating a Volumetric light with a visible material:
  1. Set all of the necessary options in the Edit dialog.
  2. Set the material in the Material Lab.
  3. **DO NOT** return to the light's Edit dialog, or a system crash may result.
- To create a total eclipse of the sun in your world, so the following:
  1. Create a sky with no Stratus or Cumulus clouds and with a sun visible on the horizon. Make the sun's intensity 50% and give it a visible ring.
  2. Create a 2D disk, colored black, that covers most of the sun. Move it back (Z axis) so that it can be resized to interfere with the light in the scene. Turn off its ability to cast and receive shadows.
  3. Make the sun's light a light gray color to mute the scene and check the Blend With Sun option in the Sky&Fog editor.
  4. Use a black Haze set at 50%. See Figure 13.1.

NOTE *If you want to create a partially eclipsed sun, use a separate Negative Boolean sphere to cut away part of the Positive 2D disk as needed.*

ANIMATION

If you are familiar with the original Star Trek episodes, you have seen this animation technique used many times. It can still be effective. I call it the Star Trek Fast-Travel Trick. Here's how to do it:

FIGURE *An eclipsed sun glows over a Bryce 3D world.*
13.1

1. Render a spaceship as seen from the rear. It can have as much detail as you prefer. Save it to disk.
2. Import the image into a paint application and use a solid white to paint out any background elements not wanted. Save the image to disk as My-Ship.TIF.
3. Using the same picture in your paint application, select the image only and fill it with a solid black. Save this image to disk as the Alpha image, as MyShipA.TIF.
4. Map the image and its respective Alpha image to a 2D vertical plane in Bryce 3D.
5. At the start of a 150-frame 30FPS animation, place the picture close to the camera. Move it back on the Z axis as far as you desire in the last frame. When the animation plays back, the ship will "travel" towards the far point of your scene.

RENDERING

- Never use the highest antialiasing option. The only time to even consider it is for extreme cases where super-fine printouts are required, or when your output is meant for high-quality movie film. Even then, think twice. This option can more than quadruple your rendering time.

- To save rendering time, use color and no texture on objects in the far background.
- Freezing the cloud plane in place (with no animated movements) can save 30% or more of your rendering time when you are working with skies that take half or more of the frame.

CAMERA

Do not fly the Camera through solid objects in an animation. It will most likely result in a system crash. Volumetric objects, mapped with volumetric materials, are of course the exception and allowed.

OBJECT CREATION

- When you need to create a complex object in an already complex scene in Bryce 3D, consider creating it away from the scene in an empty area. When finished, it can be copy/pasted into the scene. The original can be removed prior to the final scene save.
- When you need to use a render of the scene as a bitmap that will create a Terrain Object, render the scene from the top view and save it to disk. Import it into a paint application and customize it as necessary. Import it back into the Terrain Editor of Bryce 3D, and you'll have an object that was created in Bryce 3D for object creation, a circular process.
- Render a Wireframe top view of your scene for export to a paint application. There, you can use all of the application's painting options before exporting the image back to Bryce 3D. Once in Bryce 3D, the image can be used in the Terrain Editor or the Picture Editor.
- When the object you need to create for an already complex scene is very large and complex itself, consider creating it as a separate Bryce 3D project. When finished, it can be Merged back into the original scene.
- Make sure you name each item and Mesh Group in your scene. This makes it easy to find what you need when you are engaged in complex editing sessions.

MATERIALS

- Be aware that complex detailed materials, rendered without antialiasing, can cause flickering in animation playback.
- Remember that Volumetric materials, with Base Density adjusted, can serve as particle systems when animated. To simulate a particle system with Volumetric materials, use World Y axis rotation and alterations in the base Density.

- Usually, increasing the Metalicity percentage of a material also increases the intensity of the Diffuse Color component.
- Black and White Marble material, mapped to the ground plane and re-sized to about 4%, makes a great "ice floe" look.
- When a Negative Boolean is set to transfer its material to the "hole" cut in a Positive Boolean object, don't forget that the material can be chosen to emulate the heat of a cutting object. As the hole becomes visible, it can be made to range from hot (yellow or orange) to a cooled surface (any material, like stone or metal). This enhances the animated cutting effect.
- Foliage addition is one of Bryce 3D's weakest points, as there is no auto-matic way to populate a terrain with trees or other flora. One way to ac-complish this is to duplicate the terrain object, and resize it about 10% larger than the original. With the cloned terrain selected, map it with a green tree-like material that has Alpha channel "holes" in it, allowing the original terrain to show through. Where you want to see far less greenery, use a Negative Boolean to cut away a larger swath.
- Don't forget to explore the use of applying textures to the Specularity channels of an object. This allows lights that shine on the object to reveal the applied material.

Learning from Master Users

As a creative person wanting to push your level of mastery to the limit in Bryce 3D, don't neglect to study and learn from other Bryce users. There are a num-ber of professional artists and animators who have devoted years of study to Bryce, and who have moved to Bryce 3D to create stunning art and animation. You can find these users and their work noted on the Web, especially at the MetaCreations site: http://www.metacreations.com.

This book takes a look at two Bryce 3D masters, Cecilia Ziemer and Mark Smith. Both of these artist-animators have used Bryce, and now Bryce 3D, to create magazine covers, illustrations, and animated works. We are happy to share their words, advice, graphics, and project files with you. You can read their biographical information in Appendix H of this book.

CECILIA ZIEMER

Celia Ziemer comes at computer art and animation from the world of tradi-tional painting, a transition she made some years ago. She calls her section in this book "Push-Button Orogeny (Mountain Building)," and here are her own words and Bryce 3D examples.

Leaving aside atmosphere, animation, and gorgeous materials, Bryce in its

various incarnations has had a great aura of really democratic software, bypass-
ing the whole high-end/low-end gradient. It's more open-ended. Although
Bryce 3D requires more than a bare-minimum computer to run on now (and
even more RAM and more speed, 200 MHz as a bottom end for animation or
heavy use of volumetric materials), almost anyone can afford it. Even someone
who has never before used a 3D application can dive right in and begin poking
icons and making things. Making Things is unavoidable. Push a button, raise
a mountain, or lay down a quick timeline and fly the camera away. Even the
first image or animation you make won't look all that shabby.

This is the kind of positive reinforcement that creativity can feed on, little
feelings of accomplishment (even if the first accomplishment is only with a
canned mountain and a default sky) that grow into the desire to explore, to
push the edges. Make images, make movies, make textures for use in other 3D
applications, and get wild while you're doing it. Bryce 3D movies may soon be
ubiquitous, everything from home movies of Poser model electric grandmas
(textured neatly from photographs) in space stations, to professionally produced music videos, to visualizations of the ten unfurled dimensions and a
string or two.

Maybe it's the terra-cotta knobs, the big workspace, or the Organically
Grown terrains that can sometimes lead to the feeling that a world is "growing"
on the monitor. Bryce 3D helps enable the imaginative edge, the thin wall between reality and fantasy, the big "What If." What were these mountains before
they were mountains? Well, what if they weren't "that"? Perhaps they were
mountains on an undiscovered planet circling Epsilon Eridani? Or mountains
of anti-matter? What are these mountains in dreams?

NOTE *The following items have project files on the CD-ROM in the Celia folder.*

BUMPLENS, a Bizarre Project

Look at this as a loosen-up exercise, unrepentant abstract imaging, or just a
fungus among us.

1. From the Director's View, create a sphere, use the Resize Tool to enlarge
   it about twice, then lift it free of the ground.
2. From front, right, or left view rotate the camera toward the sky. (In this
   image the camera is rotated -88.19 on the x-axis, -180 on the y axis; (rotating -90 on the x-axis caused the camera to flip over).
3. Drag the camera completely inside the sphere. Set up a light and colorful sky in the Sky&Fog Palette. If you Randomize the sky, don't let fog

occlude the bottom of the sphere. Put a material on the sphere, switch to the camera, and render.

For this image I used the Pebbles shader (it's under Sand) with a bead in the Bump and both Bump and Specularity set at 100%. The only other setting is Refraction, at 25. Remember, this is Bryce 3D, so explore other ways of doing this. Play with various material components, ones with good Bump Channels, change the Refraction, add a shader to the transparency Color Channel. Change the way the material components are applied (Object Space with Symmetric Tiling is interesting, as is Spherical). You can animate this by spinning the sphere, changing the camera's field of view, animating between two materials, and have your own fungoidal light show. See Figure 13.2.

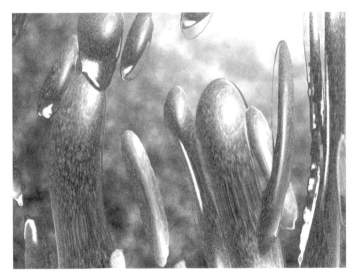

FIGURE *The Bumplens rendering.*
13.2

FLEURDEMAL: Customized Terrain Object
Why should the mountains get it all?

1. Create a Terrain and open it in the Terrain Editor. Click **New**. Click once on **Blob Maker** to, yes, make a blob; then click once on **Cross Ridges**.
2. Drag the bottom of the Clipping Bracket up about ½ inch, this isn't critical, you can adjust it later.
3. Click on Gaussian Edges, dragging to the right; you will see four petals form. It's more squash blossom than lily.

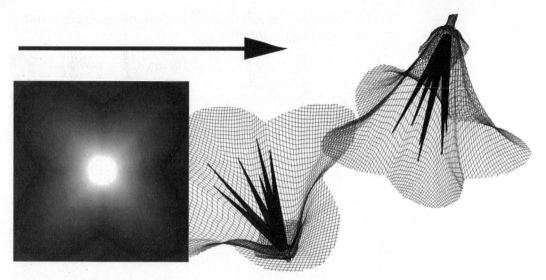

FIGURE
13.3
The form is created in the Terrain Editor, resulting in the flower models at the right.

4. From here you can smooth the flower and exit the Terrain Editor, or you can add a slight Erosion for veins, or repeat the Cross Ridges and Gaussian Edges steps for deeper petals. Once the flower is shaped, you can also drag Gaussian Edges in the opposite direction to fatten the flower.

5. Now adjust the clipping slider to clean up the crumbs. In the Working Window, ascertain the flower/terrain has no rotation, then elongate it in the y-dimension (or leave it flat if you want to duplicate it for a polyploid). See Figure 13.3.

6. I used a transparent material, but a good flower material can be made by combining Basic Altitude (the first Basic Altitude, it's morning-glory color) with low clouds, a bead in the Diffuse channels of both, Specularity of around 25%, and Transparency of 1.7%. Construction of the calyx is by the same process as construction of the flower: Blob, Ridges, Edges, then scaled down uniformly with no elongation in length. For clarity, stamens in this example are just elongated cones, grouped and aligned to the calyx. See Figure 13.4.

DAYGUY/NIGHTGUY

Dayguy is a Poser model, exported from Poser as a single piece Wavefront. OBJ, which was originally created for the purpose of trying out a Poser/De-

FIGURE *The finished flowers rendered.*
13.4

tailer texture in Bryce. It worked well but the sky worked better, so up he went, and reality went out the window. Dayguy's material is the Gradient Vein shader, right out of the box (under Psychedelic), applied as Object Space, with Volumetric enabled. Beads are in the color channels for Diffuse, Ambient, and Specular. Diffusion is set at 100%, Ambient at 45%, Specular at 100%. In the Volumetric settings, the Base Density is 100% (no bead), Fuzzy Factor is set at 218, and Speed/Quality at 59. The camera's FOV is 107. See Figure 13.5.

Nightguy, obviously, is the same Poser model. Nightguy's material is the Jerry Garcia shader applied as Cylindrical, with Volumetric enabled. Beads are in the color channels for Diffuse and Specular. Ambient color is set to a pale yellow. Diffusion is set at 59.3%, Ambient at 42.4%, Specular at 100%. In the Volumetric settings, the Base Density is 71.2% (no bead), Fuzzy Factor is set at 106, and Speed/Quality at 59. The camera's FOV is set at 70. Note the comet at the left of the big pink foot. See Figure 13.6.

This figure still accepts the Poser texture maps. If you have the maps, try combining Male Muscle Texture from the Poser Texture folder with a marble shader; put a bead in the Poser map's bump channel and set it high. For a little more weirdness look at the Male Skeleton Template with a bead in its transparency channel combined with the Alien shader.

FIGURE *The Dayguy rendering.*
13.5

FIGURE *The Nightguy rendering.*
13.6

ASHEL

This is a Metacreations' RayDream import, combined with a height map on a Symmetric Lattice object. This creature is a rough reincarnation of an old ink-dot drawing. It's the kind of thing that visually works better in 3D, with environment and atmosphere, than in tiny black dots—and I could grab the heads for free. The Poser head had a little tweak to one side of the face and a reverse nose-job in Ray Dream 5, before it came into Bryce as an .OBJ file. The shelly parts are also Ray Dream; the main carapace is a gray-scale map on a Symmetric Lattice.

Rendering time precluded the use of a Volumetric slab for the "heavy water." I used a flat plane with a transparent Waves material and custom atmospheric settings. Dark Haze makes a good deepening-distance effect and renders much faster than volumetric water. To keep the scene from going completely dark, I bounced the sun off low Stratus clouds, and changed the Ambient Light/Shadows color to gold.

The watery substance didn't look quite thick and "tunnel-y" enough so I lowered and rotated the plane to cut through and "bend" the two background terrains.

By tradition, Janus-faced figures guard gates. This guy is currently unemployed. See Figures 13.7 and 13.8.

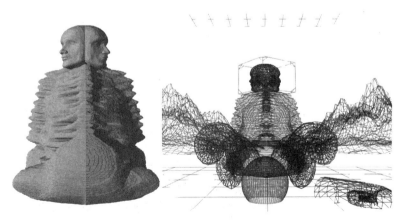

FIGURE **13.7** *The Ashel object was developed with the help of Metacreations' Ray Dream Mesh Modeler.*

FIGURE   *The finished Ashel rendering.*
13.8

BRIDGE

This is a Boolean bridge, Terrain roof. The project file for this contains one section of bridge, one cylinder tower, one roof, and a sphere holding an interesting material. See Figure 13.9.

FIGURE   *The basic rendered Bridge.*
13.9

NOTE? *You can combine, add on, duplicate, distort, drop your own creatures in. Best yet (and hence the large size): set up a entire network of bridges and towers, drop in a low-lying cloud slab or two, and animate flights under the bridges—it's not illegal in 3D.*

The bottom of the bridge is three Boolean arches, positive Stretched Cubes and negative Ellipsoids. The Ellipsoids dutifully transferred their Tech Map material to the inside of the arches.

The top of the bridge is one Brickoid with material to delineate the rails and posts, and one squashed Brickoid for the floor. For the rails and posts, the material component in channel A is Basic Grid, with a bead in its transparency. The frequency is changed (in the Editor: Transformation Tools) to x=12%, y=1%, z=0. Channel B contains the Rocky material component, for bump and diffusion. This made cables and side posts. Since the side posts (invisible in the wireframe) needed alignment to the Boolean objects, I did a patch render of the top section, then switched to Combined Mode Display and it was a snap.

First I aligned the bridge top and the three duplicate Boolean arch groups along their x axes, then selected each arch and dragged under its respective top "post."

The roof is a Terrain object. I created a new terrain, made a blob, gave it square edges, raised it as high as I could without losing the point, again squared the edges to increase curvature. Why use a Terrain having 32800 polygons when a cone would roof a tower with only 32 polygons? Try replacing the Terrain with a Cone and you'll see the whole tenor of the image change. The world of the young water strider in this example simply required a more curvilinear roof. If a conical roof is better suited to your creature (or to your RAM), ungroup and delete the roof-terrain; it won't blow up the building. See Figure 13.10.

HEIGHT MAP BUILDING: Filtered Terrain

Don't forget the filters—they're great for extracting buildings from terrains. This building began with a Blob and Cross-ridges (my favorite way to start non-mountains), was filtered, clipped, eroded, and stretched vertically. It 's roofed with another Blob that rests on a Toroid. By the time I got to the Toroid, the building looked more a place for calling down or conjuring a moon than a regular observatory (especially as the final moon was a translucent sphere). So why not look at it with crystal balls—big ones, visible from the entry? One moon-viewing sphere is in the exact center of the viewing chamber and the other, for focus, on the moonward side.

FIGURE **13.10** *The Bridge with a unique Poser figure added, the Water Strider.*

The distant moon-catcher structure is another Blobbed terrain, posterized, with paint dots added for the pillars. A translucent moon wasn't in the original plan; an orbiting ball of pure water ice would become opaque from meteor collisions, stress, and space garbage in a hurry. It just looked better, so once again, fantasy devoured reality. See Figure 13.11.

For renderings from inside, outside, and different angles on a scene, it's handy to set a one-second time line and a motion path for the camera with

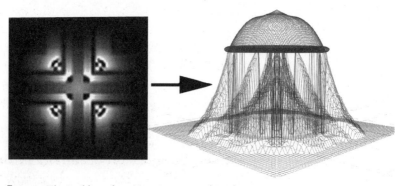

FIGURE **13.11** *The Building, from Terrain map to object base.*

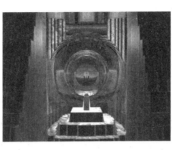

FIGURE *The Building, showing close-up detail and a final rendering in a Bryce 3D*
13.12 *environment.*

keyframes at the desired views, say 8 views. Set up the animation to render
(small) as 8 sequenced PICTs (Mac) or BMPs (Windows). Turn off your monitor, go outdoors, enjoy nature, and watch the moon.

Open the renderings in Photoshop or another image editor and find your
best view. Then in Bryce 3D, just move the timeline slider to the correspond-
ing keyframe to do the final rendering. See Figure 13.12.

ASCENE: Something to Explore

Here's a place to set up a fly-over, a drive-in (add neon to taste), a panorama, or
grab some terrains and textures. The cloud slab is stretched vertically to make
a cloud plane at the top and radiation (low lying) fog at the bottom. Explore .
. . See Figure 13.13.

See if you can spot the following things to be found in the Project file on the
CD-ROM: a sort-of jellyfish, mostly hidden in the well; three custom materials on spheres hidden behind the wall; and one flying-saucer lattice thingy
(with a neat height map) parked behind a mountain.

MARK SMITH

Mark uses his Bryce and Bryce 3D interactions to create what he describes as
"non-landscape" pieces. The rest of the text describing his work is in his own
words.

Random Thoughts on Creativity in Bryce

When I first saw images that were produced with Bryce, I , like many others
was in complete awe. The overall quality of the rendering was vibrant and intense. I really admire Eric Wenger (Bryce's creator). He was fascinated with cre-

<figure>FIGURE
13.13　*The finished rendering exemplifies the best of a mysterious and inviting Bryce 3D world.*</figure>

ating real-world landscapes and terrains, so he simply decided to code his own software for helping him generate the kind of images he had floating around in his imagination. The renderer in Bryce is a rather sophisticated raytracer. My excitement for Bryce was forged in that quality of the rendered look, but extrapolated beyond landscape generation.

I am a digital f/x artist and principal of Digital Drama. We create digital f/x for film and television. We use some of the most sophisticated and expensive software available on all the platforms including Silicon Graphics workstations. When I create on a personal level, though, I always turn to MetaCreation's Bryce and now, Bryce 3D.

When I get asked for tips on Bryce's use, I inevitably turn more philosophical than factual. For me, Bryce 3D is a very Zen-like experience. I use it as one tool from a host of tools to reach my end goal. The Bryce 3D software is a means to an end with little allegiance to any one platform or program. For me, Bryce 3D means much more than landscapes. Early on in the evolution of Bryce, no one had made this more perfectly clear than the published artists Jackson Ting and Robert Bailey. Their 100% Bryce-rendered and created image of an eighteen-wheel tractor trailer really exemplifies this. Three other artists that really inspired me personally are H.R. Gieger, William Latham, and Yoichiro Kawaguchi. Gieger was the man responsible for the creature design in the "Alien" series of films and the author of several fantastical art books such as "Necronomicon." Latham focused on computer-generated pseudo-organic iterative animation. His work can be seen in "The Conquest of Form: The Art of William Latham." Yoichiro Kawaguchi expressed his creativity in the form of uniquely flowing very organic and colorful inspirations. His video release "Luminous Visions" is beautiful.

I enjoy using Bryce to create my pseudo-organic images because of the expressive quality that the renderer provides. I rarely model in Bryce. As this book describes, Bryce can be used to create some interesting models, but they are proprietary and cannot be exported. Bryce's modeling is confined to non-standard tools like 3D displacement. The ability to import models created in other programs adds a whole dimensionality to the program. Whether importing a DXF tank for a Bryce desert or a 3DS model of a soaring bird against a Bryce-rendered sky, it opens up the program to a world of possibilities.

I rely on modeling outside of Bryce and importing my model. I use Alias PowerAnimator on the SGI. The models are used as the basis of much more complex iterated models once imported into Bryce. You just can't model an animal's horn or teardrop that well in Bryce. I like to think of this procedure as creating a "Mark" primitive. A good deal of what I have been creating in Bryce, based on my primitive, is using Bryce's Multi-replicate command. The simplest shape takes on a whole new complexity when it is multi-replicated and infused with an intriguing combination of iterated XYZ rotations, XYZ scaling, and XYZ transformation. This is a rather standard function in most 3D packages worth their salt. It would be easy enough to create this model in another program and then import the result, but it is less configurable within Bryce afterwards. A multi-replicated object created in this way is imported as whole objects and forfeits some of the accessible properties of the model. This same multi-replicated object within Bryce is all separate and distinct parts. One obvious advantage to creating this type of object in Bryce is mapping the individually cloned objects differently from the rest. A second advantage is that individually these objects can have separate Boolean properties. A tightly knit, multi-replicated series of objects with alternating Boolean properties can result in some very unexpected models.

If you are modeling a table, then it should be able to be identified as a table by others looking at your image. I am at an advantage with the creation of my imagery because what I usually create has no basis in reality. I am afforded the opportunity to do some really strange and interesting things. For the sake of experimentation, try using multiple infinite water planes. These are objects and can be rotated from their normal ground-like orientation. The confluence of multiple infinite plains with varying textures can be quite stark. The raytracer handles water quite well in Bryce. I have not seen many raytracers that take advantage of the angle at which a plane of water is viewed. Multiple parallel water planes with varying lighting between layers also can yield amazing results. When you play with multiple levels of refraction you are asking for a render time nightmare. My advice is avoid animations with it, unless you are going on vacation.

I have developed a series of pet projects called "Organix," which will take my forms into the realm of the moving image. I hope to create 40 minutes of CG animation based on my designs. During the Beta testing of Bryce 3D with animation my sole concern was the inclusion of a pivot point in the object. As it is now a movable pivot, the possibilities of using multi-replicate within Bryce is exciting. I had "Organix" in mind during this Beta cycle and was pleased by its inclusion. The possibilities of a moving mass of nested clones all moving in sync yet following its own configurations, such as Boolean interactions, is really far off from the landscape Bryce was designed for.

Use Bryce as a tool for a specific look that you may be seeking. I often take advantage of a Bryce rendering along with many other programs to create an end goal. The convenience of a mutual image file format allows you to move the image from program to program to gain the right look. Bryce 3D can even be used to generate some really cool icons or web buttons. This is why I always talk about Bryce in terms of its rendering. The beauty of the final output is what is important. I have nothing against rendering a landscape in Bryce 3D, as it is also awesome for this purpose. I used Bryce to create a backdrop image for an Alien Jellyfish that I did for the cover of May 97 *Digital Magic* magazine. The alien model was done in Alias. My best tip for anyone using Bryce is to consider using it for things other than a landscape. It would be a crime not to take advantage of it in alternate ways. See Figures 13.14 and 13.15.

Moving On

This chapter has included a number of additional hints and tips. You have also had the opportunity to learn from and to see some of the work of two amazing Bryce 3D masters, Cecelia Ziemer and Mark Smith. The next chapter completes the book. It contains information and graphics from customizable projects and sample animations on the CD-ROM designed to push your Bryce 3D work to the creative heights you've been dreaming about.

Copyright 1996 Mark J. Smith   (201)992-4213   digitaldrama@earthlink.net

FIGURE   *Mark Smith's Bryce 3D artwork is well known for its explorational design and*
13.14   *masterful alluring visuals.*

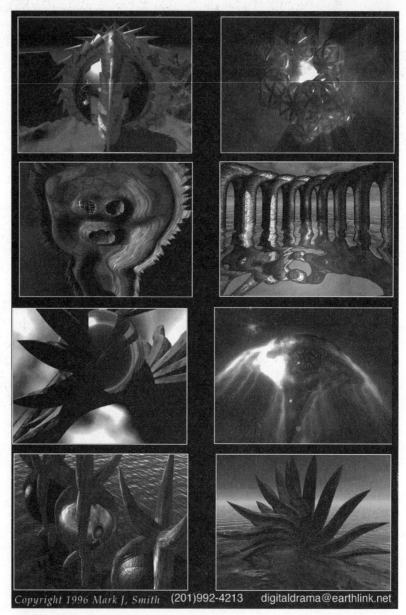

Copyright 1996 Mark J. Smith   (201)992-4213   digitaldrama@earthlink.net

FIGURE   *Mark Smith's Bryce 3D artwork is well known for its explorational design and*
13.15   *masterful alluring visuals.*

14 Special Projects

In this last chapter of the book, we will detail the Special Projects contained on the CD-ROM and their respective animations. All of these projects relate to aspects of the things the book teaches you to do, and all can be explored and customized. There are infinite ways you can alter these project files to make them your own. The projects referred to are in the Projects/CH14 folder, and the animations are in the Anims/CH14 folder on the CD-ROM.

Anthroz

The Anthroz project contains an animated Poser figure with four arms, involved in a dance. There are also two side figures, made from a Poser head and Boolean elements. The accompanying animation shows the Poser figure doing a little dance and then the side figures turning from profile to face the camera.

WHAT TO EXPLORE

Investigate the way that the Poser figure is articulated and Linked. Look at the materials assigned to the figure parts, and also to the rest of the elements in the scene. The Boolean side figures are also interesting, especially the cut-aways of the Poser heads. In each of the hands is a Linked glowing sphere, with a material you should investigate. Also look at the Torus used as a hat, with a material that makes it look like a piece of peppermint candy.

SUGGESTIONS FOR YOUR CUSTOMIZING EFFORTS

- Alter the materials used on the spheres so that they look like wooden or metal balls.
- Create an animation that shows the side figures gradually melting away and disappearing (Hint: Alter their size from the top down).
- Create a different animated movement for the Poser figure, including a jump up and off the screen.
- Make the ground material water.
- Create a stormy sky and make the sun flash from reds to blues.

See the Anthro1.mov animation on the CD-ROM, and the Anthros1.br3 Project file as well. Also see Figures 14.1 to 14.3.

Astrdz

The scene involves a ship making its way through an asteroid field. The ship has lights to help it navigate through the obstructions safely. It enters from the left and finally makes its way off-screen at the right. All the while, the asteroids are orbiting a hidden Null object, and many also spin on their own Origin Points.

FIGURE   *The articulated Poser figure.*
14.1

FIGURE   *The side figure, showing the Boolean cut-aways.*
14.2

WHAT TO EXPLORE

Look at the materials mapped to the ship. It's always nice to have a mix of random "dirty" materials and shiny metallics. Variety, in animation as in life, is the needed spice. The ship was modeled in Caligari's trueSpace on a Windows system, because trueSpace has better modeling options than Bryce 3D. Look at

FIGURE *The finished scene, showing figures in place.*
14.3

how the model is put together by ungrouping it. take a close look at the materials used on the asteroids. They really create the illusion of pock-marked space rocks. Investigate the way a Null object is used to control the global animation of the asteroid field.

SUGGESTIONS FOR YOUR CUSTOMIZING EFFORTS

- If you have the time to spare, try mapping the lights with Volumes instead of Surfaces. The rendering time increases, but the effect is more realistic and pronounced.
- Duplicate the ship and make a fleet of them fly through the scene at different rates.
- Reduce the size of the ship and make it navigate between the asteroids instead of above them.
- Create a laser beam from the ship that disintegrates some of the asteroids (Hint: Alter the transparency of targeted asteroid's materials in the Materials Lab).

See the Aster1.mov animation on the CD-ROM, and the Aster1.br3 Project file as well. Also see Figures 14.4 to 14.6.

NOTE

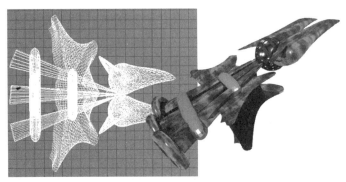

FIGURE
14.4
The ship was modeled in Caligari's trueSpace application and imported into Bryce 3D, where materials were applied.

FIGURE
14.5
Glowing spheres were Linked to the engines to simulate rocket flames.

FIGURE
14.6
A collection of rocks was added for the asteroid field. Surface lights were added to the ship.

Drive

This project makes use of a different technique to create the illusion of travel over terrain features. Instead of mapping the features to a flat plane, they are placed on the surface of a revolving cylinder. This creates some strange animated effects, but can be very useful when you want an animation to loop while traveling in a straight path. Using this method, you can create very long animated sequences that show a vehicle (or just the camera) passing through the terrain over and over again, just as in vintage movies and cartoons. The object is to place interesting objects along the way to keep the viewer interested.

WHAT TO EXPLORE

Investigate the cylinder thoroughly, observing how various elements are placed and mapped. Also explore the way that the "roadway" is kept free of obstacles. Note that the materials are NEVER applied with global mapping, since the objects are in motion, and this would result in the unwanted animation of the materials as well. Note that when a "car" or "plane" is used as a vehicle, it is locked into place, and that the camera and a light are both linked to the car. This controls both the constancy of the view and the lighting.

Do not allow object to collide with the camera, or you may suffer a system crash.

SUGGESTIONS FOR YOUR CUSTOMIZING EFFORTS

- Place obstacles in the path of the "car," and let the vehicle jump them.
- Create your own vehicle and use it to replace the vehicle in the Project file.
- Create your own elements on the cylinder, which can be tunnels and bridges.
- Move your vehicle from side to side at various points in the animation to give it more viewer interest.
- Change the cylinder's material to water to show a reflected journey.

See the Drive1, 2, and 3.mov animations on the CD-ROM, and the Drive3.br3, Drive4.br3, and Drive5.br3 project files as well. Also see Figures 14.7 to 14.9.

Freddy

Freddy is part robot and part angle, with the wings of a dove. Freddy dances for joy, and his two cloned partners in the background follow his example only part of the time. To complicate matters, a large asteroid moves across the background of the scene.

FIGURE **14.7** *With the camera placed in back of the car, the animation shows it traveling forward.*

FIGURE **14.8** *At one point in the animation, the vehicle travels through the legs of a giant ape.*

WHAT TO EXPLORE

Here's another look at an animated Poser figure, one that has been duplicated twice to add more interest. Explore the way the animated figures move, especially the wings. The wings were added from a dove model, and their movement was customized in the Motion Lab.

FIGURE *Instead of a ground vehicle you can use the same method to fly over the scene*
14.9 *with a plane or a rocket.*

SUGGESTIONS FOR YOUR CUSTOMIZING EFFORTS

- Alter the movements of all of the Poser figures to your own liking.
- Use the animated figure to fly over a terrain geography that you create.
- Replace any of Freddy's body parts with your own selection of elements.

See the Fred.mov animation on the CD-ROM, and the Fred.br3 Project file as well. Also see Figure 14.10.

FIGURE *Doing the Freddy dance.*
14.10

Logoz

You normally think of Bryce 3D as a creative platform for developing enhanced natural worlds, but you can also use it to develop and animate other types of projects. One of the most called for project types in the broadcast media is Logo animation. Logos are corporate or institutional symbols or identification text lines that introduce products or concepts to an audience. Bryce 3D allows you to create animation styles for logos that other 3D applications are hard pressed to compete with. Let's take a look at four Logo animation examples: Alchemy (materials transformations), BustUp (a Logo that fades to an explosion), FlyFog (a Logo that flys up through the fog), and TerraTrans (a Logo that is transformed and animated in the Terrain Editor).

WHAT TO EXPLORE

Alchemy

This is a process that Bryce 3D makes simple, though it takes ten times as much effort in other 3D applications. Basically stated, the idea is to map different materials to a targeted object (in this case, a logo) at different keyframes of an animation. You can customize the materials in the Materials Lab any way you like, using any or all of the options. The idea is to allow the final targeted material to be identical with the character of your logo. You can explore the materials used in this example, but when it comes time to use this procedure on your own logo, use materials that appeal to you and that help define your logo's character.

BustUp

This logo animation option uses two objects superimposed over one another to define the logo. The first is a terrain map of the logo as you would expect to see it, while the second is a rough stand-in composed of a series of rocks. You could use primitive objects instead of rocks, as long as they are placed in some relative position so they match the original logo's outline. The original logo changes color for the first third of the animation, and then becomes 100% transparent. The stand-in object does the reverse, being 100% transparent for the first third of the animation, and then 100% opaque for the rest. When the stand-in logo makes its appearance, the Dispersion tool is used to break the pieces apart. Explore the way this is accomplished in the Logo3.br3 project.

FogReveal

In media jargon, any hidden object in front of the camera that suddenly or gradually makes itself visible is said to go through a "reveal." Bryce 3D has some of the most elegant ways of creating reveals. This is a basic but effective one, sim-

ply using a 100% fog on the first frame and clearing the fog on the last frame.
Though simple to generate, the effect is good enough for very high-end uses.

TerraTrans

Creating animations by tweaking an object in the Terrain Editor should be a
process that is quite familiar to you by now. The complexity that can be initiated
here is directly relevant to audience interest, since you can never really run out of
unique ideas using this method. The only thing to pay attention to is that the
animation should end up showing the logo intact. How you get there and what
effects you apply over time in the Terrain Editor are completely up to you.

SUGGESTIONS FOR YOUR CUSTOMIZING EFFORTS

Alchemy

- Use your own logo in place of the one in this example project and create
  your own selection of materials along the way.
- Turn off all the lights and use a material with specular swatches of color
  at the first frame then bring the lights up on the last frame, and display
  the diffuse color or pattern.
- Use the same material from start to finish, but vary the size and/or rotation.

BustUp

- Use smaller-sized logos as elements of the stand-in logo, so when it
  breaks up, it displays smaller cloned logos flying off.
- Use reflective glass spheres as the stand-in object, and watch how they interact when dispersed.
- Do this animation in reverse, allowing a gathering of disparate parts to
  form the final logo.

FogReveal

- Use just the fog height at 100% to reveal the logo.
- Use Haze instead of fog (or in addition to it) to accomplish the reveal.
- Change the color of the fog during the animation for a more psychedelic
  effect.

TerraTrans

- Use a Terrain Editor animation that shows the object going from flat to
  3D surfaced (Hint: Use the height tool).

- Use the Erode tool on the first frame and smooth out the logo on the last frame.
- Use the Elevation Brush to paint "holes" in the logo that smooth over as the animation progresses.
- Use the Invert operation at the start of an animation, reverting to normal at the end. This makes the logo look like it is emerging from a solid block of material (use a stone or wood material to map it).

See the animations Logo1, 2, 3, and 4.mov on the CD-ROM, and the Logo.br3 Project file as well. Also see Figures 14.11 to 14.14.

NOTE

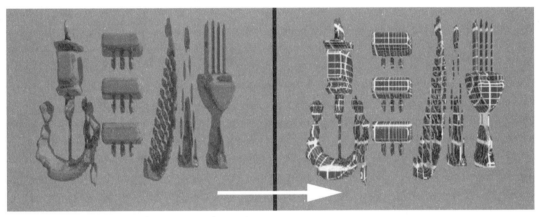

FIGURE   *Different materials fade into one another as the animation progresses.*
14.11

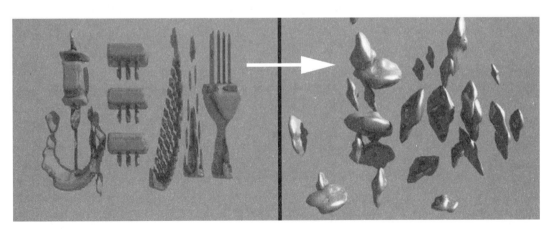

FIGURE   *The logo breaks up into a scattered group of rocks in this example.*
14.12

FIGURE *Out of the misty fog, the logo enters the scene.*
14.13

FIGURE *Twisting morphing convolutions attend to the logo's dance.*
14.14

Rktway

Sometimes the simplest shape can be all that's needed to evoke an animated world in Bryce 3D. In this case, a primitive squashed sphere was used as the ship design. This allows the viewer to appreciate the terrain object more by not cluttering the scene with too many complicated objects. As the animation progresses, three ships exit the tunnel and fly in different directions. A light inside the tunnel pulses on and off.

WHAT TO EXPLORE

Look at the way that a Torus was used to outline the tunnel exit. You might even want to look inside of the terrain object, either from the tunnel or from inside one of the cave openings on the side. Explore how different paths were used to add variety to the flights of the three ships. Look at the placement of the radial light in the tunnel, the way it pulses, and the way it is blocked by the ships exiting in front of it.

SUGGESTIONS FOR YOUR CUSTOMIZING EFFORTS

- Use the Motion Lab to cause the radial light to flash more during the animation, or with a different pulse.
- Create five more ships, so a whole squadron exits from the tunnel.
- Use the camera to fly over the scene from above while the ships are exiting the tunnel.
- Place different models in the tunnel to fly out: kitchen appliances, Poser heads, animals, and so on.

See the Rktzaw.mov animation on the CD-ROM, and the Rktzawy.br3 Project file as well. Also see Figures 14.15 and 14.16.

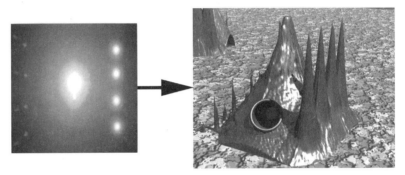

FIGURE **14.15** *The lens flare image on the left created the terrain object on the right in the Bryce 3D Terrain Editor.*

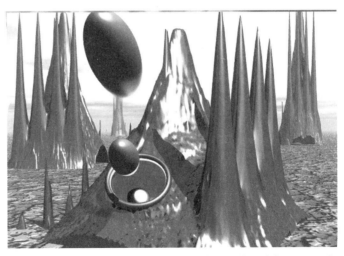

FIGURE **14.16** *The finished animation shows three lozenge shaped ships exiting from the tunnel in the terrain object.*

Spcwrp

Spacewarp takes a look at the uses of camera lens f/x, much like those covered in Chapter 7 of the book. Startling animations can be created when you move a lens to create moving f/x. The result is a true warping of the space in the scene, useful as a stand-alone effect, a transition between scenes, or a view ready to be composited into a narrative about a space warp journey. This project and the sample animation utilize two simple 3D forms in a scene, a cube and a sphere. This demonstrates the process and the f/x, allowing you to apply the same principle to a more complex Bryce 3D scene.

WHAT TO EXPLORE

Study the shape of the lens object in the scene. It is composed of Boolean objects, which can be selected and moved. Rotate the lens so that it is convex instead of concave and render a scene. Note the differences. There is no limit to the quantity of Boolean objects that can be combined (grouped) to create a camera lens. The lens can be moved over the camera, or in front of it. When used in front of it, standard use dictates that you alter the FOV so that it does not range outside of the lens. If the FOV is larger than the lens area, you will see a border unaffected by the lens f/x surrounding the warped area. This can, however, be exactly what you want in certain circumstances. Also note that the lens is commonly mapped with a 100% transparent material, typically glass. It doesn't have to be that way, as you can explore very different mappings.

SUGGESTIONS FOR YOUR CUSTOMIZING EFFORTS

- Use a variety of primitive objects to create a lens, from cubes to spheres and more. Note that each has its own signature lens f/x.
- Create a lens whose Boolean components do not overlap in the beginning of an animation and gradually coincide as the animation progresses.
- Create a lens that is bump mapped, and note how the inconsistencies in the "glass" affect what you see through the camera.

See the Spcwrp.mov animation on the CD-ROM and the Spcwrp.br3 Project file as well. Also see Figures 14.17 and 14.18.

Tunnelz

The story: Two beings from an advanced civilization are ready to explore another dimension and prepare themselves by fine-tuning their chair-transits for the journey. They sit back, adjust the controls in the darkened room, and open the doorway to the dimensional tunnel. Slowly the doorway opens, and one by one they speed through a long tunnel, to exit into a world light years distant.

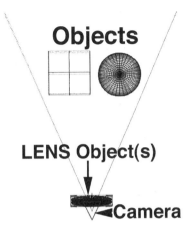

FIGURE   *As seen from the top view, this figure illustrates the basic placement of camera,*
14.17 *lens, and targeted objects.*

FIGURE   *With the unaffected scene shown at the upper left, the other three views show*
14.18 *how radically the view can be altered through the use of lens flx.*

There are infinite ways you can create tunnel animations in Bryce 3D, and tunnel animations are some of the most popular in use in films. Whether it's a time vortex or a dimensional passageway, creating a tunnel that vehicles or actors fly through remains a popular and attractive effect. This project shows one such example.

WHAT TO EXPLORE

Take a good look at the vehicles, the chairs into which the Poser forms sit. The vehicles are created by combining a series of Bryce 3D object primitives. The Poser figure was stretched and altered a bit in Poser itself before being exported to Bryce 3D, giving her a somewhat alien look. Note that a simple sphere was used as her hairpiece. The tunnel is a long hollow cylinder, with a series of glow lights attached to the sides. The lights revolve while the vehicle travels down the tunnel, adding the feeling that we are not in Kansas anymore.

On the other side of the tunnel is the destination world. This is marked by a ring of stones, above which floats a tetrahedron. Study the material applied to the tetrahedron, and also to the stones. The "Puddles" material was used to map the ground. The two chair vehicles orbit the tetrahedron at the conclusion of the animation. The room that the vehicles leave from is a completely segmented two-room apartment.

SUGGESTIONS FOR YOUR CUSTOMIZING EFFORTS

- Place a camera in front of one of the chairs to create an animation that shows a view from the front.
- Alter the destination dimension, creating your own Bryce 3D world in its place.
- Place your own Poser figure in the chair vehicle, adjusting the animation as necessary.
- Design a different vehicle for the dimensional journey.

NOTE

See the Tunnel.mov animation on the CD-ROM and the Tunnel.br3 Project file as well. Also see Figures 14.19 to 14.22.

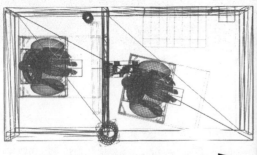 

FIGURE **14.19** *The design of the room that the vehicles exit from is shown on the left (top view), while the rendered first frame is at the right.*

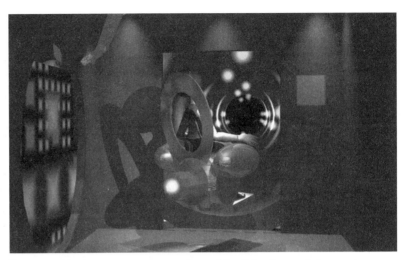

FIGURE *As the door opens, you can see the revolving lights that mark the tunnel.*
14.20

FIGURE *As the chair travels down the tunnel, a light linked to the chair creates*
14.21 *interesting shadows on the walls.*

FIGURE   *Reaching their destination, the actors orbit a floating tetrahedron over an alien*
14.22   *landscape.*

Volco

This scene features one example of how effective 2D mapped animation sequences can be. It displays a fireball that seems to be coming from the mouth
of a volcano. The fireball is a sequence of images taken from the Pyromania
CD-ROM collection and mapped frame by frame in the Materials Lab to a
2D picture plane. Care was taken to create the Alpha masks first, to show the
bitmapped images in full brilliant color.

WHAT TO EXPLORE

Notice that the fireball loops several times, as customized in the Materials Lab
Picture Editor. Changing the order of the mapping will result in a very different animated fireball. The face on the doorway of the volcano started off as an
innocent picture of a friend of mine and was tweaked in the Terrain Editor into
a more malevolent portrait. Gold material is used throughout, with green
Specularity and a reddish light, giving the gold green and red highlights. The
figure sitting on top of the doorway is a Poser import colored metallic blue.
The background volcanoes are Boolean constructs. Explore their design. The
movement of the animation is a Hollywood standard "pan and truck," meaning a look around the scene followed by a movement into it. Also take time to
explore the material used to map the "moon" in the background.

SUGGESTIONS FOR YOUR CUSTOMIZING EFFORTS

- Move the camera in for an even closer look at the fireball movement, but never veer from the frontal view while doing it.
- Animate the doorway opening to reveal a treasure inside (Hint: Use a negative Boolean to cut a hole in the volcano).
- Duplicate the 2D animated sequence of fire for the background volcanoes.
- Move the camera from a close-up to a very distant shot at the end of the animation.

See the Volco 1 and 2.mov animations on the CD-ROM and the Volco.br3 Project file as well. See Figures 14.23 to 14.25.

FIGURE **14.23** *The evolution of the volcano door, from the building stones through the application of the gold material.*

FIGURE **14.24** *The explosion seems to emanate from the volcano.*

FIGURE *Here, the scene is shown as the camera pulls back.*
14.25

Zland

This project is by far the most extensive one in the book. I called it "Zland" because I wanted it to be listed last. In Bryce 3D terms, it covers hundreds of
acres. The general theme is that of an island hideaway, a peaceful place to es-
cape to when the real world gets too upsetting. There is a long river that leads
to an inlet. On one side of the inlet is a beach with two huts on stilts, over-
looking a pier. A few dugouts are resting on the sand, while a family looks out
over the water to the other side. In the water on the other shore are two elephants basking in the sun, while behind them an animated waterfall displays its
beauty. The voyage into this hidden place is provided by another dugout, nav-
igated by a Poser figure in a turban. The voyage traverses the river and winds up
next to the pier. The animation took two days to render at 320 x 240 with antialiasing off.

WHAT TO LOOK FOR

There's lots to investigate here. The sheer size of this project and the number of
ways you can further customize it mean that everything you look at can be the
motivation for deeper exploration. Let's start with the water plane. If you alter
the transparency or turbulence of the water, you will automatically create a very
different story than the one the audience is asked to intuit by the presentation
as it is now put together. The land masses that straddle the inlet are con-

structed from a mix of large rocks and terrain objects. Look at each grouping and the materials that address it.

The dugouts on the shore, and the one that acts as our touring vehicle, are Boolean constructs of the simplest kind. The material that texturizes them looks like a cross between wood and wicker, so you should look at it in the Materials Lab. The huts on stilts that form the village habitat in the background were crafted in Ray Dream and exported to Bryce 3D. If you wanted to, you could set up a rendering camera inside one, and record a view looking through the window. The Poser figures standing on the pier and the figure that pilots the animated dugout can also be explored thoroughly, as well as ungrouped and recomposed. Take a look at the material composition of the "beach areas." Some look like rock, and others like sand. Explore the textures used to create the material that is used to map the pier posts, one of the most stunning materials in this project.

The waterfall is a separate item that warrants closer inspection. Instead of a plain cylinder being used for its construction, it was crafted from a Symmetrical Lattice object. This was done so the cylindrical shape could be notched, so that when it was mapped with a water texture and animated, the notches would show irregularities that make the water appear more randomly placed and "real." The elephants are from the Acuworlds Bryce 3D library collection, available separately. The Zland1.mov animation focuses upon just the waterfall.

SUGGESTIONS FOR YOUR CUSTOMIZING EFFORTS

- Alter the path of the animated dugout. You can even make it go around the perimeter of the island from the outside, before entering the inlet.
- Clone the Poser figures on the shore and place a tribe of onlookers in the scene.
- Place a hut at the top of the mountain that overlooks the inlet, acting as a special temple next to the shrine that stands there now.
- Make one of the mountainous terrains a volcano, adding sparks and animated fireballs as necessary.
- Import fish models to populate the water world and animate them.
- Change the animated craft to a submarine. You can build it using Bryce 3D primitive objects, grouping them together.
- Do a camera flyover animation, allowing your audience to appreciate this huge scene from above.
- Build a protective sea wall at the opening of the river, allowing the water in the inlet to be fresh instead of salty. Create an animated door that opens to allow dugouts and other craft entry.

- There is an oar attached to the right hand of the boatman. Animate his arms and the oar so he can be seen as rowing the dugout.

See the Zland1.mov and Zland2.mov animations on the CD-ROM, and the Zland.br3 project file as well. Also see Figures 14.26 to 14.29.

NOTE

FIGURE
14.26 *Some of the elements of the Zland world.*

FIGURE
14.27 *An aerial view of Zland, showing the waterfall in the lower left of the picture. The village can be seen below, with the pier. The inlet is at the right, and you can make out the dugout beginning its journey.*

FIGURE *Alternate views of the figures on the pier.*
14.28

FIGURE *The village, the boatman, and the waterfall*
14.29

In Conclusion　　As far as your initial exploration of this book, we are at journey's end. You can always return to those sections of the book that need more study, or to clarify your Bryce 3D work. Hopefully, you have found that the book and the material on the CD-ROM that accompanies it have added more depth to your Bryce 3D world creating capabilities. Perhaps a few items have even pushed you to explore new areas of endeavor. Thank you for purchasing this book, and may your Bryce 3D worlds be worlds of continual discovery.

APPENDIX

CD-ROM
Content

T his book comes with a CD-ROM bursting with content for you to explore, customize, and use as part of your Bryce 3D work.

As a value-added benefit to both Mac and Windows users, there are demo versions of both Terran Interactive's MediaCleaner Pro and Ulead's MediaStudio Pro. This book was created using both a Pentium and a PowerMac system, and both of these applications were used to fine tune the Bryce 3D animations. Depending on whether you are working on a Pentium or PowerMac, take a look at either or both MediaCleaner Pro (Mac) and/or MediaStudio Pro (Windows) on the book's CD-ROM.

There are project files relating to the tutorial sections in each chapter in the Project folder. A number of unique materials are contained in the Materials folder, and you can also load and save hundreds of customized materials by loading each project, and using the Materials Lab to save materials to your own disk library. Bryce 3D is an animation application, and for that reason, we have created **80 animations** (as QuickTime movies) that you can play back for creative exploration, as well as your own entertainment. This is one of the major value-added features offered by this book over any other Bryce 3D book on the market. The movies are in the Anims folder on the CD-ROM, and their content is detailed below.

If you are a Windows user, you will need QuickTime for Windows in order to view these movies. If you don't already have it installed on your system, you can download it from Apple's QuickTime Web site, at http://www.apple.com/quicktime/.

NOTE

Name of Movie Folder	Name of Movie	Description of Movie
1. Anims/Other	Curtin1.mov; 1.4 MB	Rock in back of animated changing transparent material.
2. Anims/Other	Explos1; 264K	Pyromania explosion.
3 & 4. Anims/Other	Island1.mov; 1.8 MB Island3.mov; 2.2 MB	Prop plane flights over island.
5. Anims/Other	Linkers1.mov; 948K	Linked birds in fog.
6. Anims/Other objects.	Optilus1.mov; 1.6 MB	Light Gel projection and inserted sky plane over moving Boolean
7–9. Anims/Other	RobatX4.mov; 1.9 MB RobatX5.mov; 1.9 MB RobatX8.mov; 1.9 MB	Primitives robot in three animations.
10. Anims/Other	Explo-singles (BMP); 996K	Pyromania BMP singles of explosion.
11. Anims/Other	Ants1.mov; 2.5 MB Ants2.mov; 2.6 MB	Import models, ants simple anim (no parts).
12–14. Anims/Other	BlThru1.mov; 1.1 MB BlThru2.mov; 1.1 MB BlThru3.mov; 1.9 MB	1. Camera target Ball. 2. Camera Link Ball. 3. Camera IS Ball.
15. Anims/Other	City_02.mov; 5 MB	Two rockets over terrain citymap.
16 & 17. Anims/Other	Clouds1.mov; 1 MB Clouds2.mov; 848K	Camera points at moving clouds.
18. Anims/Other	DetFly1.mov; 4.1 MB	Up from sea over table and out.
19-23. Anims/Other	ET2-6.mov; 1, 2.2, 3, 2.9, 3.1 MB	ET ship from different angles. Light is attached to bottom of ship.
24. Anims/Other	Fish_2A.mov; 5.3 MB	Fish in Water cage. Note materials.
25. Anims/Other	Gel1.mov; 1.2 MB	Great Gel projection thru spotlight.
26. Anims/Other	Grower1.mov; 848K	Animated Terrains on end- grow & short.
27. Anims/Other	H2OFly1.mov; 4.6 MB	Complex flyover of water and sunflower object.
28. Anims/Other	Header1.mov; 848K	Ulead Media Studio 5 post f/x of head with orbiting stuff.
29. Anims/Other	Literz1.mov; 1 MB	Great ship in dark with moving volume spotlights.
30. Anims/Other	Mazer1.mov; 1 MB	Great flythrough of camera behind ball through maze.
31. Anims/Other	MyBrc3.mov; 1 MB	Poser figure animated.
32–34. Anims/Other	Psr1,2,3.mov; 1.4, 1.5, and 1.6 MB	Different views of Poser 3D figure bouncing ball.
35. Anims/Other	Spinny1.mov; 432K	Simple orbit of cube around sphere.
36–40. Anims/Other	TM1-TM5.mov; 736K, 720K, 768K, 768K, 944K	Terramorph animations showing 5 different morphs.
41. Anims/Other	Boolhl1.mov; 1.9 MB	Holes cut in infinite plane above reveal sky and birds overhead.
42. Anims/Other	Jelloh1.mov; 992K	Transparent Torus jiggles to reveal light changes behind.
43. Anims/Other	Mandy1.mov; 1.2 MB	Mandala of birds flying around disk with image sequence mapped on it.

Name of Movie Folder	Name of Movie	Description of Movie
44. Anims/Other	Ploperz.mov; 368K	Plop rendering animation in upper right corner of image.
45. Anims/Other	Reveal1.mov; 1.4 MB	Boolean Sphere cuts wall to reveal scene.
46. Anims/Other	Cosclam1.mov; 1.2 MB	Clam shell opens and pearl flies out.
47. Anims/Other	Skely.mov; 1.4 MB	Poser skeleton animated with terrain-morphed headpiece.
48. Anims/CH6	Fig6_1.mov; 1.2 MB	Camera shows animated vertical sky in back of object.
49. Anims/CH8	Aurora1.mov; 1.3 MB	Aurora Borealis f/x.
50. Anims/CH8	Liqrk.mov; 1.2 MB	Rock with animated material.
51. Anims/CH8	Mud1M.mov; 1.7 MB	Boiling Mud.
52 & 53. Anims/CH8	Skywash1 & 2.mov; 2 MB	Sky animation, and same animation with vortex effect.
54. Anims/CH9	Camdrl1.mov; 850k	Camera attached to Boolean object drills hole to reveal scene.
55 & 56. Anims/CH9	Citbool1 & 2.mov; 850k	Boolean Negative and Intersect f/x.
57. Anims/CH9	Linky1.mov; 1.2 MB	Linked objects fly and disperse.
58. Anims/CH9	Solsys1.mov; 1 MB	Multiple planets orbit a sun.
59. Anims/CH10	Runz1.mov; 500k	Figure has animated legs and materials.
60. Anims/CH11	Mthrp.mov; 600k	Globe has animated and layered materials.
61. Anims/CH12	Ballfl.mov; 1.6 MB	Flying ball.
62. Anims/CH12	Disnull.mov; 1.8 MB	Orbiting objects are controlled by a Null object.
63. Anims/CH12	Gwellm.mov; 1 MB	Null object controls gravity well.
64. Anims/CH14	Anthro.mov; 2.9 MB	Bryce 3D/Poser animation.
65. Anims/CH14	Aster.mov; 2.9 MB	Ship makes its way through asteroid field.
66–68. Anims/CH14	Drive1,2, and 3.mov; 2.6MB, 2.8MB, 3.3 MB	Rotating cylinder scene with car and plane.
69. Anims/CH14	Fred.mov; 992k	Three Poser figures combined with imported parts and animated.
70–73. Anims/CH14	Logoz1, 2, 3, and 4; 1027k, 613k, 1634k, 2261k	Logo f/x animations.
74. Anims/CH14	Rktzaw.mov; 2.7 MB	Three ships emerge from terrain object and fly in different directions.
75. Anims/CH14	Spcwrp.mov; 2 MB	Animated camera lens f/x.
76. Anims/CH14	Tunnel.mov; 5.4 MB	Two Poser beings cross the dimensional divide through a tunnel.
77 & 78. Anims/CH14	Volco 1 and 2.mov; 3.3 and 2.3 MB	Exploding volcano in a composite scene.
79 & 80. Anims/CH14	Zland 1 and 2.mov; 2.8 and 4.8 MB	Dugout navigator journeys through scene with waterfall, elephants, and small village.

B
Web Output

Internally, Bryce 3D files can be rendered as 360 degree Panoramas for use on the Web. They have to be translated to Apple's QuickTime VR format first. Contact Apple's Web site for downloading the appropriate translators and the QuickTime VR module: http://www.apple.com.

Windows users can use MediaStudio Pro (a try-out version is included on the CD-ROM) to translate AVI animations into GIF animations for the Web. Mac users can do the same with any application that reads QuickTime movies and writes GIF animations. Both Mac and Windows users can use any suitable application that writes out GIF or JPEG (and Progressive JPEG) files to post Bryce 3D pictures to the Web. There are also new technologies coming on board that allow you to post PICT, BMP, and TIFF pictures to the Web, as well as QuickTime animations. The reader should research computer graphics magazines and the Web to keep informed concerning these new options.

APPENDIX C

Useful Add-ons

There are a number of applications you will want to investigate to make your Bryce 3D experience even more exciting. Here are a few.

Tree Professional (Windows & Mac)

http://www.onyx.com

Though Bryce 3D does a number of things quite well, it falls pretty flat when it comes to designing tree objects. The present way Bryce 3D allows you to generate trees in your scene, from Boolean objects or trees created by manipulating the material in the Materials Lab, takes far too much rendering time. Tree Professional from Onyx Software is one of the best answers, and it is available for both Mac and Windows users.

TreePro has more options than any other foliage generating application. It comes with a library of hundreds of tree forms and rendered 2D graphics. The pre-rendered graphics can be used when you need to place groups of trees in the background, written to 2D picture planes in Bryce 3D. The tree 3D models can be used when you need to have the tree visible from different views as a full 3D object. TreePro allows you full design options for Broadleaves (deciduous), Conifers, and Palms. You can also easily create some pretty interesting alien tree forms.

TreePro has a small chainsaw-shaped icon that allows you to prune branches off of any tree model, customizing it exactly to your specifications. In addition, a complete leaf phylotaxy is included, as are controls for shaping every aspect of the tree. Tree models are saved out of TreePro as DXF models, just right for Bryce 3D imports. As you might imagine, a large tree covered with leaves can take up a lot of space on your hard drive, and could even choke Bryce 3D when imported. But not to worry, since TreePro allows you to trim the DXF file with several options before saving the DXF model, displaying the DXF polygon count before the model is committed to storage. TreePro can also build bushes and other tree-like objects. TreePro is a perfect Bryce 3D companion.

Net Toob (Windows)

http://www.duplexx.com

If you are running Bryce 3D on a Windows system and would like to have a utility that displays your Bryce 3D animations at larger than saved sizes, investigate Net Toob from Duplexx Software. A demo version of Net Toob can be found at hundreds of places on the Web, or, you can contact Duplexx directly with the URL given above. Net Toob allows you to play your Bryce 3D animation at Normal, Double, and Full Screen sizes, at speeds ranging from 10 to 400%. You can also use Net Toob to save your Bryce 3D AVI, QuickTime, or MPEG animations as screen savers.

MetaSynth (PowerMac)

http://www.uisoftware.com

Eric Wenger, the creator of Bryce, continues to develop software for the arts. One of his latest creations is MetaSynth, an application that allows you to create music from graphics files. It requires a PowerMac running at 120 MHz or better, with 1.5 MB of free hard disk space. With MetaSynth, you can create sound tracks for your Bryce 3D animations.

MetaSynth translates visual data into audio data. The vertical axis of an image relates to pitch, and the horizontal axis represents duration. Brightness of a pixel relates to the volume of a sound, and its color shift is translated into where the stereo sound is placed in space (Red=left, Yellow=center, and Green=right). You can develop Bryce 3D images, save them as PICT files, and load them into MetaSynth where they will be translated into sounds. You do not need special sound cards to "play" a graphic file in MetaSynth. Everything is contained in the software, including a large number of Synthesis and Playback engines. In addition, you can load your own Sound Designer or AIFF sound samples into MetaSynth. For audiophiles, Eric Wenger's MetaSynth is as intense a creative environment as Bryce 3D.

Other MetaCreations' Applications

In addition to developing and marketing Bryce 3D, MetaCreations also has a number of additional graphics and animation applications under its wing. Your Bryce 3D work can benefit from the output of each of these other applications.

Poser

This book looks at Poser output quite a number of times for the development of Bryce 3D art and animations. Poser 2 was used to develop the animated figures used in the Bryce 3D projects. Poser 3 was released after the book was completed, but offers even more than its version 2 predecessor for Bryce 3D work. Use Poser to:

- Develop human and animal articulated models for Bryce 3D animation.
- Ungroup Poser exports in Bryce 3D when you need separate parts like heads, hands, etc.
- Animate Poser models in Poser, and then import the single frame sequences into Bryce 3D for 2D plane animations and bitmap textures.

Important! Poser 2 was used to craft the humanoid models in this book, but just after the book went to press, Poser 3 was released. Poser 3 is one of the most full-featured creative applications ever to hit the market. It allows you full control over character animated features (eyes, mouths, lip phoneme alterations, and more), and also allows you to design and animate animals. If you animate your figures in Poser 3, and save them as single-frame sequences, the resulting frames can be written to 2D Picture Planes in Bryce 3D. You can also import Poser 3 OBJ and 3DS files, and animate the parts in Bryce 3D. Poser 3 is an absolute must for any Bryce 3D artist or animator.

Painter   MetaCreations' Painter is the most full featured painting application on the
                           planet. Using it for various Bryce 3D associated tasks makes your Bryce 3D
                           work shine. Use Painter to:

- Develop bitmap textures for creating Bryce 3D materials in the Materials Lab. Use the Painter output as full bitmap based materials, or as bitmap components in a texture stack.
- If you are creating 2D artwork in Bryce, meant for gallery prints or desktop publishing associated tasks, be sure to investigate the uses of the Painter Image Hose for spraying various image details on top of your Bryce 3D output.
- Import your QuickTime and AVI animations directly into Painter, and use its collection of effects to alter the entire animation.

Ray Dream   Ray Dream 5 has spectacular modeling and file transfer capabilities, all of
                           which are very useful to the Bryce 3D artist and animator. Use Ray Dream to:

- Develop and customize models in the Meshform other modeling modules for specific Bryce 3D projects.
- Translate imported DXF models into 3D Studio or WaveFront OBJ models for export to Bryce 3D for smooth rendering and animation.
- Translate any of Ray Dream's huge collection of 3D models for use in Bryce 3D.

Infini-D   Another 3D modeling and animation solution from MetaCreations, Infini-D
                           can be used to:

- Model objects for export to Bryce 3D.
- Create particle effects with one of the industry's leading particle effects generators. Export to Bryce 3D, for mapping image sequences onto 2D planes.

PowerGoo   PowerGoo is one of the most addictive morphing applications around. Use it
                           to:

- Export an animated sequence of frames to Bryce 3D, for use on 2D planes.

- Import a finished Bryce 3D movie, and add morphing-warping effects in PowerGoo.

Kai's PowerTools

PowerTools is a plugin for Photoshop, PhotoPaint, and most other bitmap augmentation applications. As a collection of f/x modules, use PowerTools to augment and customize any images headed for your Bryce 3D environment.

Final Effects Complete

When your Bryce 3D animation is finished, you may want to add some post production effects in Adobe's After Effects. Final Effects Complete is a plugin for After Effects that allows you to add an infinite number of image transitions and effects to your Bryce 3D animations.

Stay abreast of all MetaCreations wares by visiting www.metacreations.com frequently.

APPENDIX

3D File Format Translators

There are a number of applications that allow you to translate 3D file formats from selections that Bryce 3D cannot import to those it can. This opens up your Bryce 3D worlds to thousands of available models. You should own at least one of these applications, in order to make your Bryce 3D work open to CD-ROM and other 3D application model collections.

Amapi (Mac & Windows)

http:www.amapi.com

Amapi is a full-fledged 3D design system in its own right, allowing you to create models from scratch. But Amapi can also be used as a 3D file translator, an intermediate step in getting your favorite models into Bryce 3D. Amapi can import Amapi, 3DS, 3DMF, Artlantis Render, DXF, IGES, Illustrator 3, PICT, and VRML 1 files. It can export Amapi, 3DS, 3DGF, 3DMF, Artlantis Render, **Bryce 2**, Clipboard, DXF, FACT, HPGL, IGES, Illustrator, Light-Wave, PICT, PovRay, Ray Dream, Renderman, STL, Strata Studio, trueSpace, and VRML 1 formats.

NuGraf/ PolyTrans

http://www.okino.com

Okino Computer Graphics markets both the NuGraf Rendering System and PolyTrans (a subset of the NuGraf Rendering System). Both are loaded with import and export capabilities to help you place models into your Bryce 3D world. The NuGraf software is also render intensive, while PolyTrans is dedicated more toward being a bridge between file formats. Get more details by going to the Okino Web site: http://www.okino.com.

Import formats include 3DS, Alias Triangle, Detailer, DXF, NFF, IGES, Imagine, LightWave, Pro Engineer, 3DMF, SoftImage, Stereo Lithography, Strata StudioPro, trueSpace, USGS DEM, and OBJ.

Export formats include 3DS, 3DMF, Detailer, DirectX, DXF, LightScape, LightWave, OpenGL, POV, Pro/E SLP, Renderman, SoftImage, STL, Strata StudioPro, trueSpace, VRML, and OBJ.

There are other 3D geometry converters on the market, but these two are the best for your Bryce 3D work.

NOTE

Post-Production Utilities

Any number of post-production utilities can be used to further customize your Bryce 3D animations outside of Bryce 3D itself. The MediaStudio application (try-out) version on the CD-ROM is an excellent example. If you are a Windows user, load this application on your hard drive and give it a spin. You'll find that MediaStudio Pro can create all sorts of f/x for your Bryce 3D movies. In addition to MediaStudio Pro, there are two other utilities you might want to consider when it comes time to add a little pizzazz to your Bryce 3D movies. They're both from Adobe.

http://www.adobe.com

Adobe Premiere

Premiere allows you to string animations together to create a longer sequence. It also fosters the use of transitional f/x between animation segments, with many libraries included and more available as plugins. Contact Adobe for more details and pricing.

Adobe After Effects

Adobe After Effects is used to add f/x to your animations. For instance, instead of taking up precious rendering time to add fire coming from the nozzle of a rocket in Bryce 3D, you can add it later in After Effects with the right plugin. After Effects ships with dozens of plugin f/x, and another 60 are available as part of a special Production Bundle add-on. Hundreds more are available from independent vendors. These include the Final Effects Complete volumes from MetaCreations, used to create the animated waterfall in Jan Nickman's Planetary Traveler. Contact Adobe for more details and pricing.

MainActor for Windows OS2/95/NT

If there is one utility you must have for translating just about any animation format into another, or into single frames, it is MainActor from MainConcept in Germany. Nothing else works as well, or as fast. For animations, you simply select the files that make up the animation. MainActor then loads the files and allows you to preview the animation. Adjusting the speed of the animation, should the default timecode be too small or too large, is a matter of selecting a menu item and typing in a new timecode. Creating the animation file is then a matter of saving the animation in the format you desire. Sophisticated animations can be created in seconds with MainActor.

MainActor supports more animation formats than any other tool in its class, and we are constantly adding more. And with the MainActor Developer Kit, it is easy for developers to create loader/saver modules for other formats. The openness of the MainActor design means you won't be stranded as new formats come into use. Power users know that scripting is an essential element of a powerful tool and MainActor offers a proprietary scripting language, REXX. Like MainActor, REXX is a language that is designed for both beginners and power users. It has a natural-language syntax (i.e., even non-programmers can read a REXX program and get an idea of what it is doing) and it is very extensible. The REXX scripting in MainActor makes it possible to do just about anything you can do manually from the program's user interface. This makes it much easier to perform certain tasks such as creating animations

MainActor Load Formats

AVI: Cinepak, Intel Indeo v2.1/v3.1/v3.2./, Microsoft RLE, Microsoft Video 1; Motion JPEG: Support of animations generated by video capture hardware (i.e., have missing Huffman tables. This feature has been tested with animations generated by FAST, Matrox and Mire hardware), Ultimotion, Uncompressed; BMP: RunLength Encoded, Uncompressed; Dt: Type 1 and Type 2; FLI/FLC: ByteRun, Byte Line Coding, Clear Screen, Uncompressed, Word Line Coding: GIF: LZW, GIF Animation LZW; IFF Anim 3/5/7/8/ J: ByteRun, Delta 3/5/7/8/ J; IFF Picture, ByteRun; JPEG Picture: (supports pictures with missing Huffman tables); MPEG Audio: Layer I/II/II1; MPEG Animation: MPEG I & II, Supports Audio; PCX Picture: RunLength Encoded; PNG/PPM/PGM/PBM; QuickTime Animation: Sound, Apple Animation, Apple Graphics, Cinepak, Intel Indeo v2.1/3.1/v3.2, Motion JPEG; TGA Picture: RunLength Encoded, Uncompressed; WAV Sound: Pulse Code Modulation

Output Formats   AVI Animation: Sound, Cinepak (Windows Only), Intel Indeo v3.1 (OS/2 Only)/v3.2/v4.1 and v5.0 (Both Windows Only), Microsoft RLE; Motion JPEG: Software; Motion JPEG Hardware; Ultimotion (OS/2 Only), Uncompressed; BMP: Uncompressed; FLC Animation: ByteRun, Word Line Coding; FLI Animation: ByteRun, Byte Line Coding; GIF Picture: LZW; GIF-Anim Animation: LZW; JPEG; MacPICT; MPEG Audio; MPEG Audio Layer II; MPEG Animation: MPEG-I PAL (Supports Audio), MPEG-I NTSC (Supports Audio), MPEG-II PAL, MPEG-II NTSC; PNG: PPM/PGM/PBM; QuickTime Animation (Supports Sound): Cinepak (Windows Only), Intel Indeo v3.1 (OS/2 Only)/v3.2 (Windows Only)/v4.1 (Windows Only); Motion JPEG; TGA Picture: RunLength Encoded, Uncompressed; Video Data Binary (Splits the video data from animations), Video Data; WAV Sound: Pulse Code Modulation.

MainActor $60.00 US
(PowerMac version in the works)

MainConcept, GbR Moenig/Zabel
Hermann-Heusch-Platz 3
52062 Aachen
Germany

Tel: 49 (0)241-4090444
Fax: 49 (0)241-4090445

BBS: 49 (0)241-4090446

orders@mainconcept.de
support@mainconcept.de
markusm@mainconcept.de

APPENDIX

G
CD-ROM
Content
Libraries

There are hundreds of available CD-ROMs that contain 3D models, textures, and background graphics, with more being released each month. We certainly can't even begin to touch on all of them, but here are some you might want to check out for your Bryce 3D work.

CloudScapes

ImageClub Graphics: http://www.imageclub.com/digitalvision/

This CD-ROM contains 100 thematically related cloud images that can be mapped to a 2D Picture Plane in Bryce 3D. The CD is both Mac and Windows compatible.

H2O

ImageClub Graphics: http://www.imageclub.com/digitalvision/

This CD-ROM contains 100 thematically related images of water that can be mapped to a 2D Picture Plane in Bryce 3D. You can also use a number of these images as bitmap textures and even tile them for effect. The CD is both Mac and Windows compatible.

LightROM 5

Graphic Detail: (502) 363-2986

LightROM 5 contains hundreds of models in the LightWave and 3DS formats, including textures and image maps. The LightWave models will have to be translated to a format that Bryce 3D can comprehend in a separate translation application. The 3DS models can be loaded directly into Bryce 3D.

**Replica
Technology**

http://www.replica3d.com

Replica Tech produces dozens of unique CD-ROMs, each one loaded with 3D models and their image maps. They come in many formats, but to get the models into Bryce 3D you will have to translate them in an object translation utility. Three that might be of high interest for Bryce 3D users are the Camelot, Interior Design, and Wright Collections. The Camelot Collection contains all that you need to simulate a dark ages world, with castles and inner chambers, all intricately detailed and ready to place and render. The Interior Design CD-ROM is packed with rooms of decor, and the Wright Collection pays homage to the work of Frank Lloyd Wright.

MetaCreations

http://www.metacreations.com

Contact MetaCreations for the availability and pricing of additional CD-ROM libraries that extend the capacities of Bryce 3D.

APPENDIX

Master User Bios

H ere is the biographical information from the two Bryce 3D masters whose work is detailed in Chapter 13.

Cecilia Ziemer

Cecilia Ziemer a freelance artist who made the jump from 2D on canvas and paper to 3D on the computer about six years ago. She is a frequent contributor to 3D Artist magazine. Her 3D work has also appeared in *Artistry*, *Computer Graphics World*, *New Media*, and *3D Design* magazines, and the *Ray Dream 5 F/X* book (R. Shamms Mortier, Ventana Press, 1997), the *Ray Dream Handbook* (John Sledd and Craig Patchett, Charles River Media, 1997), and in *Looking Good in Color* (Gary W. Priester, Ventana Press, 1995).

She has had several one-woman shows of her paintings in Texas, New Mexico, and California. She did topographical models for the Oakland Museum's Natural History department, scientific illustration (mostly pen and ink, and airbrush), and an occasional political cartoon for the now defunct *Indian Citizen* newspaper. Although her previous work was grounded in nonobjective painting, she now works primarily with science fiction, fantasy, and visionary themes. She works on both Windows NT and Power Mac platforms, using 3D Studio Max, Bryce 3D, Infini-D, Ray Dream Studio, Poser, Photoshop, and Painter. She lives in Sunnyvale, California, and enjoys showing you some of the weird worlds around and within us.

ziemer@pop.batnet.com

Mark Smith

Mark Smith is a digital FX supervisor at Digital Drama in Newark, New Jersey. Digital Drama has produced digital visual FX for MCA/Universal, Trimark

Pictures, Concorde/New Horizons, SHOWTIME, SABAN, Gramercy Pictures and HBO. He can be reached at:

digitaldrama@home.com
http://members.home.com/digitaldrama

DIGITAL DRAMA

Digital Drama is a full-service computer graphics, animation, and digital painting facility on Routes 1&9 South, conveniently located across from Newark International Airport, in Newark, New Jersey. While putting its creative mark on a host of major corporations, Digital Drama has maintained a close relationship with the Hollywood creative community as well. Often times, the technological envelope gets pushed to the edge during the grand special effects sequences in Hollywood filmwork. Inevitably these techniques are carried over to new uses in corporate work. It remains an asset to stay rooted in film.

Our combined talent base has worked on everything from the most popular video games to the trenches of Hollywood. This diversity becomes the most powerful tool for the corporate environment today. The end goal is to provide the most memorable, thoughtful, and eye-catching content available. Whether it is outrageously load or subtly clever, images speak volumes over words.

The latest hardware and software from industry leaders makes up our stable of tools. Hardware and software on-site includes: Silicon Graphics Octane, Indigo, and Indy workstations give us the power to stay on top. We also employ Macintosh PowerPC and Windows NT workstations to remain completely compatible and ultra cross-platform. Our Software is the most sophisticated on the planet. We utilize the power of Alias/Wavefront Power Animator 8.5, A/W Composer 4.5, SoftImage Extreme 3.7, 3D Studio MAX 2.0, LightWave 5.5, Elastic Reality, Adobe After Effects 3.1, and so much more. Digital Drama is always on the cutting edge of software technology. Our membership in several high profile hardware and software Beta programs affords us the inside track on what's cool, powerful, and trendy.

Recent Film and Creative Media Clients

MCA/ Universal Studios, Gramercy Pictures, Polygram Home Video, HBO, Showtime Cable, Trimark Pictures, Saban Entertainment, FOX Home Entertainment, Capital Arts Entertainment, Concorde New Horizons, Broadway Video/Comics. We have established a wide area of expertise in the field of digital imagery. Our wide range of partnerships run the gamut of the digital spectrum. Our new alliance with Validia Animation Studio has given us a new perspective into traditional 2D cell animation! This completes the circle of what is possible and what we can produce at Digital Drama.

Bryce Update

During the preparation and production of this book, Bryce 3D went through a revision. Ity was too late to fold all of the fixes and new attributes into the body of the book, so we are presenting them here for your awareness. Please note that all of the items involved in the upgraded Bryce 3D do not negate the tutorials or hints and tips contained in the book, but that the new Bryce 3D material just adds to the functionality and usability of Bryce 3D. many of the revisions will be invisible to you, since they just make things work cleaner and faster. Contact MetaCreations at http://www.metacreations.com for the availability and other information related to this upgrade.

Enhancements

Here is an overview of the new enhanced features, and the fixes, in the new Bryce 3D.

MORE MAC PARITY

Parity with the Mac 2.1 version of Bryce has been increased, which is good news for experienced Bryce users who have saved out files in the older format. The best of what each version has to offer can be handshaked, while at the same time improving on it with the newer Bryce 3D options. This ranges all the way from importing old scenes to how the wireframe views are drawn.

NEW PREVIEW MODES

In most places that nano-renders exist (materials lab, materials presets, etc.), you can now choose what object to use, and even edit the camera. A couple of new objects have been added to the list as well as a new mode, which uses the actual object you have selected. The new objects are Pyramidî, Circle and

Square. The new mode is called Actual Selection. In this mode, even booleans and triangle meshes are represented accurately. This is VERY useful for applying textures in world space and getting true results in the nano-render.

NEW MATERIAL MAPPING MODES

The mapping mode menu in the materials lab now contains a few new features. First, Scale Pict Size now works exactly as it should. If selected, it scales pict textures instead of tiling them with increasing frequency. Both of these modes use the textures scale (which can be set through the frequency slider, or the texture transformation scale tool) as input. Next, Centered Transforms, only works with parametric mapping modes. It forces the texture's transformations (applied with the texture transformation tools) to be applied around the center of the object's surface. The Decal Colors mode is also new. It blends a texture's color with the affected component's base color, using the texture's alpha channel to control the amount of blending. This can make decaling effects much easier to achieve. The last new mode is called Alpha Scaling. Normally, if you drive a component's value with a texture, the texture's alpha channel will set the value without regard to the amount that was set using the componentís slider. With alpha scaling turned on, the amount set with the slider will scale the amount provided by the texture's alpha channel. This gives you more subtle control over the influence of the texture on the material component's value.

CLICK-LIST SELECTION

If you hold down Control (Windows) or Command (Mac) while clicking an object to select/deselect it, you will get a list of all objects under the pointer. This makes life a lot easier in complex scenes. This lets you not only view the selection status of all the listed objects, but change it as well. Again, this aids in dealing with large scenes.

SELECTION PALETTE

A couple of enhancements were made in the selection palette. Path objects now have their own menu item (list) along with groups and triangle mesh objects. This makes selecting them much easier in a crowded scene. When selecting objects with the family name menu, you now have a choice of sorting styles. If you hold down the Control (Windows) or Command (Mac) key, the list will be sorted alphabetically. Otherwise, if you hold no modifier keys, the list will be arranged in order of family position (from 1 thru 25).

NEW I/O PLUG-INS

A few new plug-ins have been added. The 3D Studio loader is now available on the MAC side as well as for Windows platforms, and both platforms now have plug-ins for generating movies as a sequence of images. For the PC, you get a BMP sequence and for the MAC you get a PICT sequence.

OVERRIDE DROP-TO-BOXES

A new item has been added to the wireframe resolution menu: Auto LOD. When checked, objects will automatically draw as boxes if it takes too long to draw the scene. If you uncheck this item, this behavior will stop. This can be useful when trying to accurately position objects, with respect to others, in a large scene.

TRANSLATION IN CURRENT SPACE

By holding down the X, Y or Z keys, you can move objects along the selected axis with respect to the camera. This works regardless of the editing mode you have selected through the edit palette. In other words, if you hold down the X key and drag an object, it will only be able to move left and right. For the Y key, up and down, and for the Z key, in and out. This can be a great time saver when positioning objects in an animation.

GROUP ORIGIN EDITING

Group origin editing was prevented in the original release of Bryce3D, but now it has been enabled. You can now freely edit (reposition) a group object's origin, just like any other object. This is a very useful revision, because the Origin Point acts as the core focus when transformations are needed.

EASIER PICT LIBRARY IMAGE LOADING

Now you can simply click on an empty slot to load a new image. This is much easier than the older method and now functions like the original version of Bryce.

LIGHT EDITOR (DARK LIGHTS & MORE INTENSITY RANGE)

The light editor now lets you make a light's intensity negative, which results in a light which removes energy instead of adding it. If your scene looks great except for one or two bright spots, just place a darklight near the bright spots to even the lighting. Also, light intensity can now go much higher (and lower) to accompany lights which use squared falloff. Lights which are very far away can also benefit from extended intensity.

Other Fixes

In addition to improving native scene loading/saving, enhancements were made in the importing of old Bryce scenes. For instance, pict textures now appear in the pict library dialog after being loaded from an old Bryce scene. Sky & Time memory dots now load and save correctly with all Bryce3D scenes. The animation system, in general, including the auto-keying mechanics, has been greatly improved.

The propagation controls, located in the object attributes dialog (LINK tab), are designed to offer customizable control over what transformation properties as passed along within a hierarchy (from parent to child). The child object defines what properties it wants to accept from its parent. That is what the propagation settings define. This control is very powerful and offers the animator much more flexibility in defining hierarchical motions. This is now working as designed.

There was a possible crash when rendering from the inside of a slab which has beenfixed. Overall, rendering quality is better.

PC CODEC PROBLEMS

The PC release of Bryce3D had CODEC crashing problems on some platform configurations. Aall have been addressed.

TERRAIN EDITOR

The copy/paste and blending operations (PICTURES tab) now properly work with the native image size. Before, the operations would always be performed in the resolution of the preview (72×72 pixels).

About the Author

R. Shamms Mortier has written and illustrated over 600 articles on computer graphics and animation for national and international publications, and has also authored eight books on the same subjects. His biweekly column in TV Technology magazine covers the latest trends and technologies in the industry. He has a Masters degree in Education, and a PhD in interdisciplinary studies. His computer graphics and animation studio, Eyeful Tower Communications in Bristol, Vermont, serves regional and national clients.

Index

Ask a Tough Question. Expect Solid Direction.

Help on the Horizon. Arnold Information Technology points corporations and organizations to information that get results. Access our experienced professionals who can help senior managers identify options and chart a course.

Since 1991, we've proven we can help in a range of capacities:

BUSINESS DEVELOPMENT
- Knowledge Management
- Competitive Intelligence
- Marketing & Sales
- Acquisitions & Mergers
- Patent Evaluations
- Technology Startups

INFORMATION TECHNOLOGY SERVICES
- Intranets, and Extranets
- Web-based Technologies
- Database Management
- Digital Work Flow Planning
- Information Engineering

ACTION FROM IDEAS. We helped build the service known as the Top 5% of the Internet, found at www.lycos.com. Our latest competitive intelligence tool can be explored at abcompass.com. It builds a personal daily news feed that only you receive.

A TEAM WITH STRATEGIC VISION. Our seasoned consultants can build, research, prototype, budget, plan, assess, and tackle some of the toughest jobs in information technology. Our managers have taken a leadership role in U.S. corporations and elsewhere in the world.

GET WHERE YOU WANT TO GO. TODAY.
We move corporations and organizations into the future. Our work spans a variety of industries, including publishing, telecommunications, government agencies, investment banks, and startups. We welcome confidential, informal discussions of your challenges and opportunities.

CONTACT:

Stephen E. Arnold, President
Arnold Information Technology
P.O. Box 320
Harrods Creek, Kentucky 40027
Voice: 502 228-1966
E-Mail: ait@arnoldit.com
Facsimile: 502 228-0548